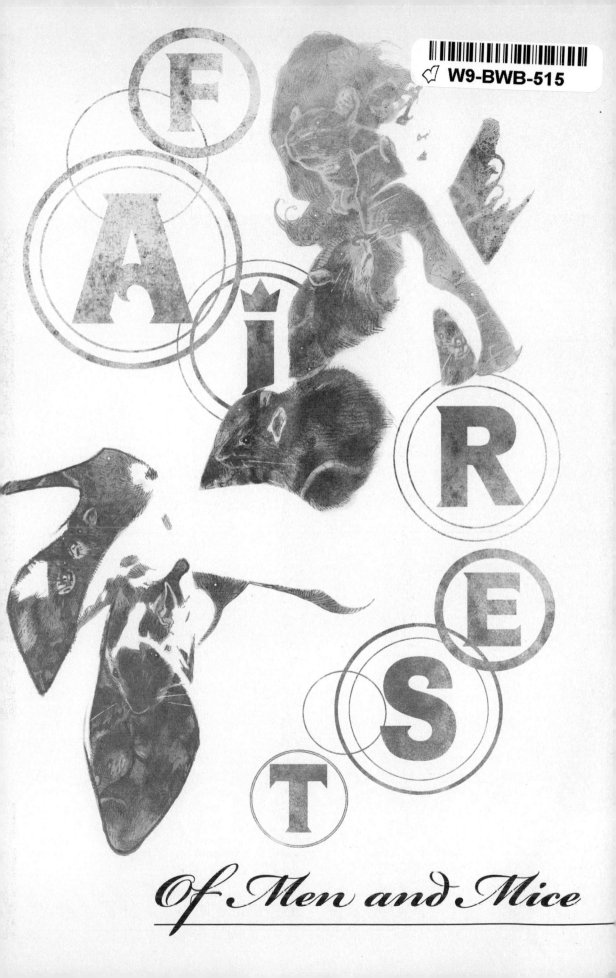

FAIREST

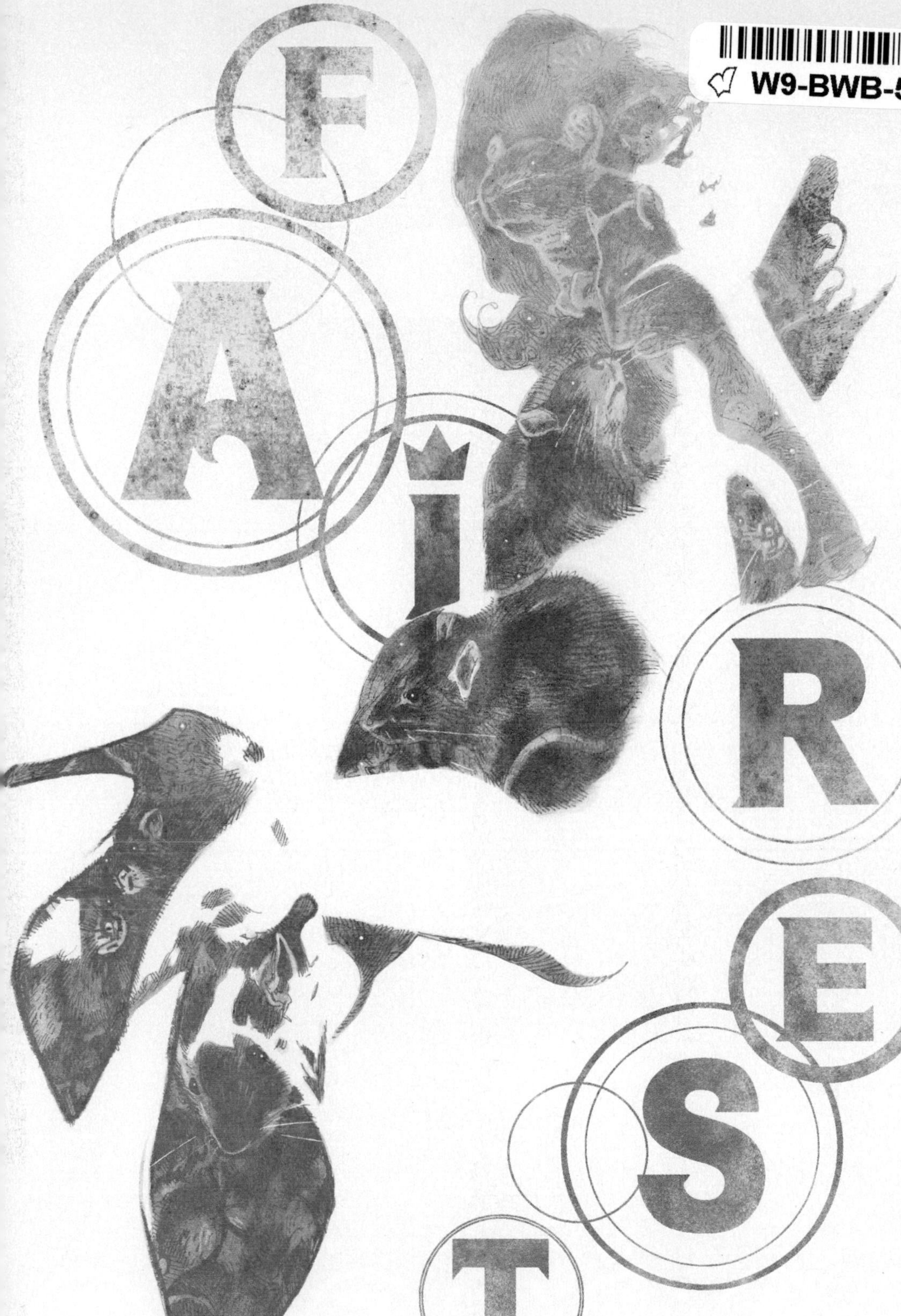

Of Men and Mice

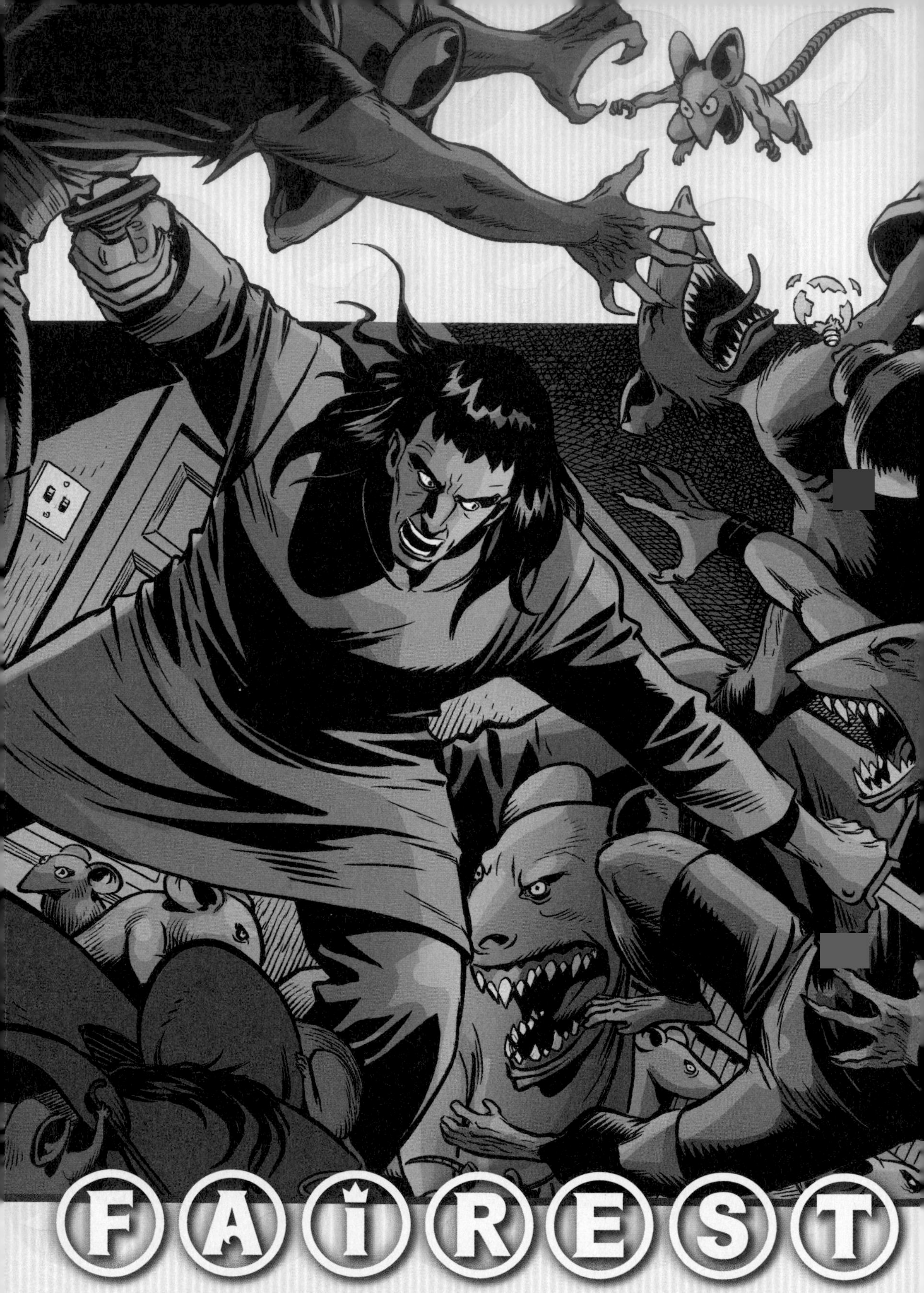

FAIREST

Of Men and Mice

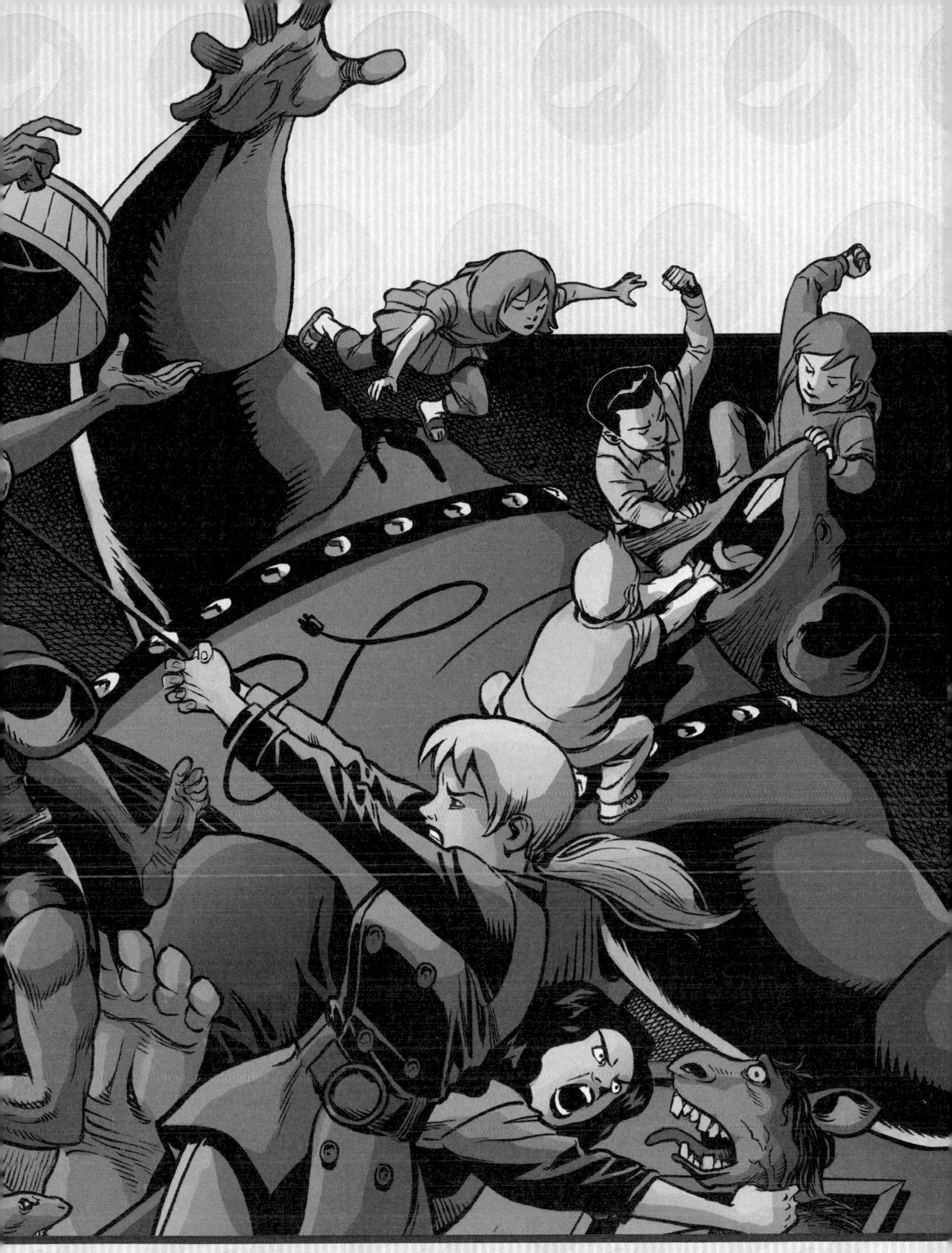

Marc Andreyko
WRITER

Shawn McManus
ARTIST

Lee Loughridge
COLORIST

Todd Klein
LETTERER

Adam Hughes
COVER ART AND ORIGINAL SERIES COVERS

FAIREST CREATED BY **Bill Willingham**

Gregory Lockard *Editor – Original Series*
Scott Nybakken *Editor*
Robbin Brosterman *Design Director – Books*
Curtis King Jr. *Publication Design*

Shelly Bond *Executive Editor – Vertigo*
Hank Kanalz *Senior VP – Vertigo & Integrated Publishing*

Diane Nelson *President*
Dan DiDio and **Jim Lee** *Co-Publishers*
Geoff Johns *Chief Creative Officer*
Amit Desai *Senior VP – Marketing & Franchise Management*
Amy Genkins *Senior VP – Business & Legal Affairs*
Nairi Gardiner *Senior VP – Finance*
Jeff Boison *VP – Publishing Planning*
Mark Chiarello *VP – Art Direction & Design*
John Cunningham *VP – Marketing*
Terri Cunningham *VP – Editorial Administration*
Larry Ganem *VP – Talent Relations & Services*
Alison Gill *Senior VP – Manufacturing & Operations*
Jay Kogan *VP – Business & Legal Affairs, Publishing*
Jack Mahan *VP – Business Affairs, Talent*
Nick Napolitano *VP – Manufacturing Administration*
Sue Pohja *VP – Book Sales*
Fred Ruiz *VP – Manufacturing Operations*
Courtney Simmons *Senior VP – Publicity*
Bob Wayne *Senior VP – Sales*

DC Comics, 1700 Broadway, New York, NY 10019
A Warner Bros. Entertainment Company
Printed in the U.S.A. First Printing. ISBN: 978-1-4012-5005-8

Library of Congress Cataloging-in-Publication Data

Andreyko, Marc.
    Fairest. Volume 4, Cinderella, Of Men and Mice / Marc Andreyko. Bill
Willingham. Shawn McManus.
        pages cm
    ISBN 978-1-4012-5005-8 (paperback)
    1. fairy tales—Comic books, strips, etc. 2. Graphic novels. I. Willingham,
Bill. II. McManus. Shawn. III. Title. IV. Title: Cinderella, Of Men and Mice. V.
Title: Of Men and Mice.
    PN6728.F255A53 2014
    741.5'973—dc23
                                                            2014014678

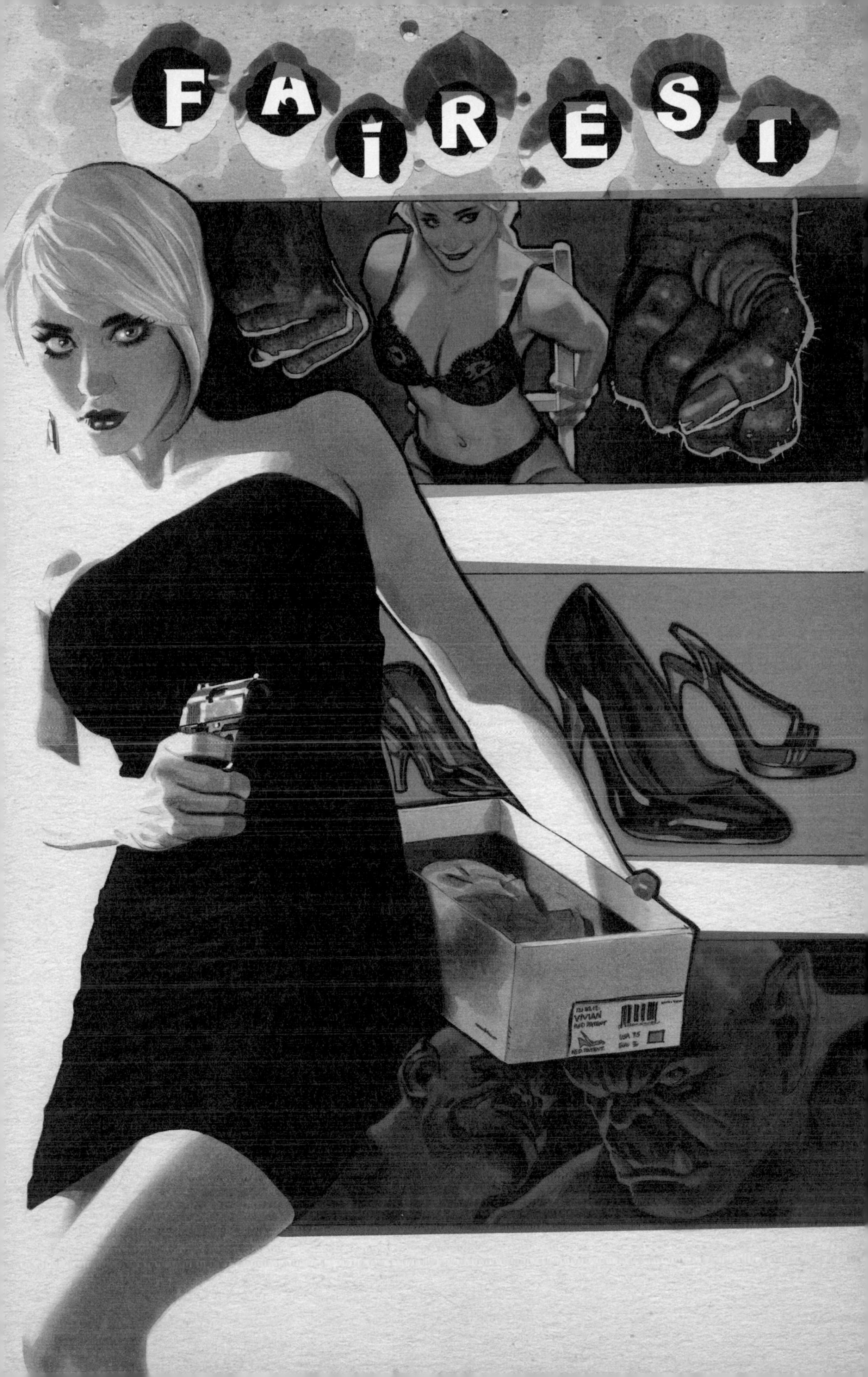
FAIREST
VIVIAN

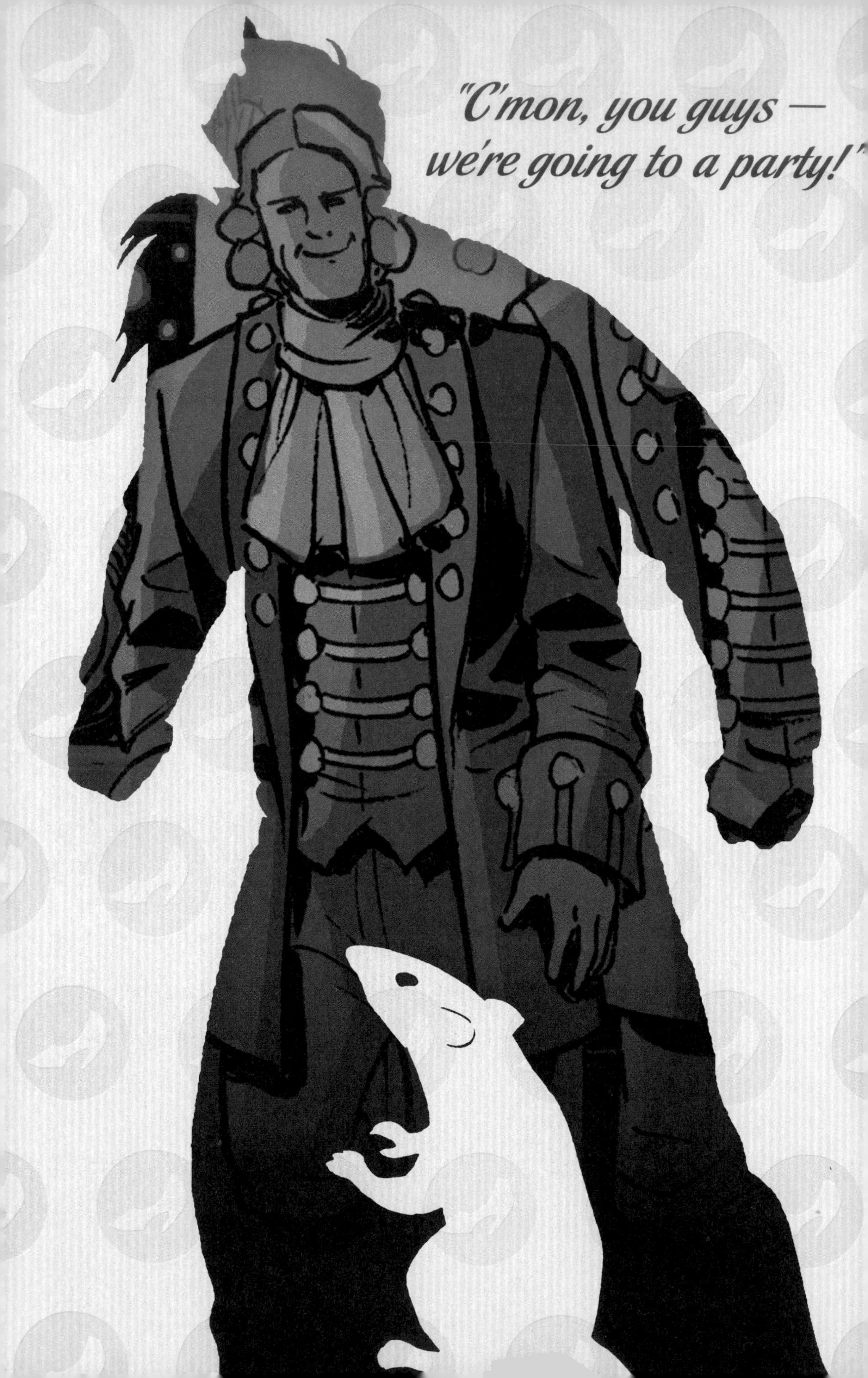
"C'mon, you guys —
we're going to a party!"

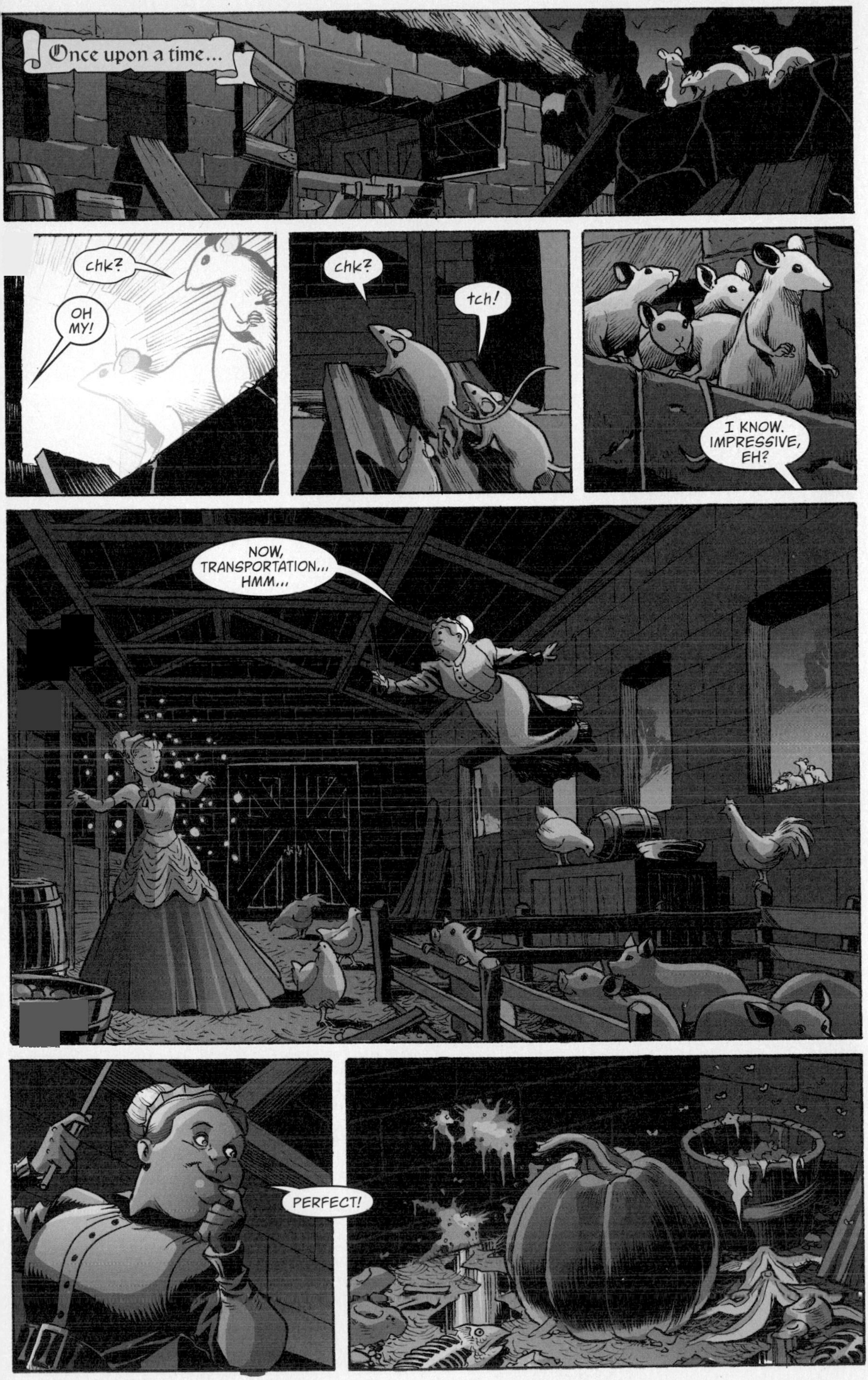
Once upon a time...
chk?
OH MY!
chk?
tch!
I KNOW. IMPRESSIVE, EH?
NOW, TRANSPORTATION... HMM...
PERFECT!

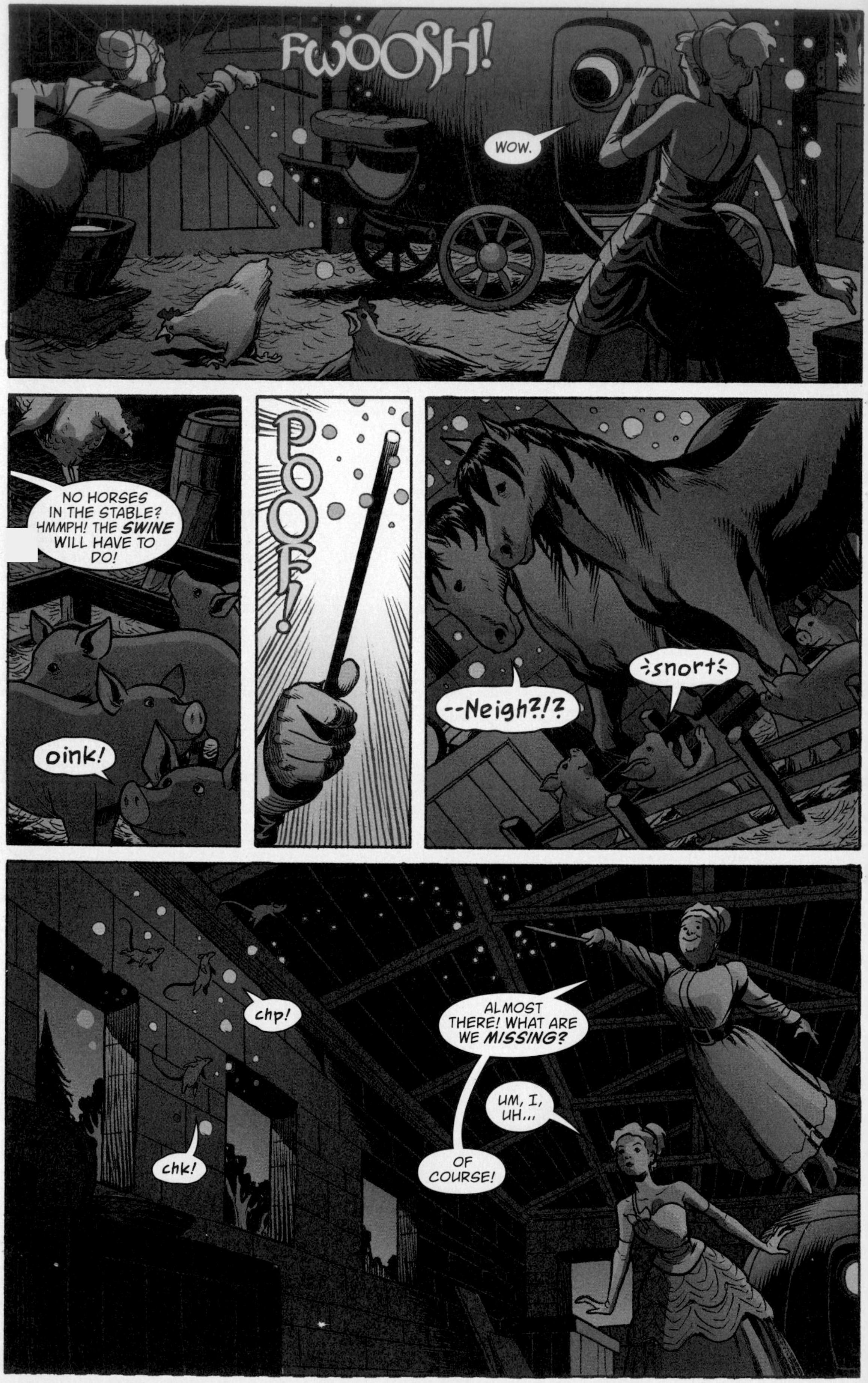
FWOOSH!
WOW.
NO HORSES IN THE STABLE? HMMPH! THE SWINE WILL HAVE TO DO!
oink!
POOF!
--Neigh?!?
snort
chp!
chk!
ALMOST THERE! WHAT ARE WE MISSING?
UM, I, UH...
OF COURSE!

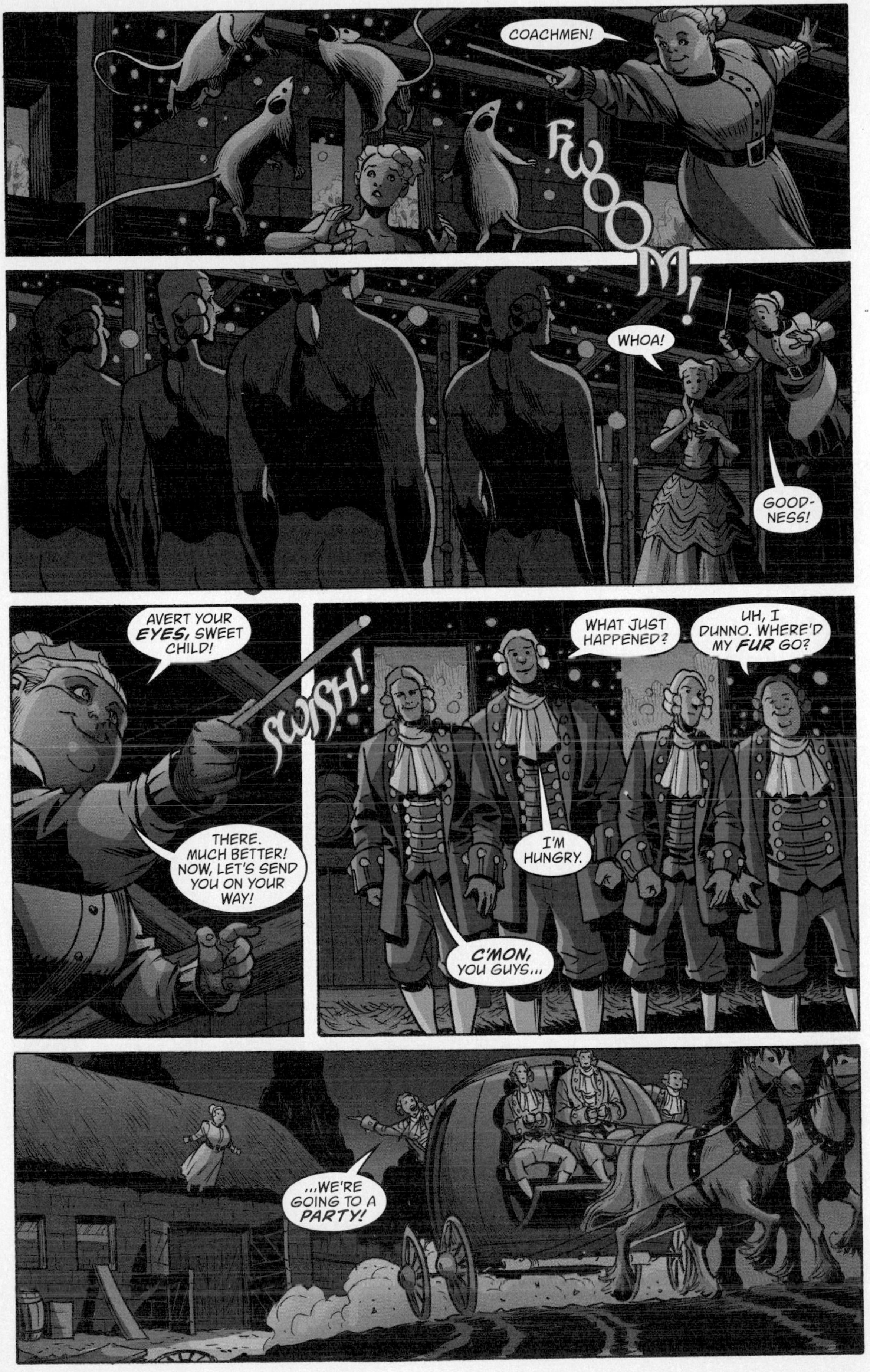
COACHMEN!
FWOOOM!
WHOA!
GOODNESS!
AVERT YOUR EYES, SWEET CHILD!
SWISH!
THERE. MUCH BETTER! NOW, LET'S SEND YOU ON YOUR WAY!
WHAT JUST HAPPENED?
UH, I DUNNO. WHERE'D MY FUR GO?
I'M HUNGRY.
C'MON, YOU GUYS...
...WE'RE GOING TO A PARTY!

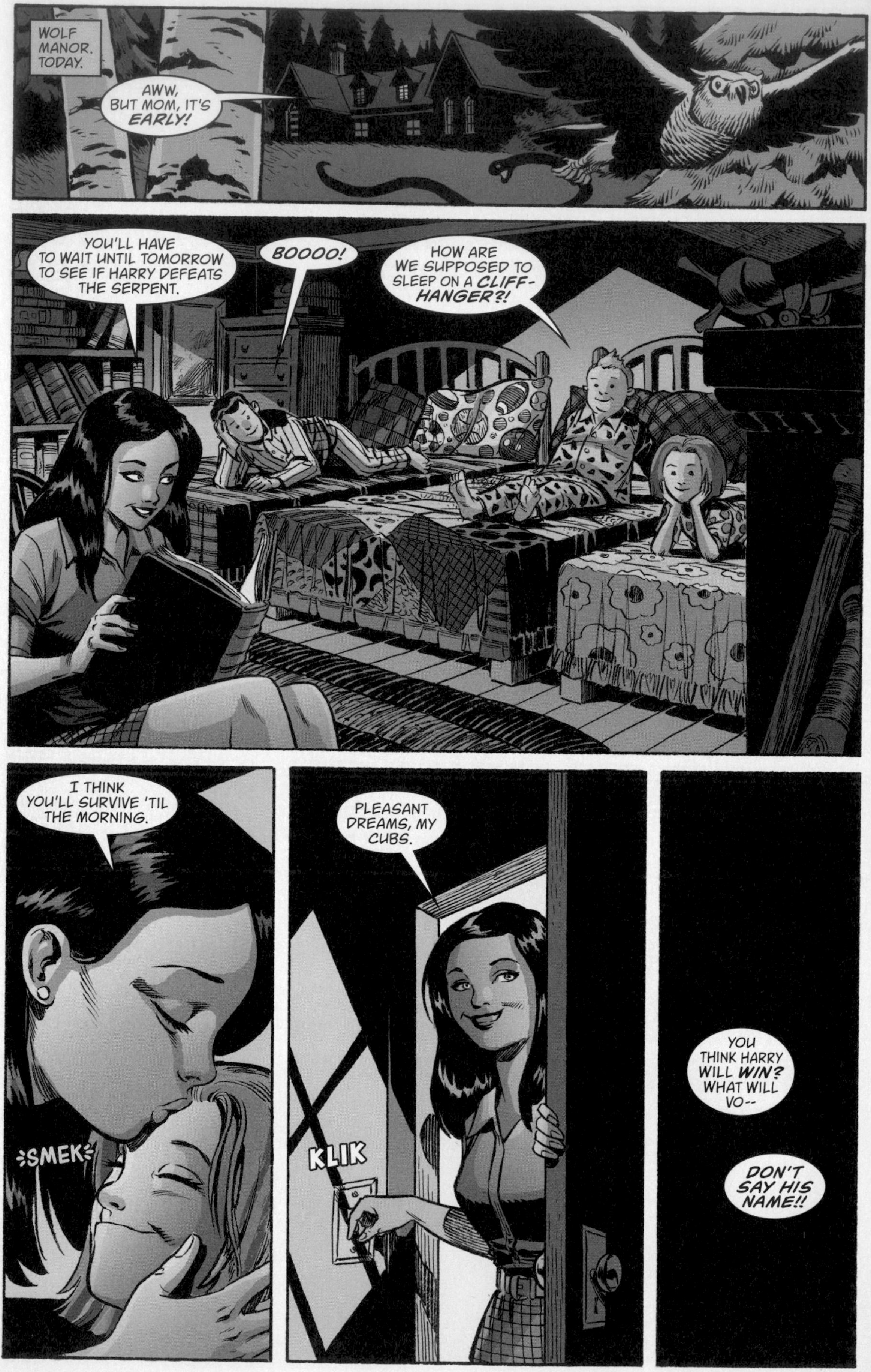
WOLF MANOR. TODAY.
AWW, BUT MOM, IT'S EARLY!
YOU'LL HAVE TO WAIT UNTIL TOMORROW TO SEE IF HARRY DEFEATS THE SERPENT.
BOOOO!
HOW ARE WE SUPPOSED TO SLEEP ON A CLIFF-HANGER?!
I THINK YOU'LL SURVIVE 'TIL THE MORNING.
SMEK
PLEASANT DREAMS, MY CUBS.
KLIK
YOU THINK HARRY WILL WIN? WHAT WILL VO--
DON'T SAY HIS NAME!!

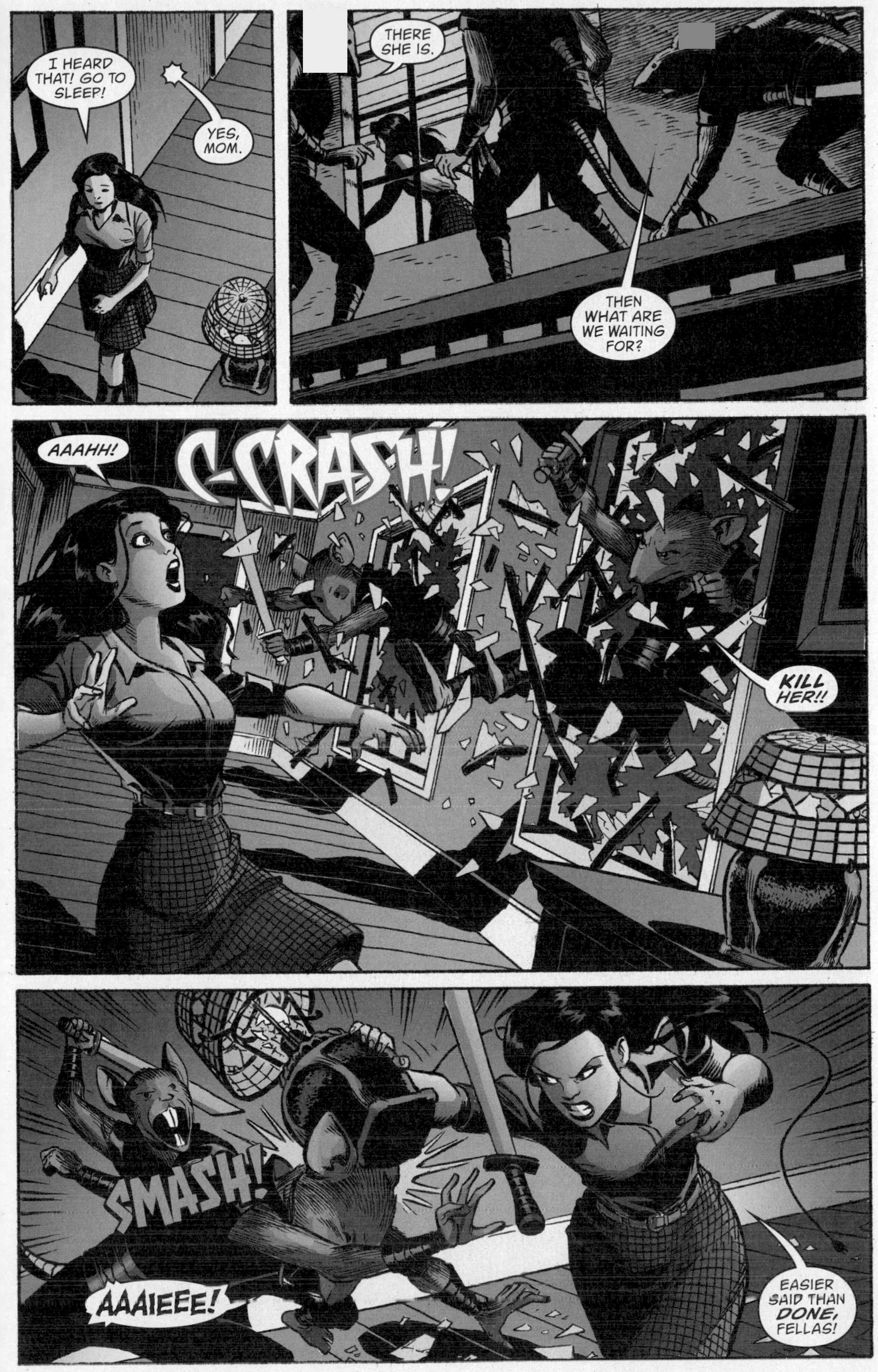
I HEARD THAT! GO TO SLEEP!
YES, MOM.
THERE SHE IS.
THEN WHAT ARE WE WAITING FOR?
AAAHH!
C-CRASH!
KILL HER!!
SMASH!
AAAIEEE!
EASIER SAID THAN DONE, FELLAS!

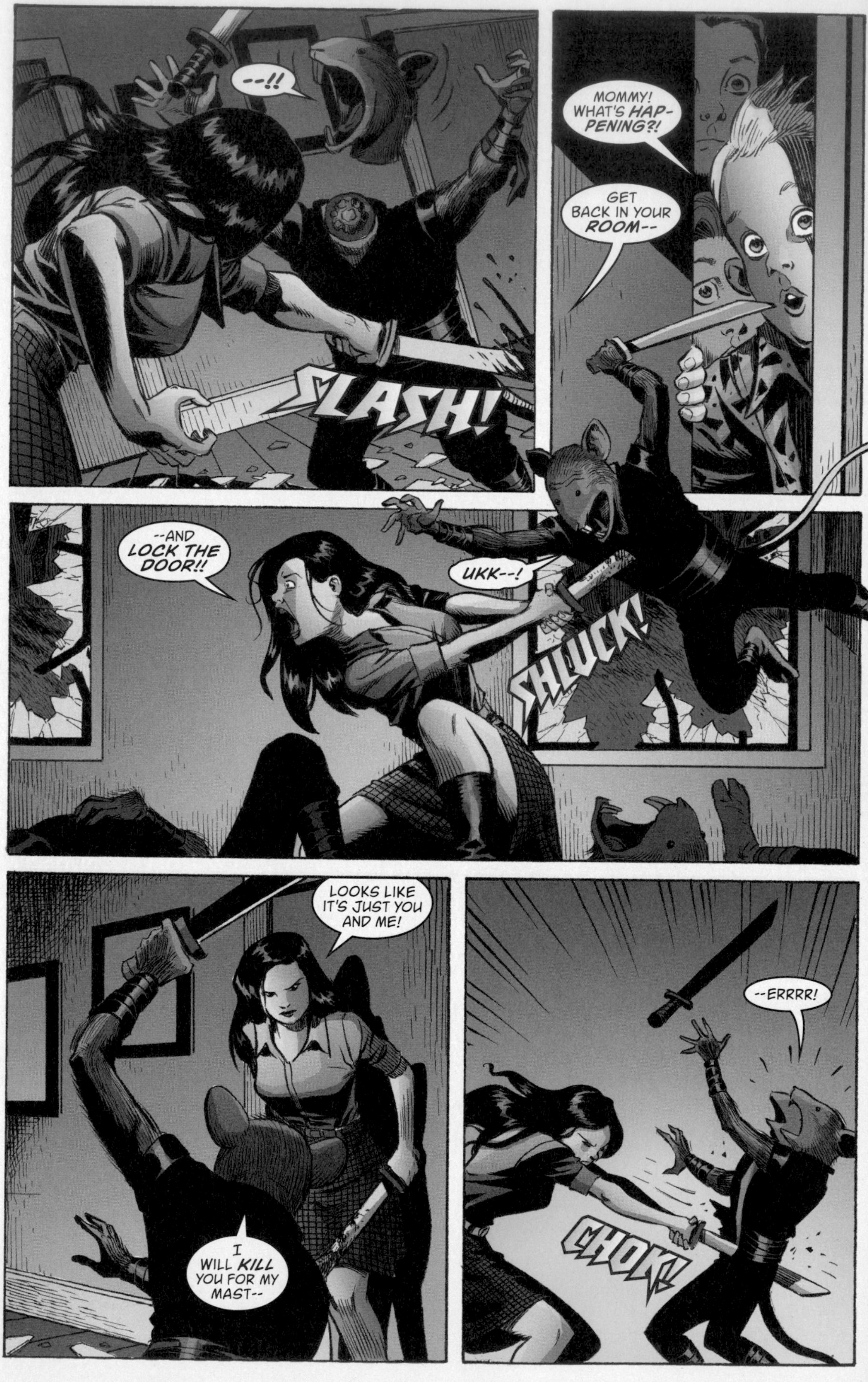
--!!
SLASH!
MOMMY! WHAT'S HAP-PENING?!
GET BACK IN YOUR ROOM--
--AND LOCK THE DOOR!!
UKK--!
SHLUCK!
LOOKS LIKE IT'S JUST YOU AND ME!
I WILL KILL YOU FOR MY MAST--
--ERRRR!
CHOK!

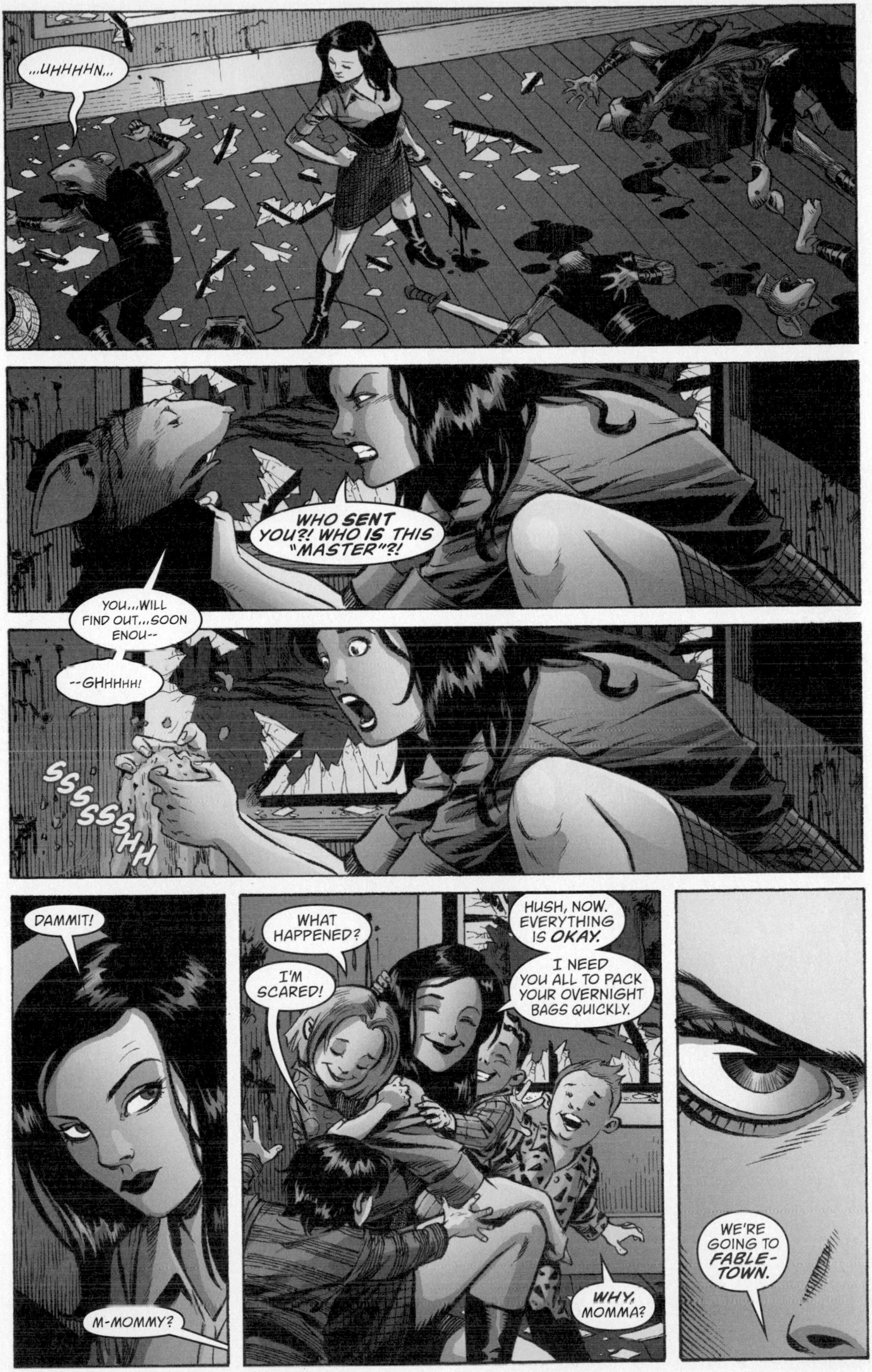
...UHHHHN...
WHO SENT YOU?! WHO IS THIS "MASTER"?!
YOU...WILL FIND OUT...SOON ENOU--
--GHHHHH!
SSSSSSHH
DAMMIT!
M-MOMMY?
WHAT HAPPENED?
I'M SCARED!
HUSH, NOW. EVERYTHING IS OKAY.
I NEED YOU ALL TO PACK YOUR OVERNIGHT BAGS QUICKLY.
WHY, MOMMA?
WE'RE GOING TO FABLE-TOWN.

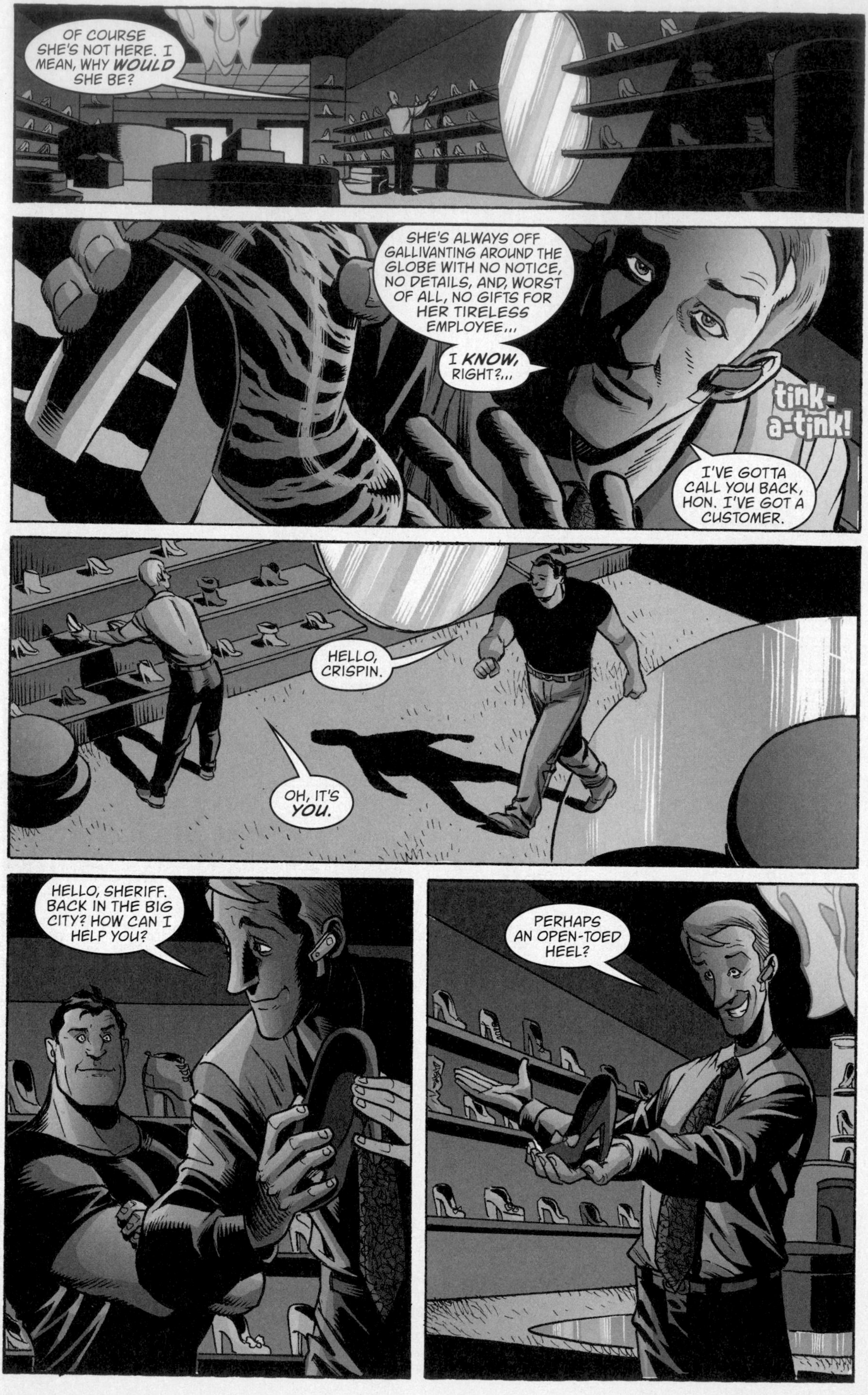
OF COURSE SHE'S NOT HERE. I MEAN, WHY WOULD SHE BE?
SHE'S ALWAYS OFF GALLIVANTING AROUND THE GLOBE WITH NO NOTICE, NO DETAILS, AND, WORST OF ALL, NO GIFTS FOR HER TIRELESS EMPLOYEE...
I KNOW, RIGHT?...
tink-a-tink!
I'VE GOTTA CALL YOU BACK, HON. I'VE GOT A CUSTOMER.
HELLO, CRISPIN.
OH, IT'S YOU.
HELLO, SHERIFF. BACK IN THE BIG CITY? HOW CAN I HELP YOU?
PERHAPS AN OPEN-TOED HEEL?

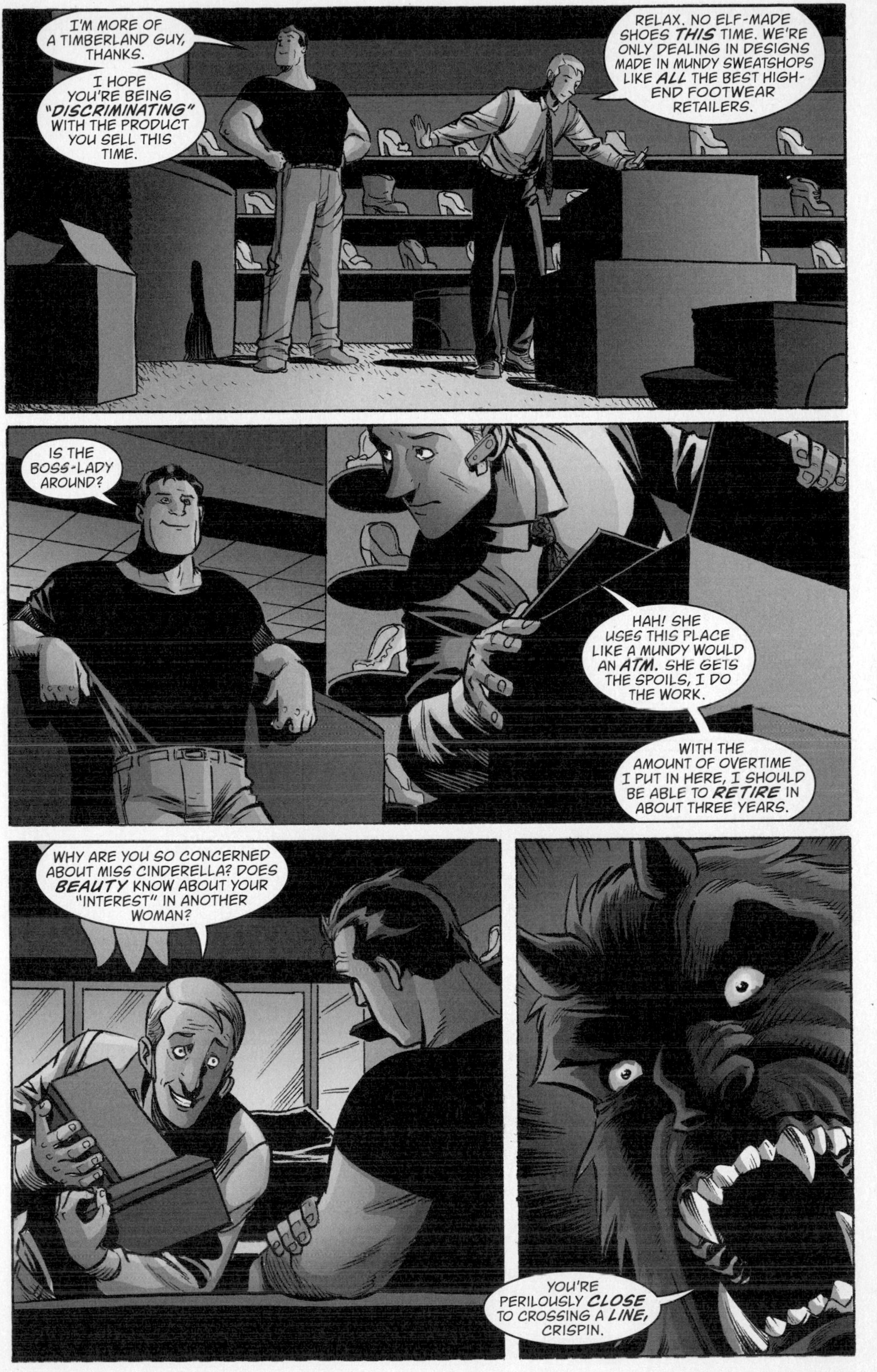
I'M MORE OF A TIMBERLAND GUY, THANKS.
I HOPE YOU'RE BEING "DISCRIMINATING" WITH THE PRODUCT YOU SELL THIS TIME.
RELAX. NO ELF-MADE SHOES THIS TIME. WE'RE ONLY DEALING IN DESIGNS MADE IN MUNDY SWEATSHOPS LIKE ALL THE BEST HIGH-END FOOTWEAR RETAILERS.
IS THE BOSS-LADY AROUND?
HAH! SHE USES THIS PLACE LIKE A MUNDY WOULD AN ATM. SHE GETS THE SPOILS, I DO THE WORK.
WITH THE AMOUNT OF OVERTIME I PUT IN HERE, I SHOULD BE ABLE TO RETIRE IN ABOUT THREE YEARS.
WHY ARE YOU SO CONCERNED ABOUT MISS CINDERELLA? DOES BEAUTY KNOW ABOUT YOUR "INTEREST" IN ANOTHER WOMAN?
YOU'RE PERILOUSLY CLOSE TO CROSSING A LINE, CRISPIN.

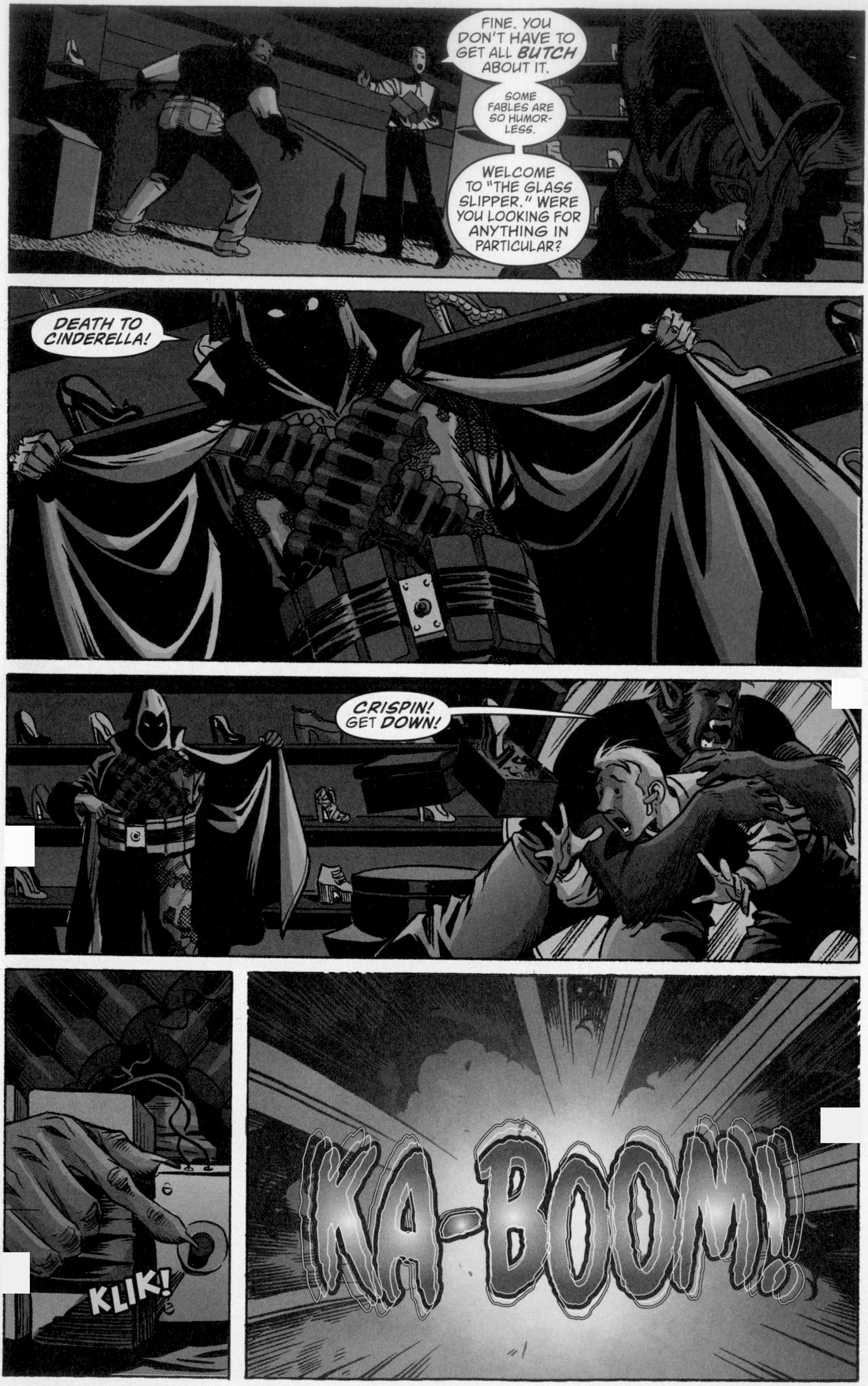
FINE. YOU DON'T HAVE TO GET ALL BUTCH ABOUT IT.
SOME FABLES ARE SO HUMOR-LESS.
WELCOME TO "THE GLASS SLIPPER." WERE YOU LOOKING FOR ANYTHING IN PARTICULAR?
DEATH TO CINDERELLA!
CRISPIN! GET DOWN!
KLIK!
KA-BOOM!

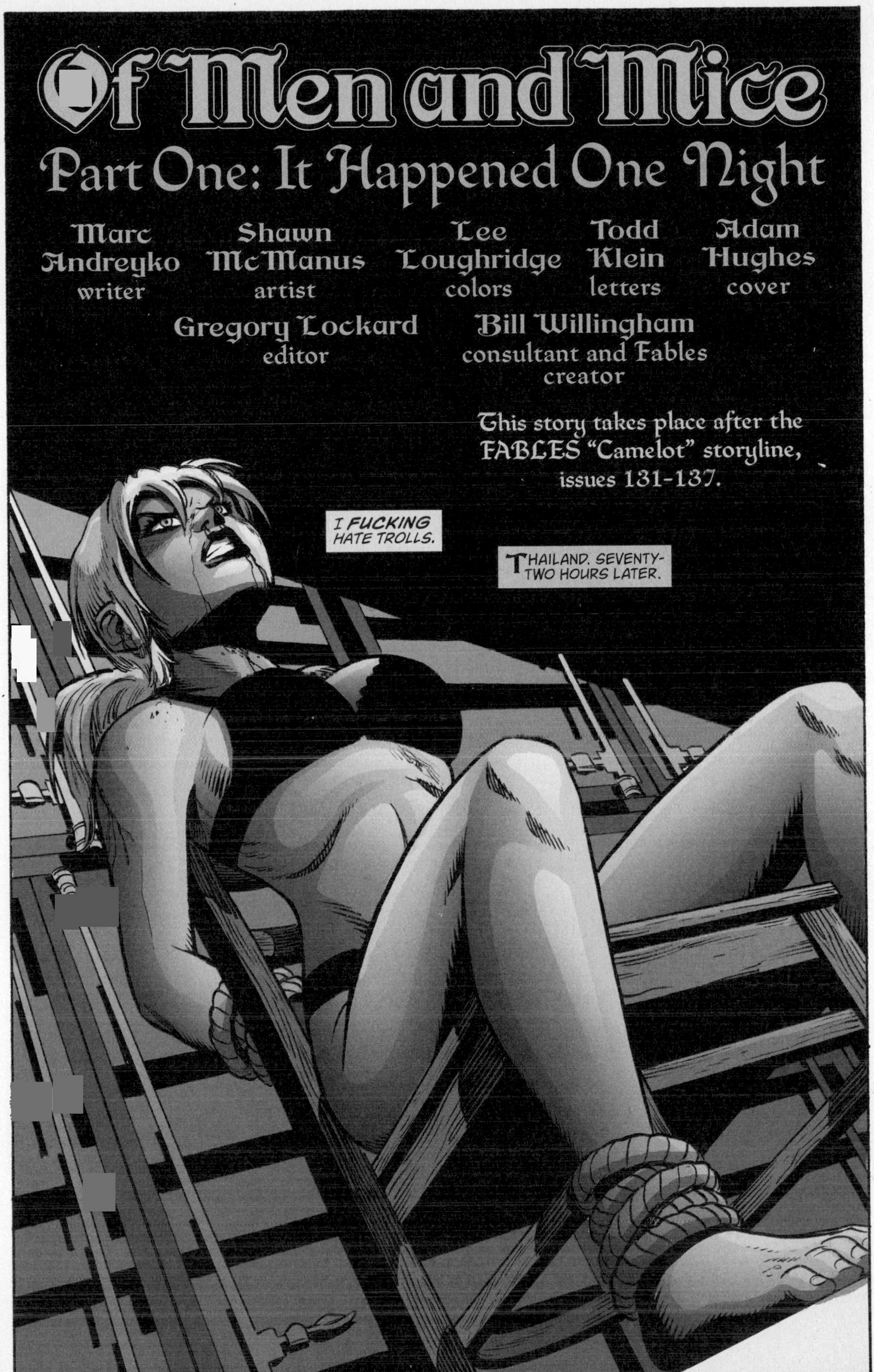
Of Men and Mice
Part One: It Happened One Night
Marc Andreyko writer
Shawn McManus artist
Lee Loughridge colors
Todd Klein letters
Adam Hughes cover
Gregory Lockard editor
Bill Willingham consultant and Fables creator
This story takes place after the FABLES "Camelot" storyline, issues 131-137.
I FUCKING HATE TROLLS.
THAILAND. SEVENTY-TWO HOURS LATER.

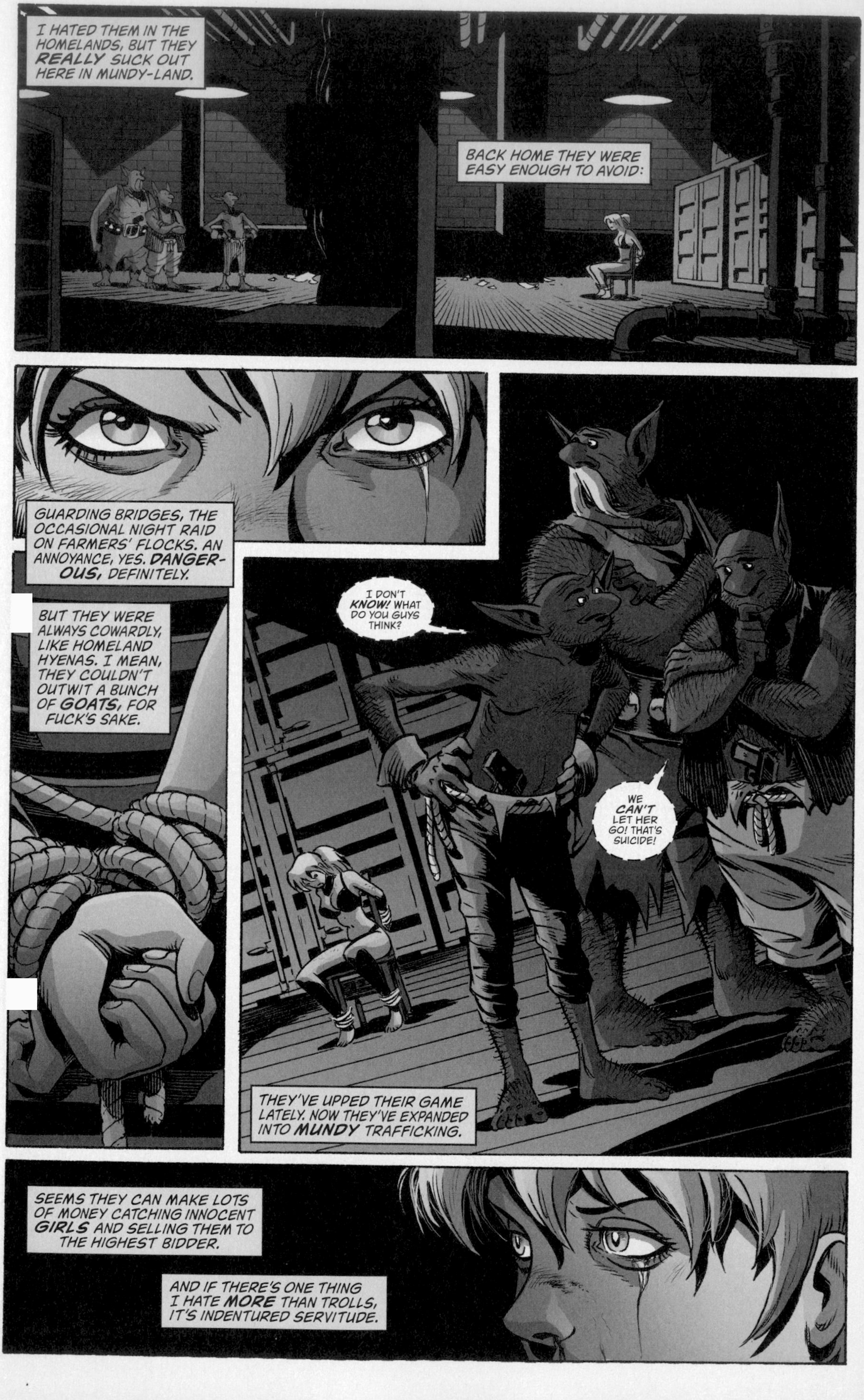

I HATED THEM IN THE HOMELANDS, BUT THEY REALLY SUCK OUT HERE IN MUNDY-LAND.
BACK HOME THEY WERE EASY ENOUGH TO AVOID:
GUARDING BRIDGES, THE OCCASIONAL NIGHT RAID ON FARMERS' FLOCKS. AN ANNOYANCE, YES. DANGEROUS, DEFINITELY.
BUT THEY WERE ALWAYS COWARDLY, LIKE HOMELAND HYENAS. I MEAN, THEY COULDN'T OUTWIT A BUNCH OF GOATS, FOR FUCK'S SAKE.
I DON'T KNOW! WHAT DO YOU GUYS THINK?
WE CAN'T LET HER GO! THAT'S SUICIDE!
THEY'VE UPPED THEIR GAME LATELY. NOW THEY'VE EXPANDED INTO MUNDY TRAFFICKING.
SEEMS THEY CAN MAKE LOTS OF MONEY CATCHING INNOCENT GIRLS AND SELLING THEM TO THE HIGHEST BIDDER.
AND IF THERE'S ONE THING I HATE MORE THAN TROLLS, IT'S INDENTURED SERVITUDE.

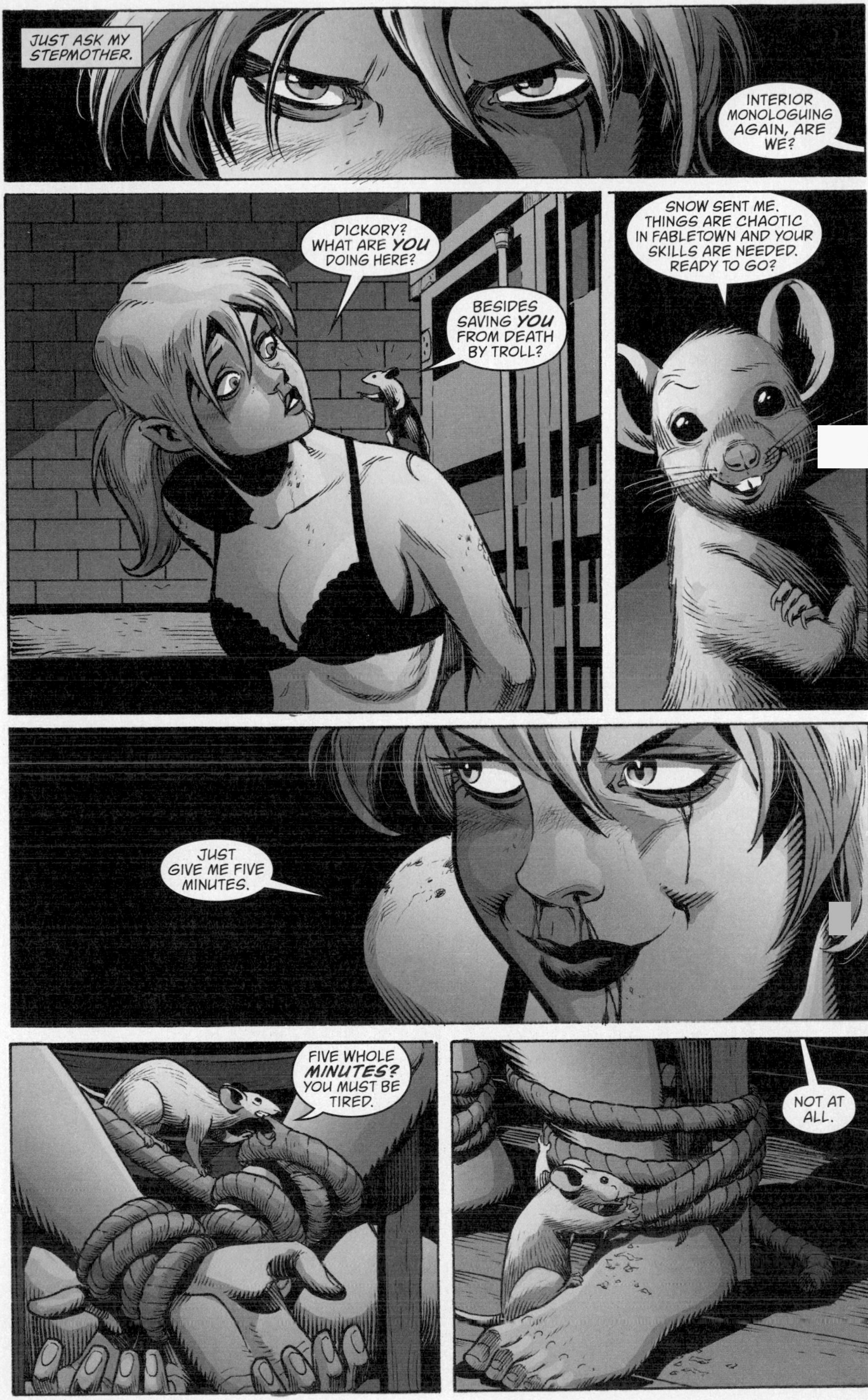
JUST ASK MY STEPMOTHER.
INTERIOR MONOLOGUING AGAIN, ARE WE?
DICKORY? WHAT ARE YOU DOING HERE?
BESIDES SAVING YOU FROM DEATH BY TROLL?
SNOW SENT ME. THINGS ARE CHAOTIC IN FABLETOWN AND YOUR SKILLS ARE NEEDED. READY TO GO?
JUST GIVE ME FIVE MINUTES.
FIVE WHOLE MINUTES? YOU MUST BE TIRED.
NOT AT ALL.

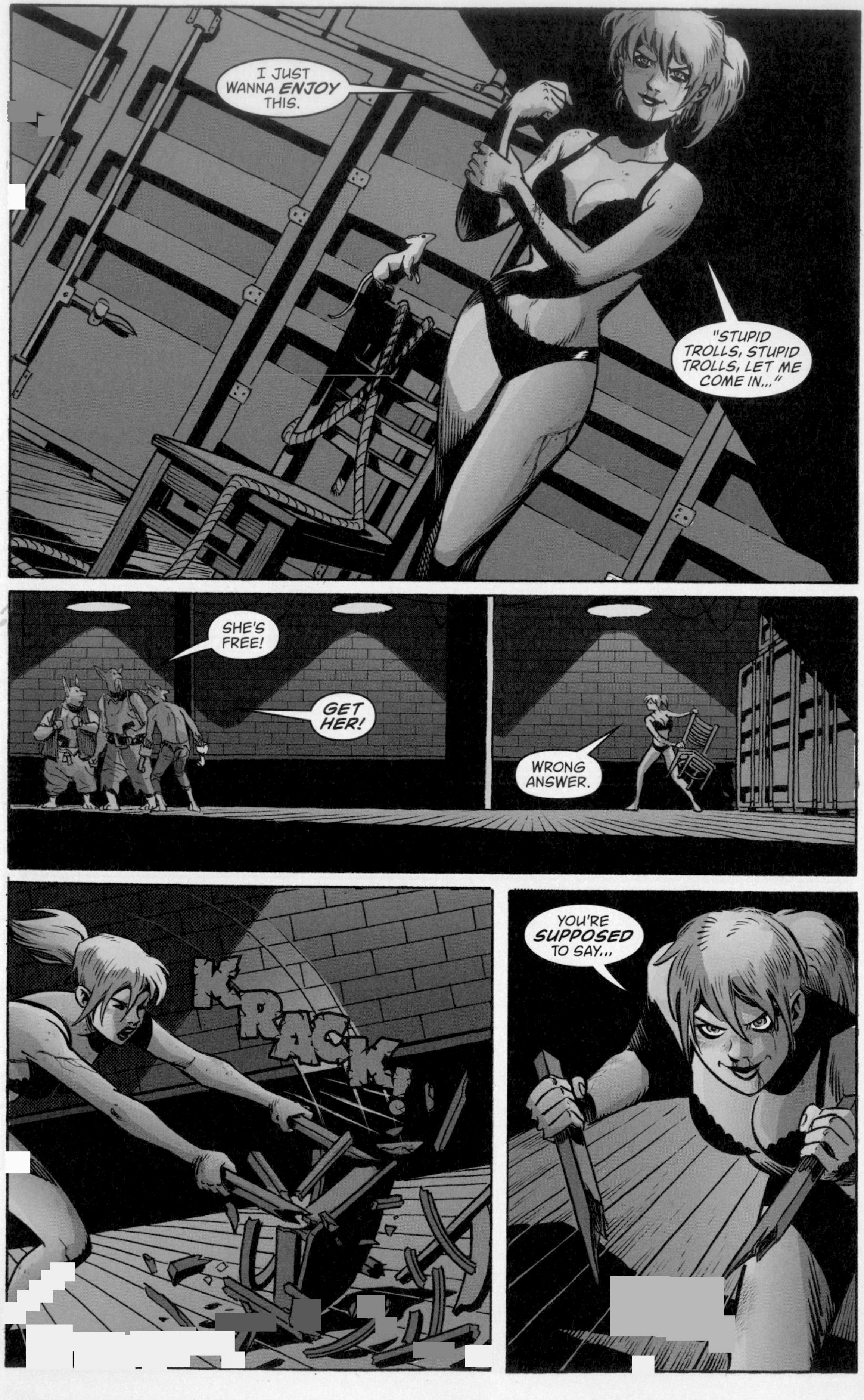
I JUST WANNA ENJOY THIS.
"STUPID TROLLS, STUPID TROLLS, LET ME COME IN..."
SHE'S FREE!
GET HER!
WRONG ANSWER.
KRACK!
YOU'RE SUPPOSED TO SAY...

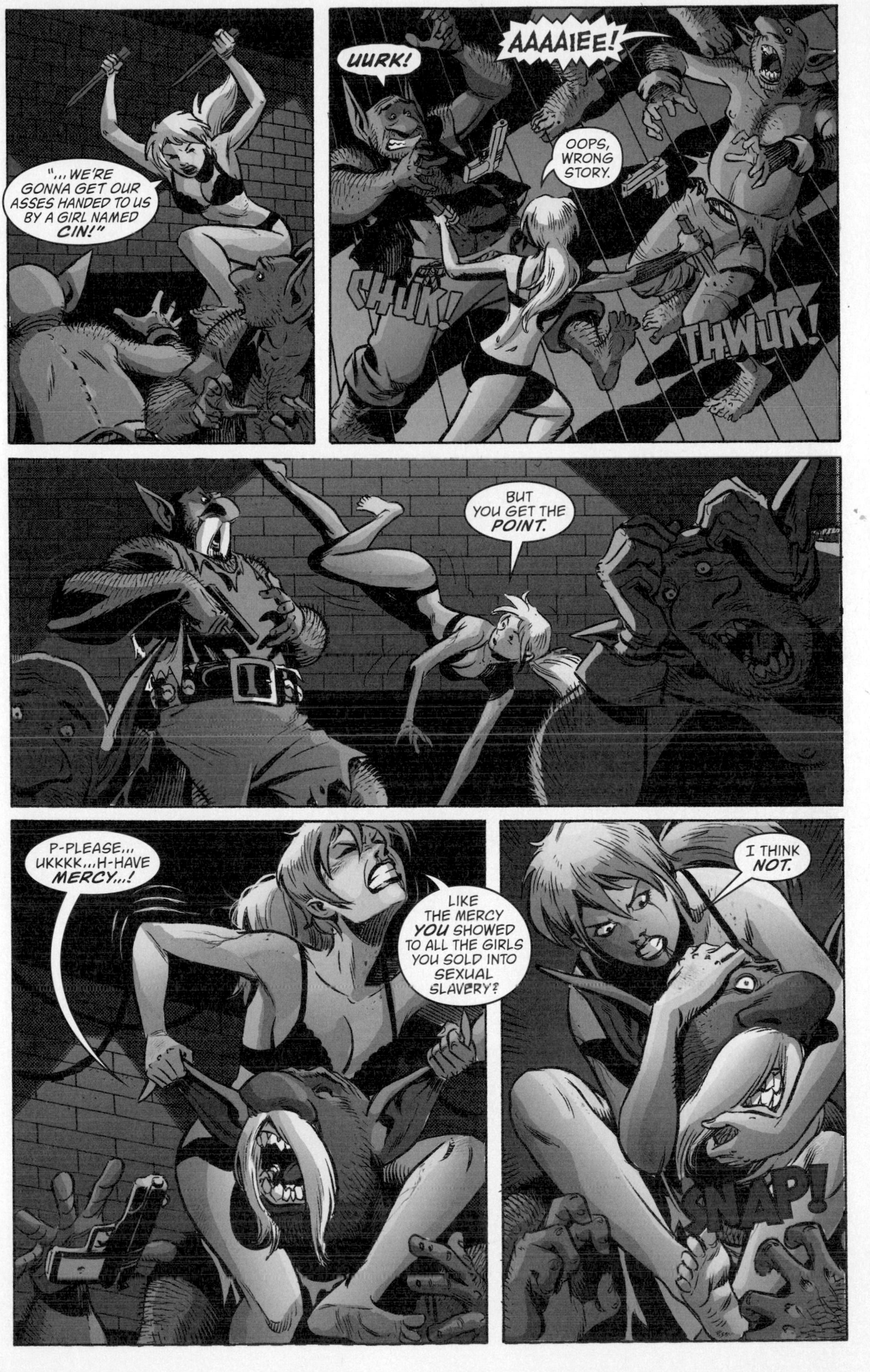
"...WE'RE GONNA GET OUR ASSES HANDED TO US BY A GIRL NAMED CIN!"
UURK!
AAAAIEE!
OOPS, WRONG STORY.
CHUK!
THWUK!
BUT YOU GET THE POINT.
P-PLEASE... UKKKK...H-HAVE MERCY...!
LIKE THE MERCY YOU SHOWED TO ALL THE GIRLS YOU SOLD INTO SEXUAL SLAVERY?
I THINK NOT.
SNAP!

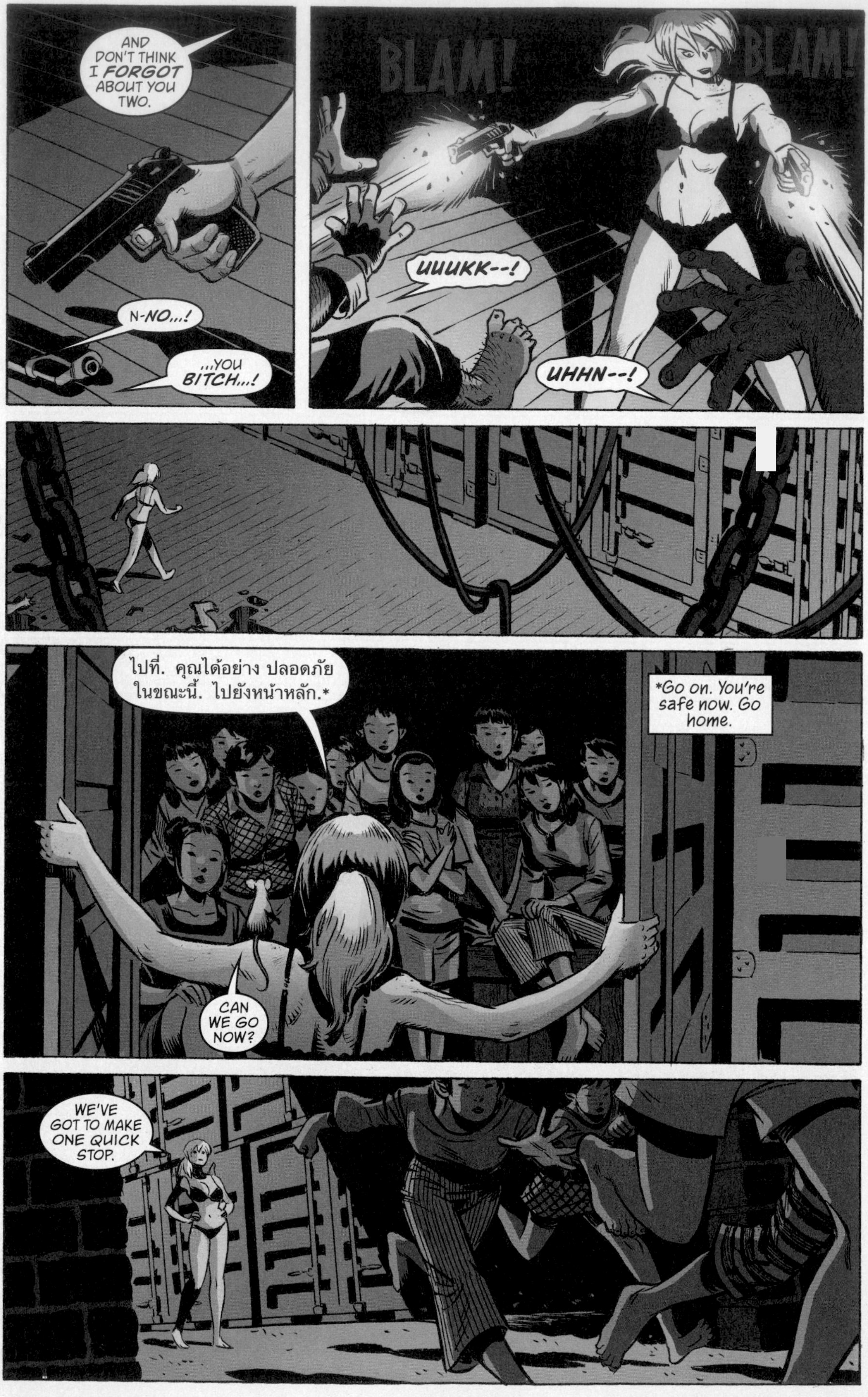
AND DON'T THINK I FORGOT ABOUT YOU TWO.
N-NO...!
...YOU BITCH...!
BLAM!
BLAM!
UUUKK--!
UHHN--!
ไปที่. คุณได้อย่าง ปลอดภัย ในขณะนี้. ไปยังหน้าหลัก.*
*Go on. You're safe now. Go home.
CAN WE GO NOW?
WE'VE GOT TO MAKE ONE QUICK STOP.

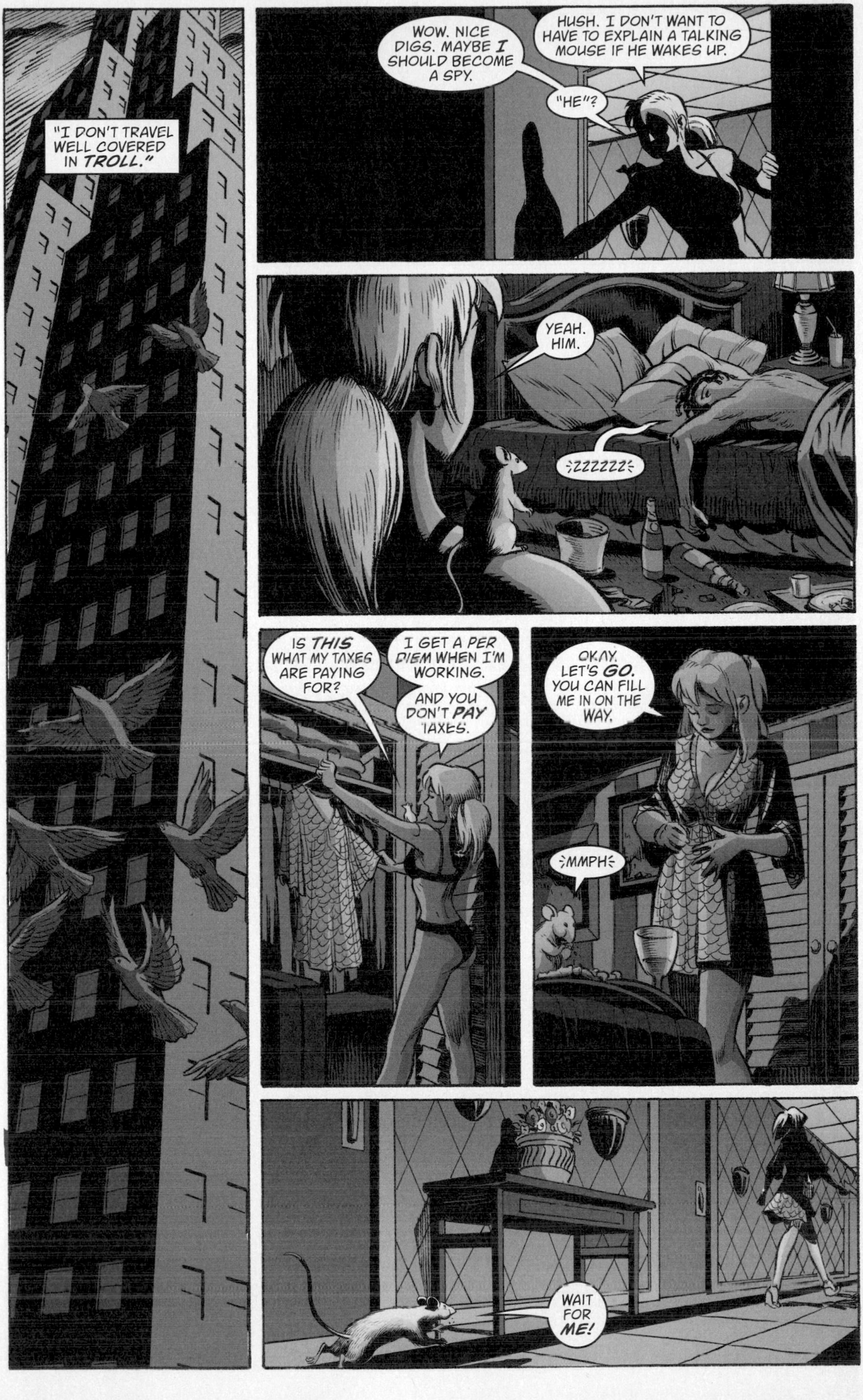
"I DON'T TRAVEL WELL COVERED IN TROLL."
WOW. NICE DIGS. MAYBE I SHOULD BECOME A SPY.
HUSH. I DON'T WANT TO HAVE TO EXPLAIN A TALKING MOUSE IF HE WAKES UP.
"HE"?
YEAH. HIM.
ZZZZZZ
IS THIS WHAT MY TAXES ARE PAYING FOR?
I GET A PER DIEM WHEN I'M WORKING.
AND YOU DON'T PAY TAXES.
OKAY. LET'S GO. YOU CAN FILL ME IN ON THE WAY.
MMPH
WAIT FOR ME!

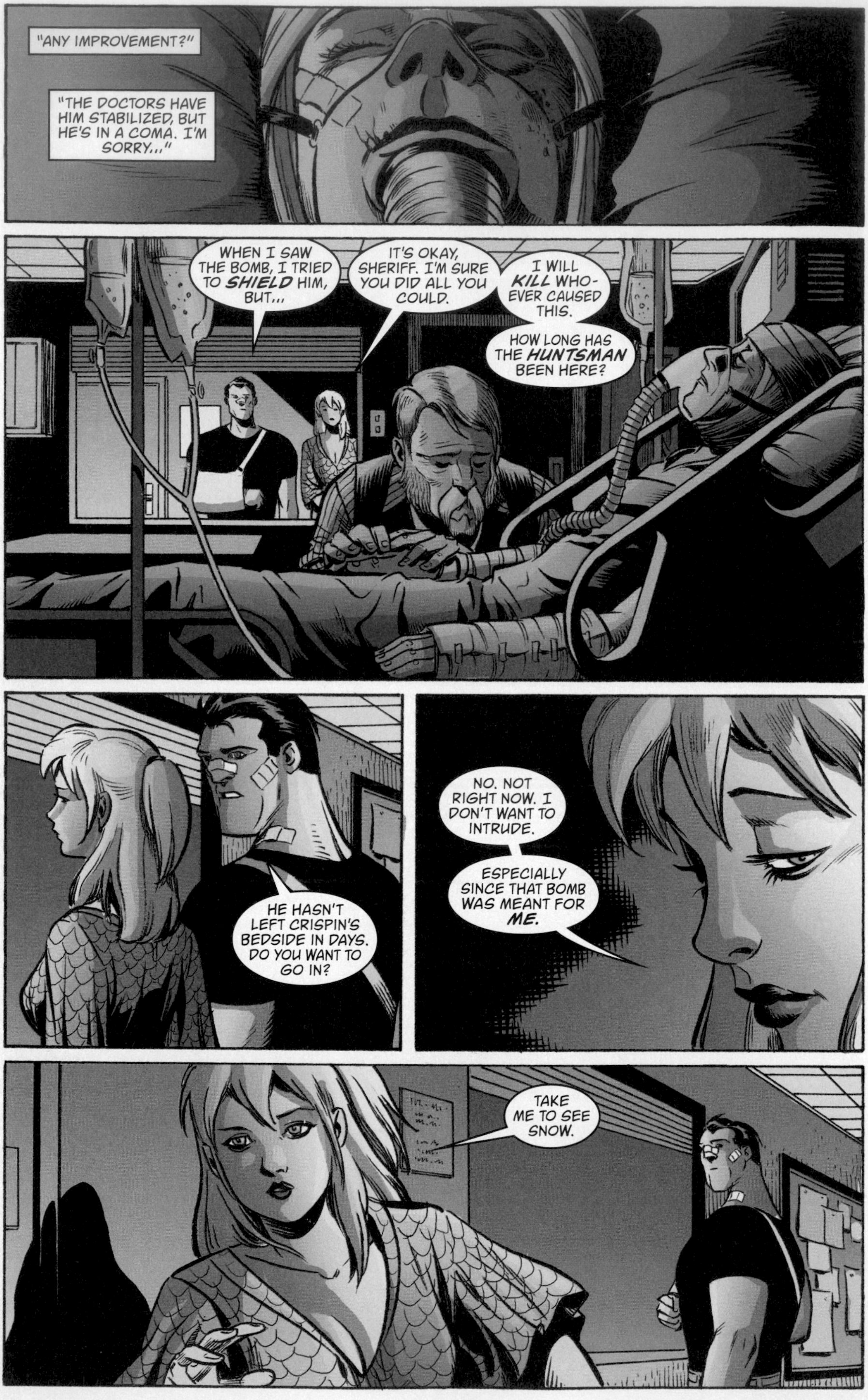
"ANY IMPROVEMENT?"
"THE DOCTORS HAVE HIM STABILIZED, BUT HE'S IN A COMA. I'M SORRY..."
WHEN I SAW THE BOMB, I TRIED TO *SHIELD* HIM, BUT...
IT'S OKAY, SHERIFF. I'M SURE YOU DID ALL YOU COULD.
I WILL *KILL* WHOEVER CAUSED THIS.
HOW LONG HAS THE *HUNTSMAN* BEEN HERE?
HE HASN'T LEFT CRISPIN'S BEDSIDE IN DAYS. DO YOU WANT TO GO IN?
NO. NOT RIGHT NOW. I DON'T WANT TO INTRUDE.
ESPECIALLY SINCE THAT BOMB WAS MEANT FOR *ME*.
TAKE ME TO SEE SNOW.

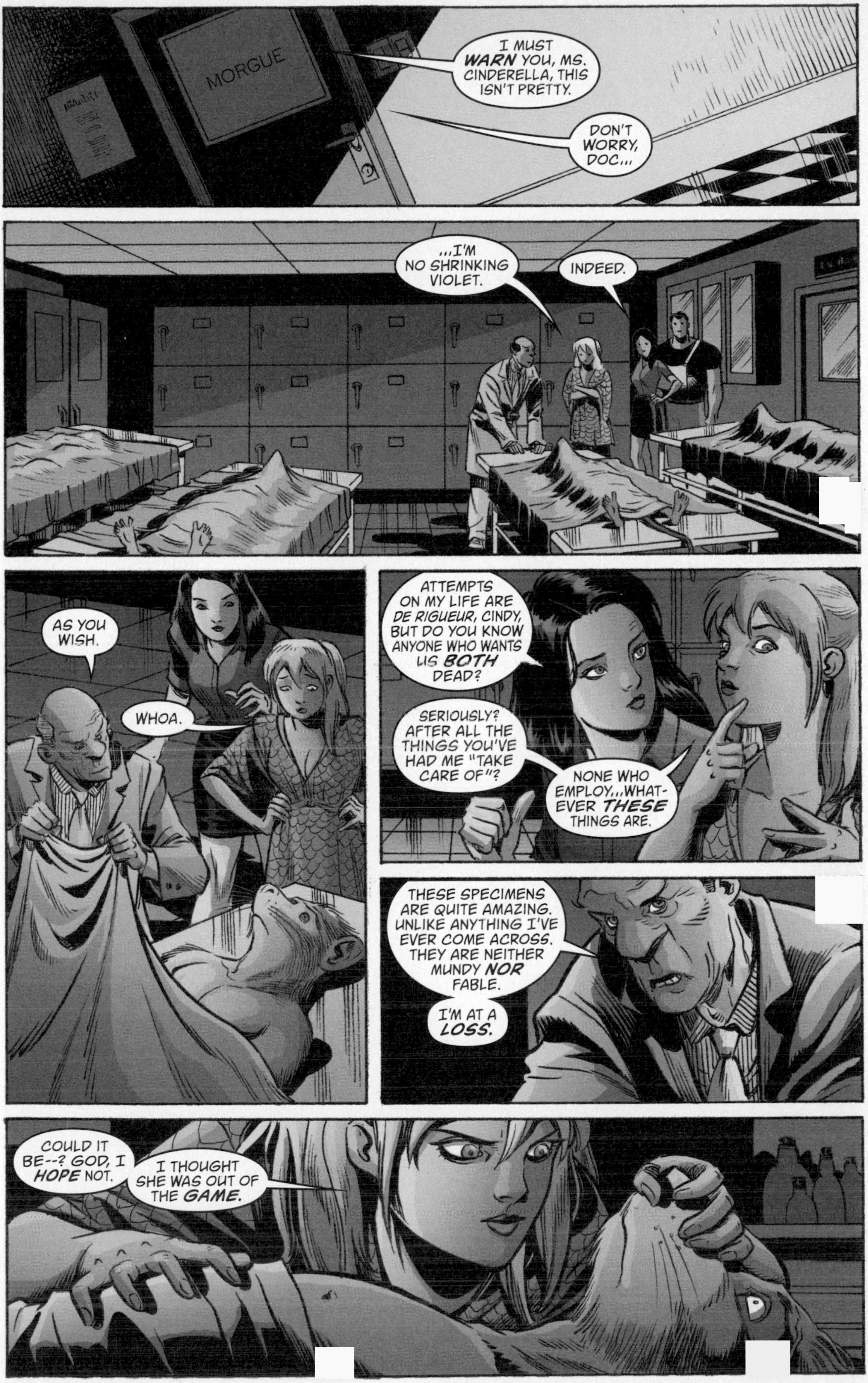
MORGUE
I MUST WARN YOU, MS. CINDERELLA, THIS ISN'T PRETTY.
DON'T WORRY, DOC...
...I'M NO SHRINKING VIOLET.
INDEED.
AS YOU WISH.
WHOA.
ATTEMPTS ON MY LIFE ARE DE RIGUEUR, CINDY, BUT DO YOU KNOW ANYONE WHO WANTS US BOTH DEAD?
SERIOUSLY? AFTER ALL THE THINGS YOU'VE HAD ME "TAKE CARE OF"?
NONE WHO EMPLOY...WHAT-EVER THESE THINGS ARE.
THESE SPECIMENS ARE QUITE AMAZING. UNLIKE ANYTHING I'VE EVER COME ACROSS. THEY ARE NEITHER MUNDY NOR FABLE.
I'M AT A LOSS.
COULD IT BE--? GOD, I HOPE NOT.
I THOUGHT SHE WAS OUT OF THE GAME.

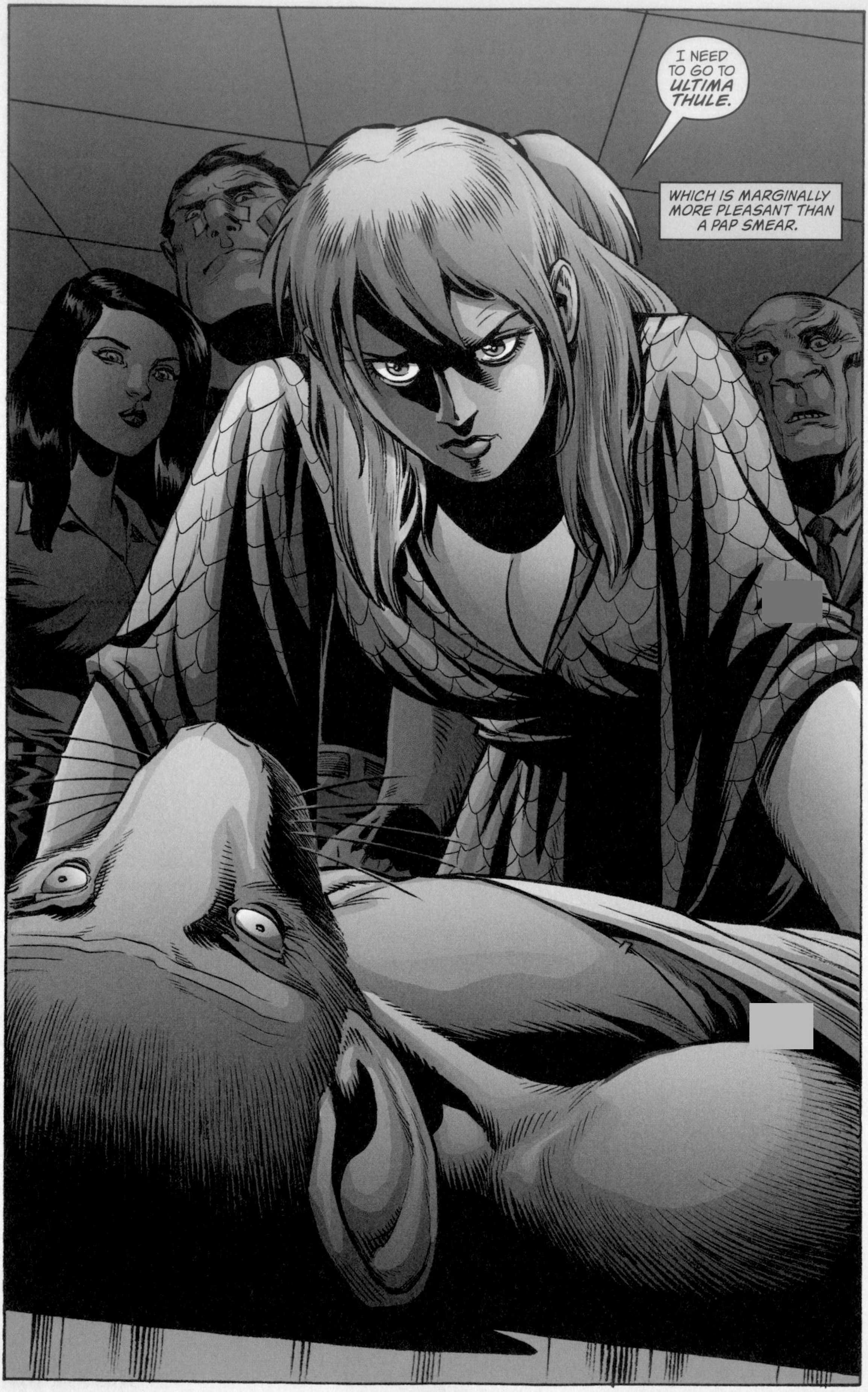
I NEED TO GO TO ULTIMA THULE.
WHICH IS MARGINALLY MORE PLEASANT THAN A PAP SMEAR.

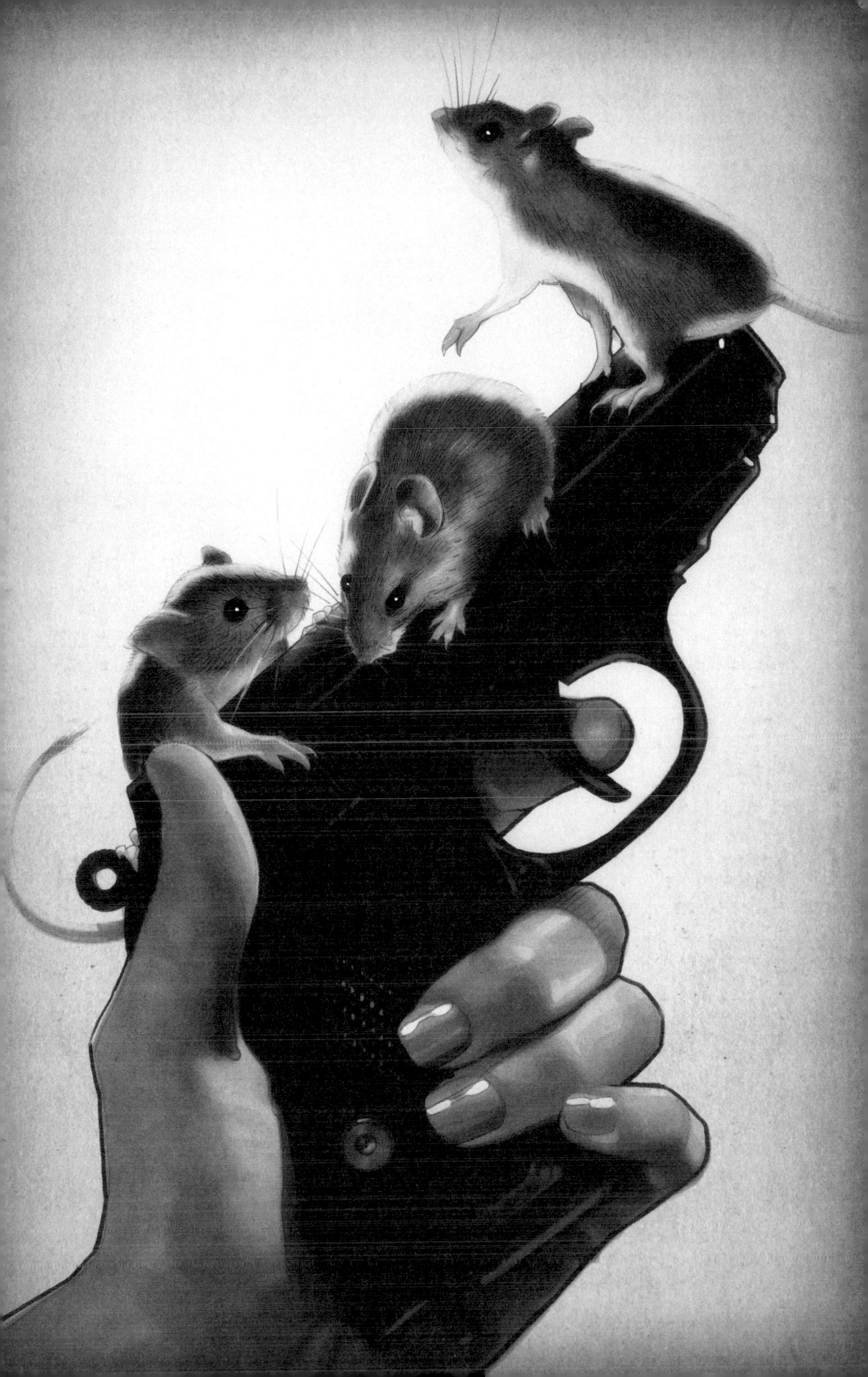

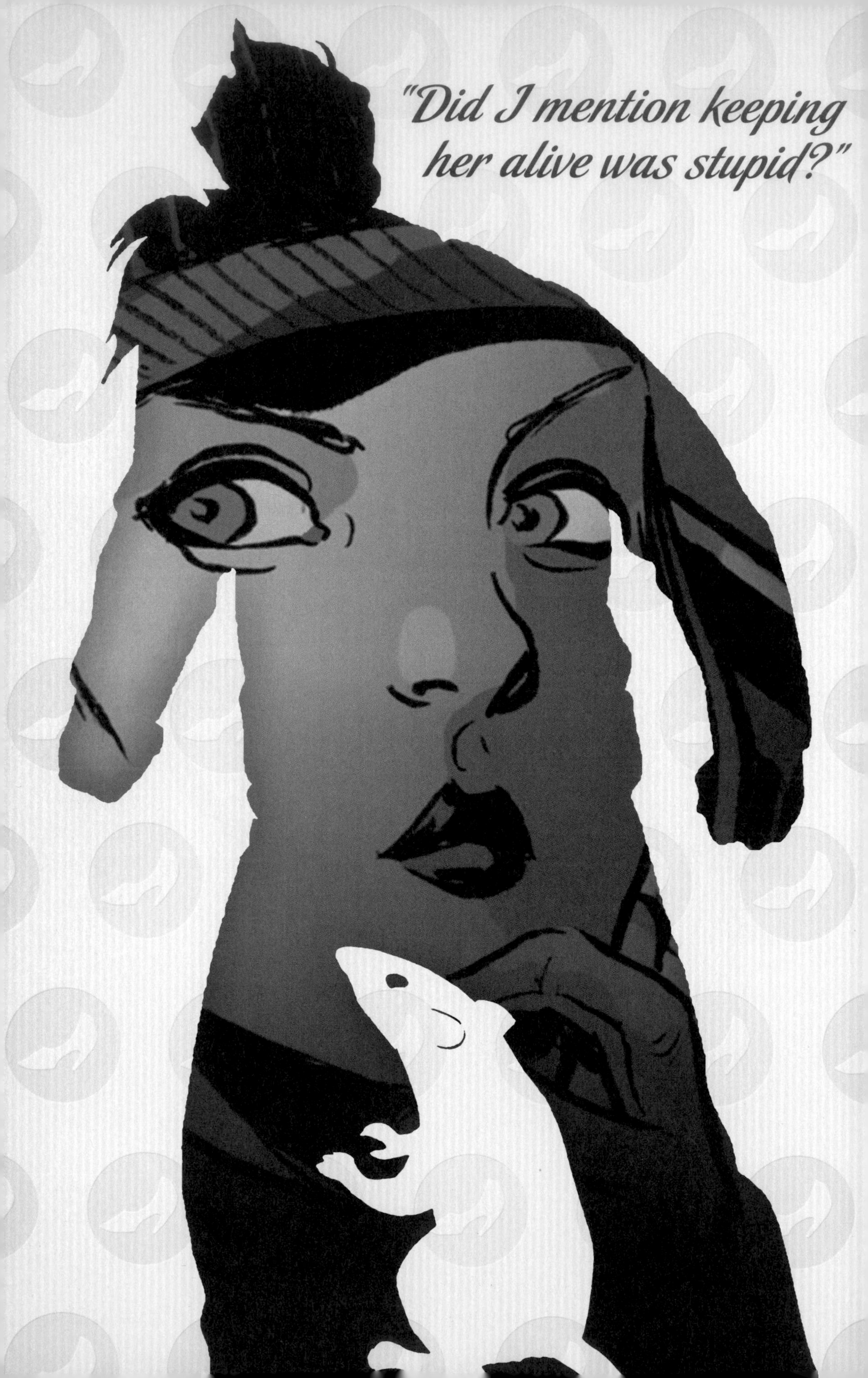
"Did I mention keeping her alive was stupid?"

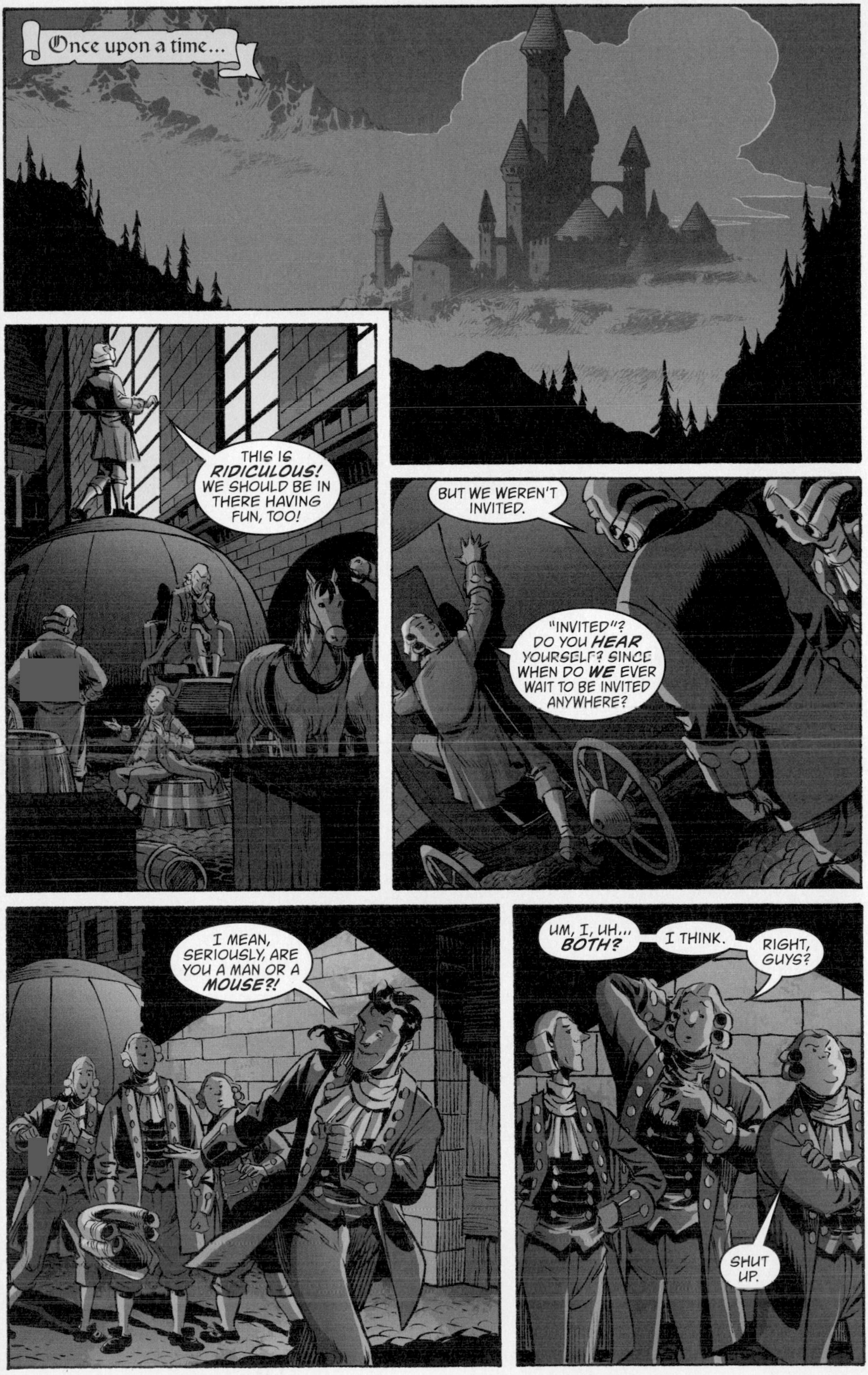
Once upon a time...
THIS IS RIDICULOUS! WE SHOULD BE IN THERE HAVING FUN, TOO!
BUT WE WEREN'T INVITED.
"INVITED"? DO YOU HEAR YOURSELF? SINCE WHEN DO WE EVER WAIT TO BE INVITED ANYWHERE?
I MEAN, SERIOUSLY, ARE YOU A MAN OR A MOUSE?!
UM, I, UH... BOTH?
I THINK.
RIGHT, GUYS?
SHUT UP.

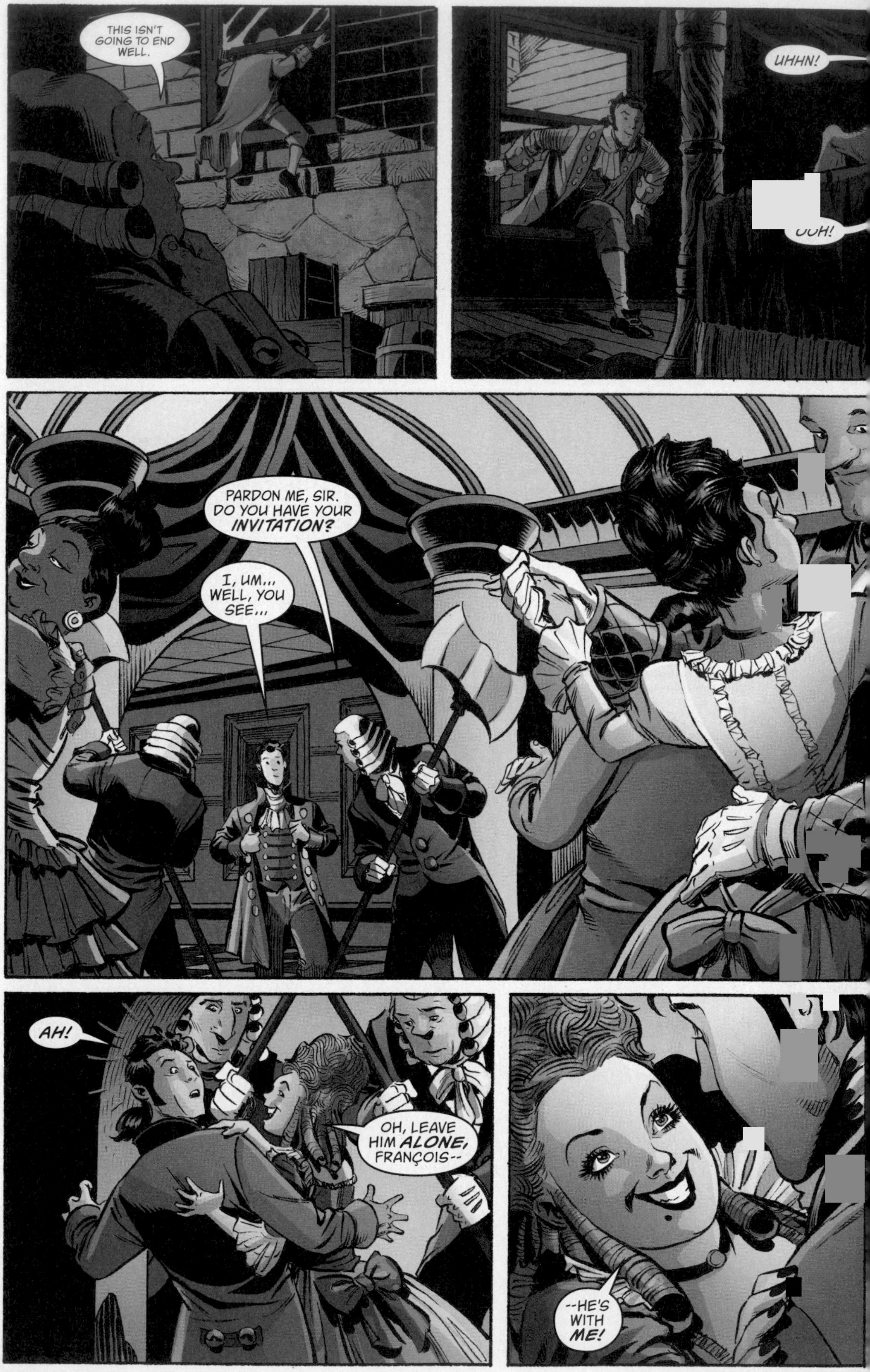
THIS ISN'T GOING TO END WELL.
UHHN!
PARDON ME, SIR. DO YOU HAVE YOUR INVITATION?
I, UM... WELL, YOU SEE...
AH!
OH, LEAVE HIM ALONE, FRANÇOIS--
--HE'S WITH ME!

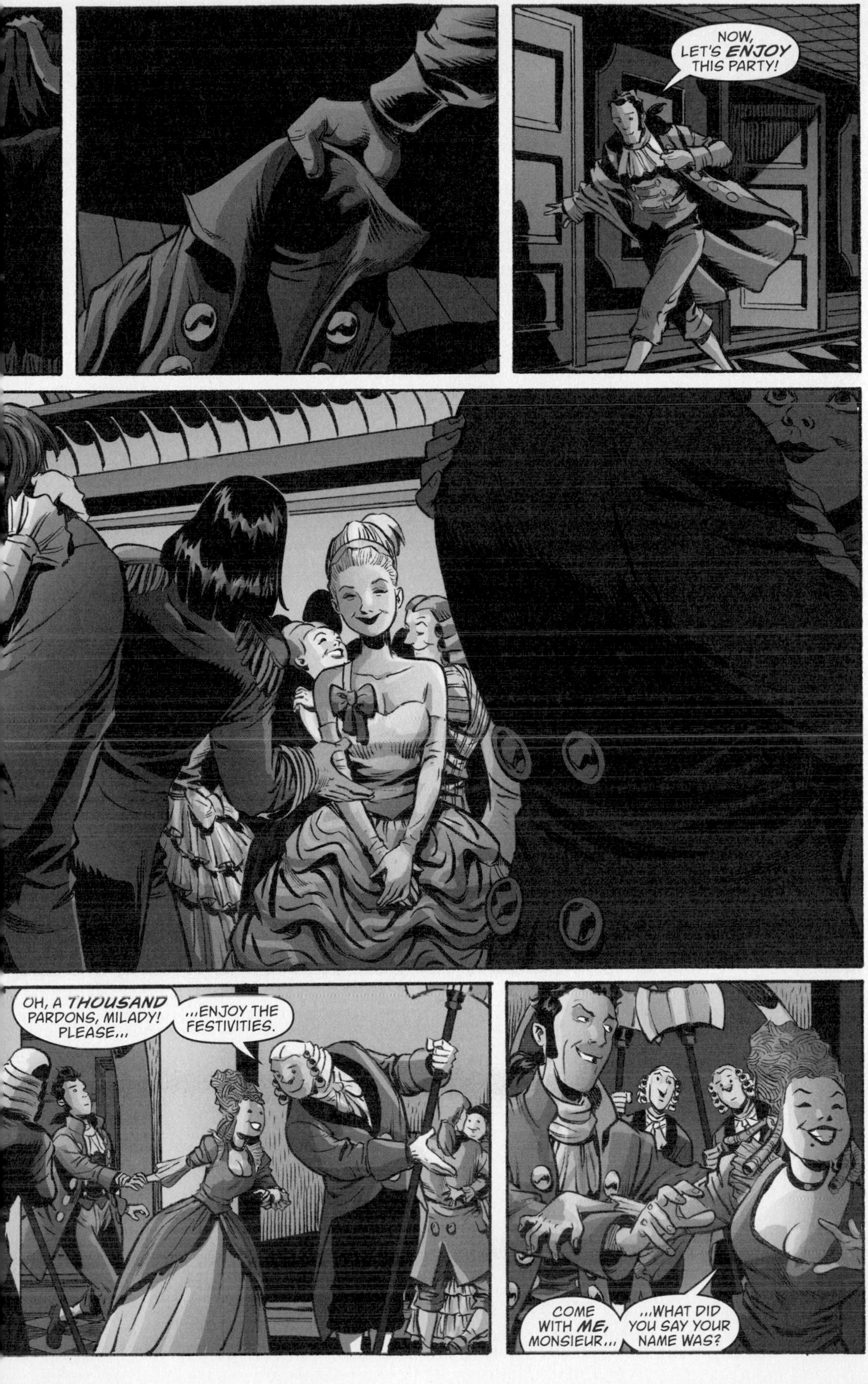
NOW, LET'S ENJOY THIS PARTY!
OH, A THOUSAND PARDONS, MILADY! PLEASE...
...ENJOY THE FESTIVITIES.
COME WITH ME, MONSIEUR...
...WHAT DID YOU SAY YOUR NAME WAS?

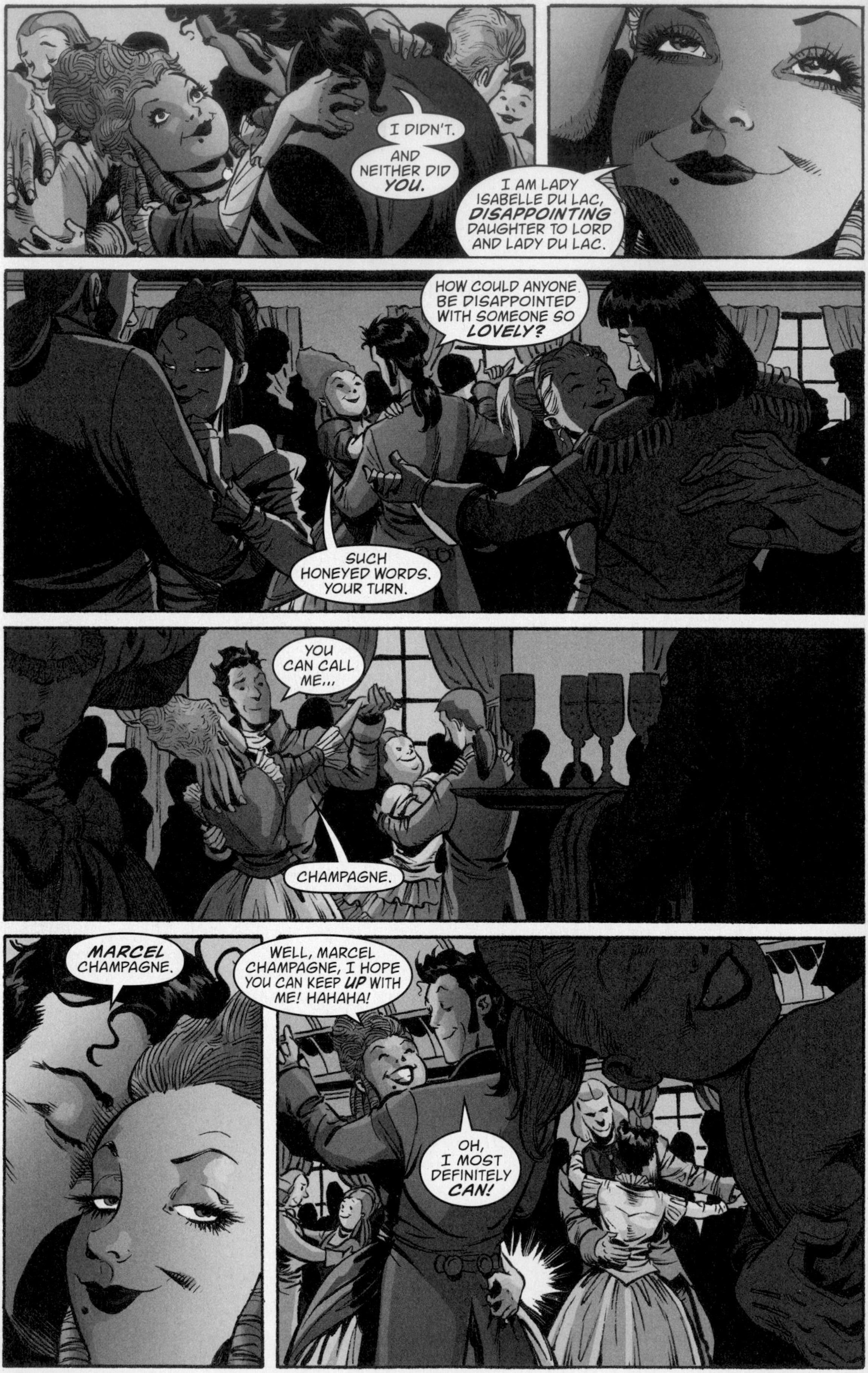
I DIDN'T.
AND NEITHER DID YOU.
I AM LADY ISABELLE DU LAC, DISAPPOINTING DAUGHTER TO LORD AND LADY DU LAC.
HOW COULD ANYONE BE DISAPPOINTED WITH SOMEONE SO LOVELY?
SUCH HONEYED WORDS. YOUR TURN.
YOU CAN CALL ME...
CHAMPAGNE.
MARCEL CHAMPAGNE.
WELL, MARCEL CHAMPAGNE, I HOPE YOU CAN KEEP UP WITH ME! HAHAHA!
OH, I MOST DEFINITELY CAN!

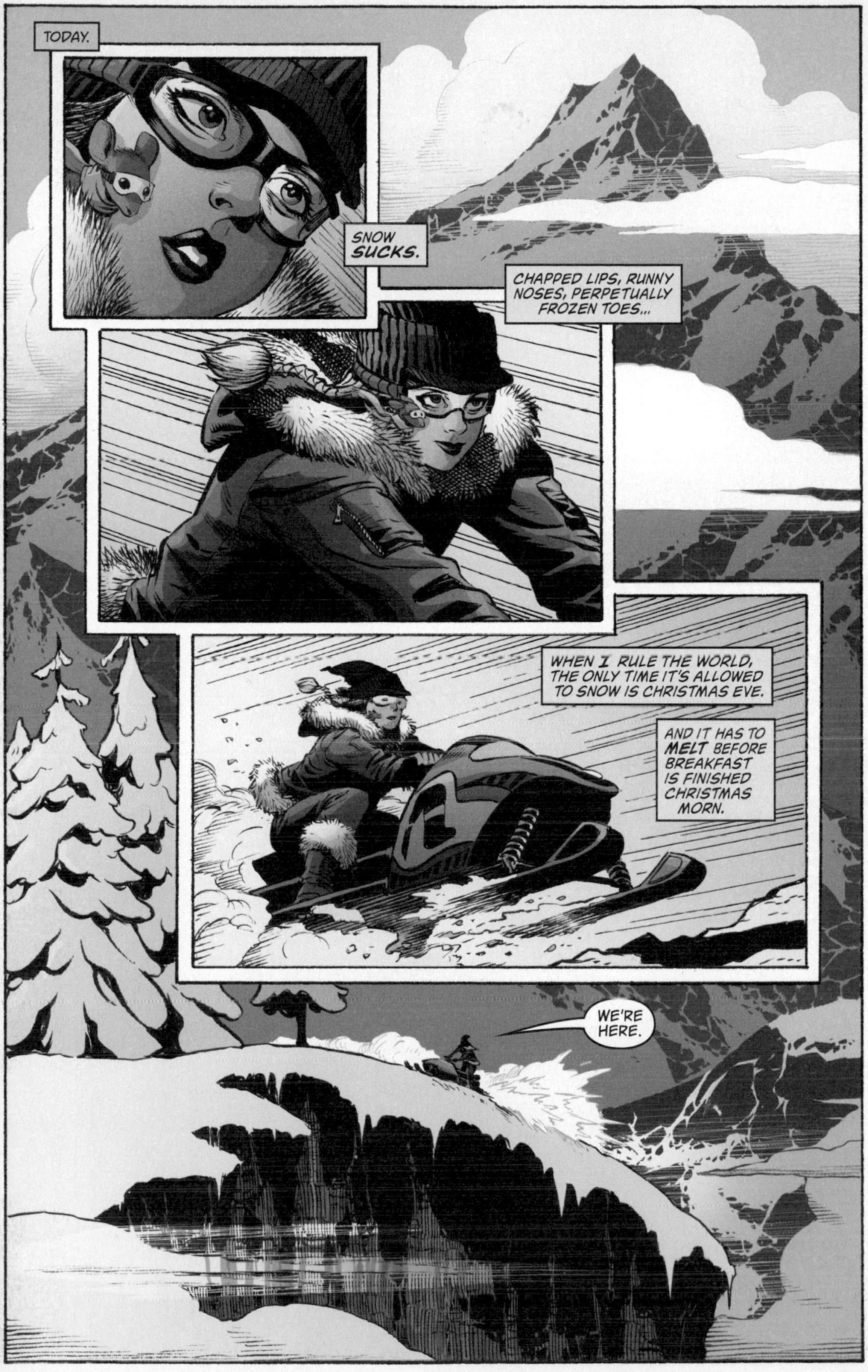
TODAY.
SNOW SUCKS.
CHAPPED LIPS, RUNNY NOSES, PERPETUALLY FROZEN TOES...
WHEN I RULE THE WORLD, THE ONLY TIME IT'S ALLOWED TO SNOW IS CHRISTMAS EVE.
AND IT HAS TO MELT BEFORE BREAKFAST IS FINISHED CHRISTMAS MORN.
WE'RE HERE.

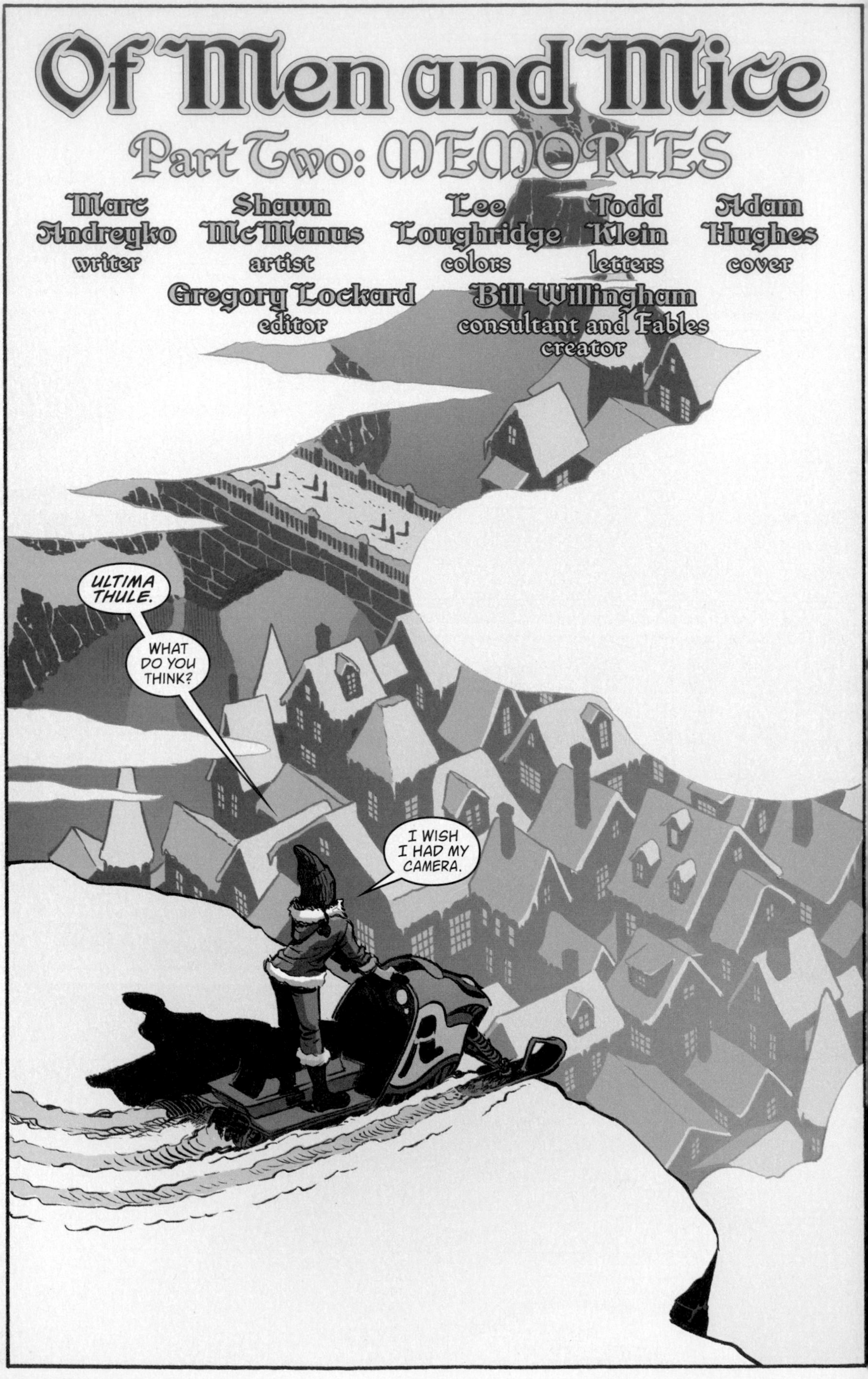
Of Men and Mice
Part Two: MEMORIES
Marc Andreyko writer
Shawn McManus artist
Lee Loughridge colors
Todd Klein letters
Adam Hughes cover
Gregory Lockard editor
Bill Willingham consultant and Fables creator
ULTIMA THULE.
WHAT DO YOU THINK?
I WISH I HAD MY CAMERA.

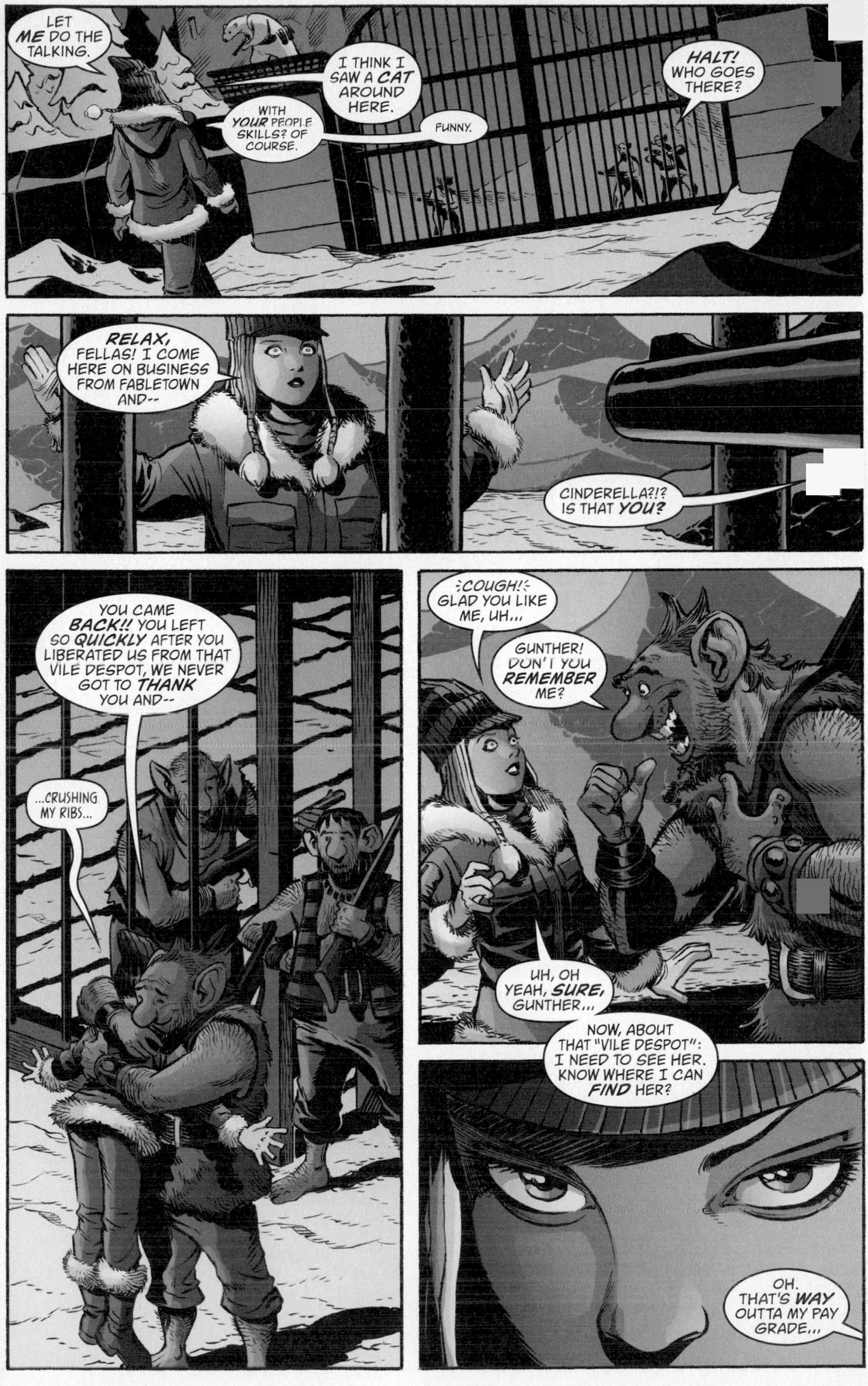
LET ME DO THE TALKING.
I THINK I SAW A CAT AROUND HERE.
WITH YOUR PEOPLE SKILLS? OF COURSE.
FUNNY.
HALT! WHO GOES THERE?
RELAX, FELLAS! I COME HERE ON BUSINESS FROM FABLETOWN AND--
CINDERELLA?!? IS THAT YOU?
YOU CAME BACK!! YOU LEFT SO QUICKLY AFTER YOU LIBERATED US FROM THAT VILE DESPOT, WE NEVER GOT TO THANK YOU AND--
...CRUSHING MY RIBS...
COUGH! GLAD YOU LIKE ME, UH...
GUNTHER! DON'T YOU REMEMBER ME?
UH, OH YEAH, SURE, GUNTHER...
NOW, ABOUT THAT "VILE DESPOT": I NEED TO SEE HER. KNOW WHERE I CAN FIND HER?
OH. THAT'S WAY OUTTA MY PAY GRADE...

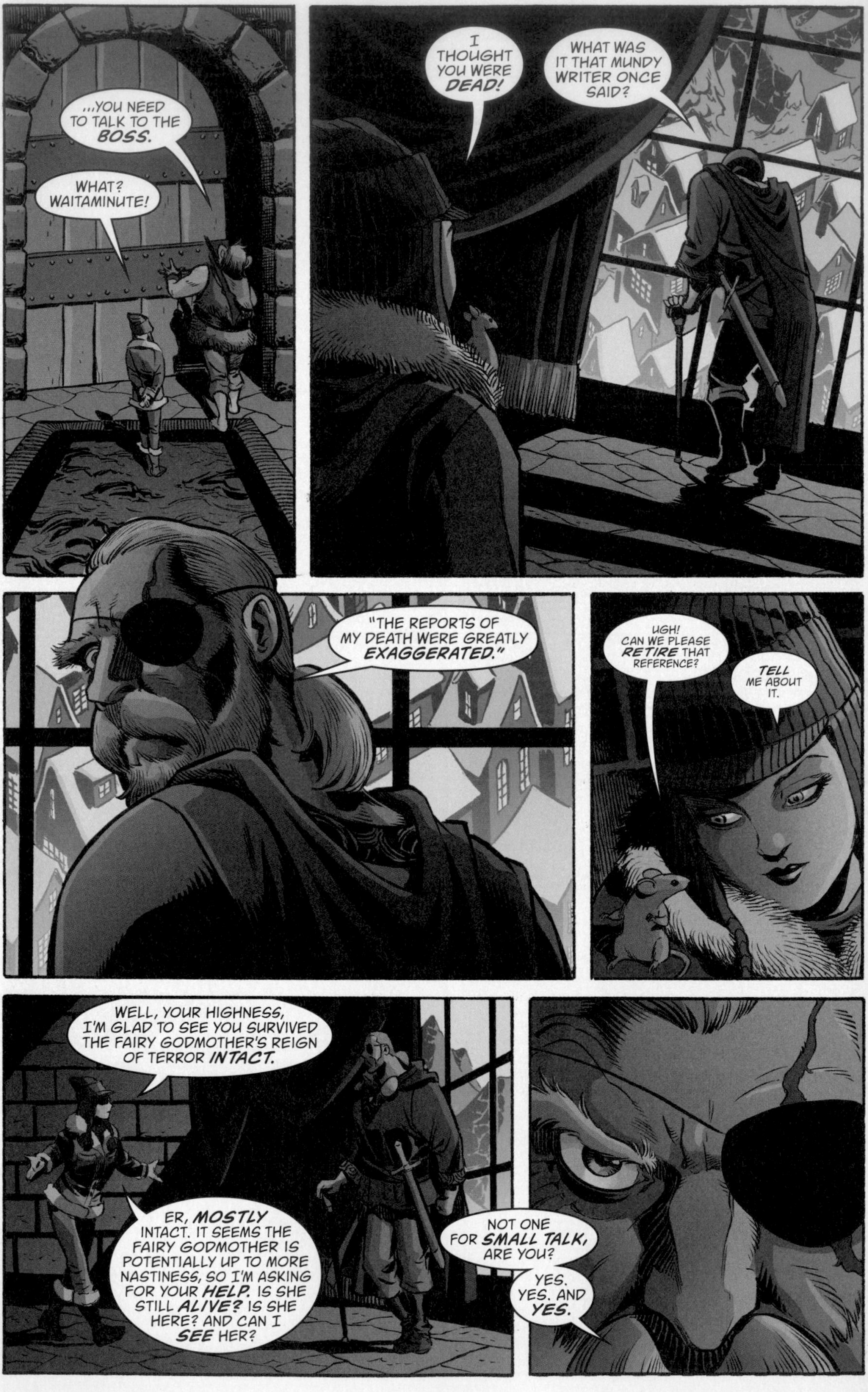
...YOU NEED TO TALK TO THE BOSS.
WHAT? WAITAMINUTE!
I THOUGHT YOU WERE DEAD!
WHAT WAS IT THAT MUNDY WRITER ONCE SAID?
"THE REPORTS OF MY DEATH WERE GREATLY EXAGGERATED."
UGH! CAN WE PLEASE RETIRE THAT REFERENCE?
TELL ME ABOUT IT.
WELL, YOUR HIGHNESS, I'M GLAD TO SEE YOU SURVIVED THE FAIRY GODMOTHER'S REIGN OF TERROR INTACT.
ER, MOSTLY INTACT. IT SEEMS THE FAIRY GODMOTHER IS POTENTIALLY UP TO MORE NASTINESS, SO I'M ASKING FOR YOUR HELP. IS SHE STILL ALIVE? IS SHE HERE? AND CAN I SEE HER?
NOT ONE FOR SMALL TALK, ARE YOU?
YES. YES. AND YES.

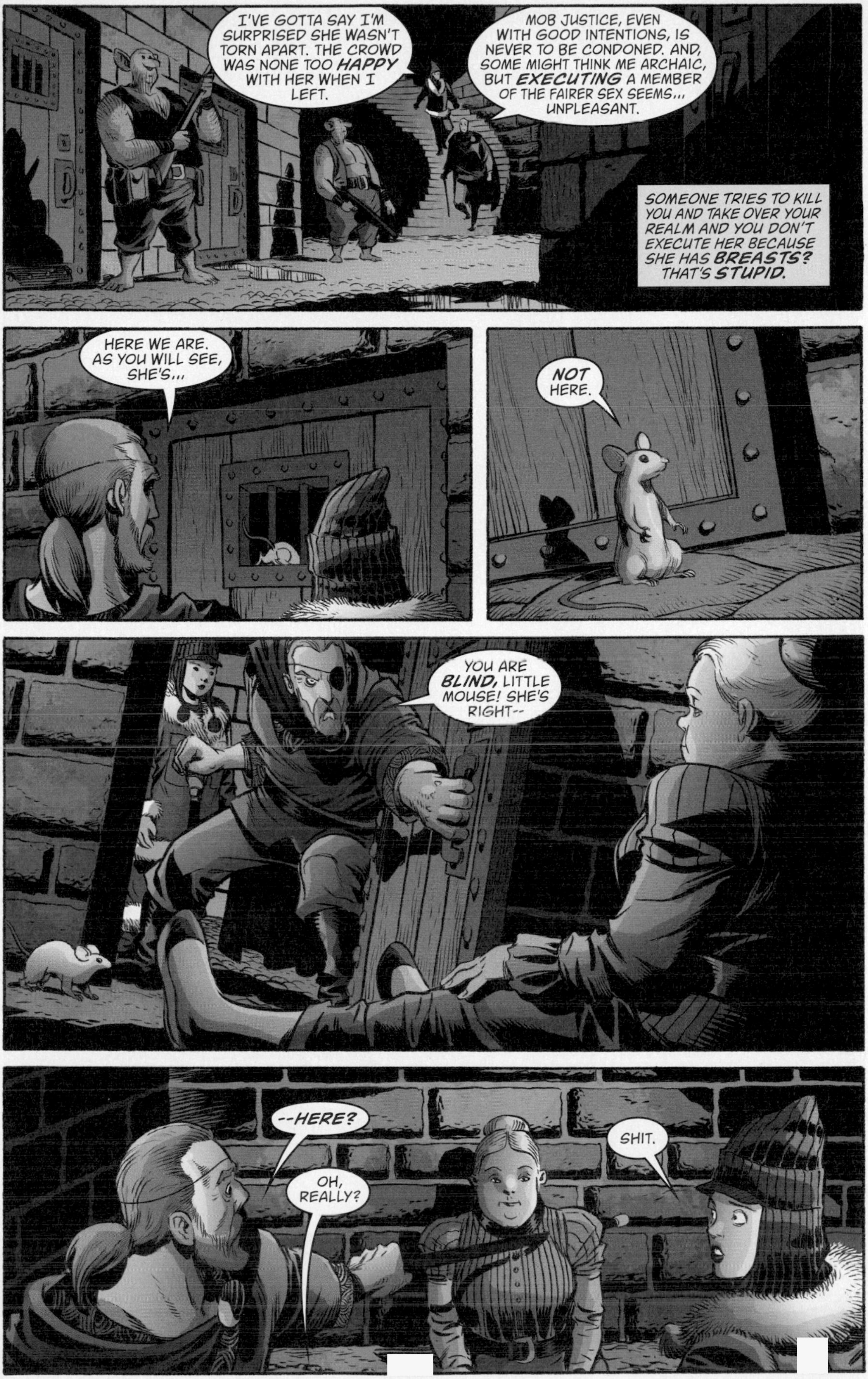
I'VE GOTTA SAY I'M SURPRISED SHE WASN'T TORN APART. THE CROWD WAS NONE TOO HAPPY WITH HER WHEN I LEFT.
MOB JUSTICE, EVEN WITH GOOD INTENTIONS, IS NEVER TO BE CONDONED. AND, SOME MIGHT THINK ME ARCHAIC, BUT EXECUTING A MEMBER OF THE FAIRER SEX SEEMS... UNPLEASANT.
SOMEONE TRIES TO KILL YOU AND TAKE OVER YOUR REALM AND YOU DON'T EXECUTE HER BECAUSE SHE HAS BREASTS? THAT'S STUPID.
HERE WE ARE. AS YOU WILL SEE, SHE'S...
NOT HERE.
YOU ARE BLIND, LITTLE MOUSE! SHE'S RIGHT--
--HERE?
OH, REALLY?
SHIT.

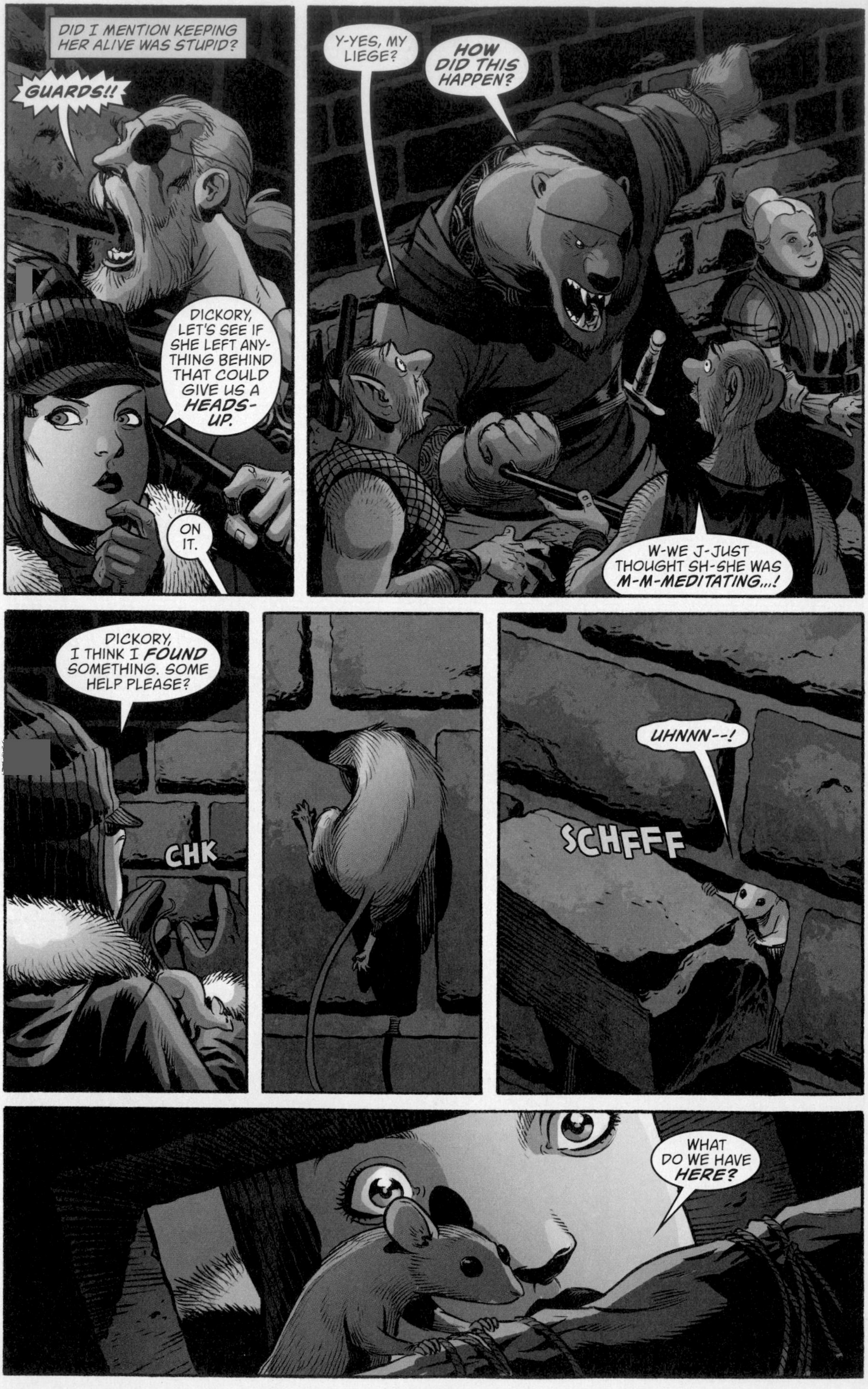
DID I MENTION KEEPING HER ALIVE WAS STUPID?
GUARDS!!
DICKORY, LET'S SEE IF SHE LEFT ANYTHING BEHIND THAT COULD GIVE US A HEADS-UP.
ON IT.
Y-YES, MY LIEGE?
HOW DID THIS HAPPEN?
W-WE J-JUST THOUGHT SH-SHE WAS M-M-MEDITATING...!
DICKORY, I THINK I FOUND SOMETHING. SOME HELP PLEASE?
CHK
UHNNN--!
SCHFFF
WHAT DO WE HAVE HERE?

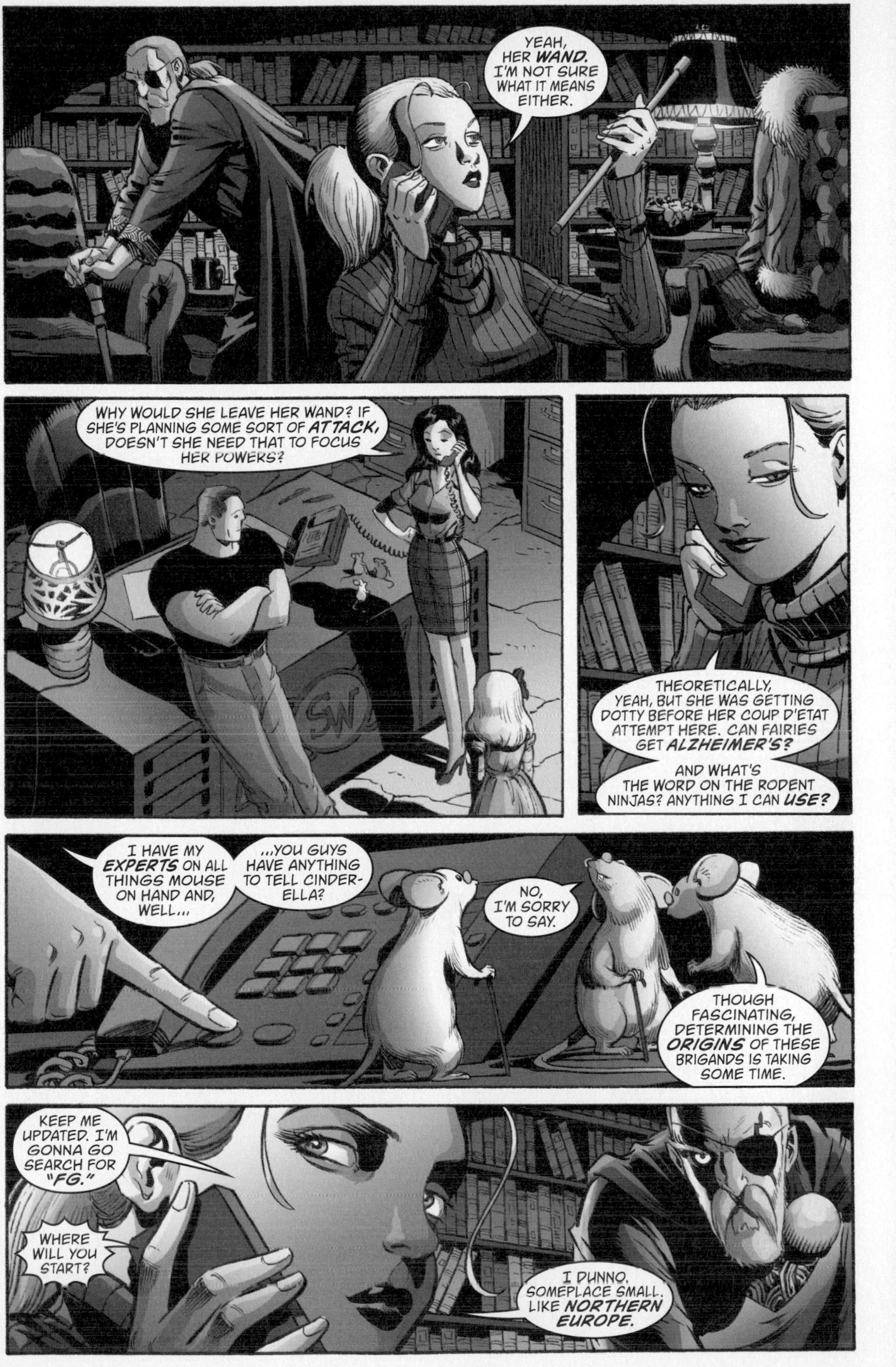
YEAH, HER *WAND*. I'M NOT SURE WHAT IT MEANS EITHER.
WHY WOULD SHE LEAVE HER WAND? IF SHE'S PLANNING SOME SORT OF *ATTACK*, DOESN'T SHE NEED THAT TO FOCUS HER POWERS?
THEORETICALLY, YEAH, BUT SHE WAS GETTING DOTTY BEFORE HER COUP D'ETAT ATTEMPT HERE. CAN FAIRIES GET *ALZHEIMER'S?*
AND WHAT'S THE WORD ON THE RODENT NINJAS? ANYTHING I CAN *USE?*
I HAVE MY *EXPERTS* ON ALL THINGS MOUSE ON HAND AND, WELL...
...YOU GUYS HAVE ANYTHING TO TELL CINDERELLA?
NO, I'M SORRY TO SAY.
THOUGH FASCINATING, DETERMINING THE *ORIGINS* OF THESE BRIGANDS IS TAKING SOME TIME.
KEEP ME UPDATED. I'M GONNA GO SEARCH FOR *"FG."*
WHERE WILL YOU START?
I DUNNO, SOMEPLACE SMALL. LIKE *NORTHERN EUROPE*.

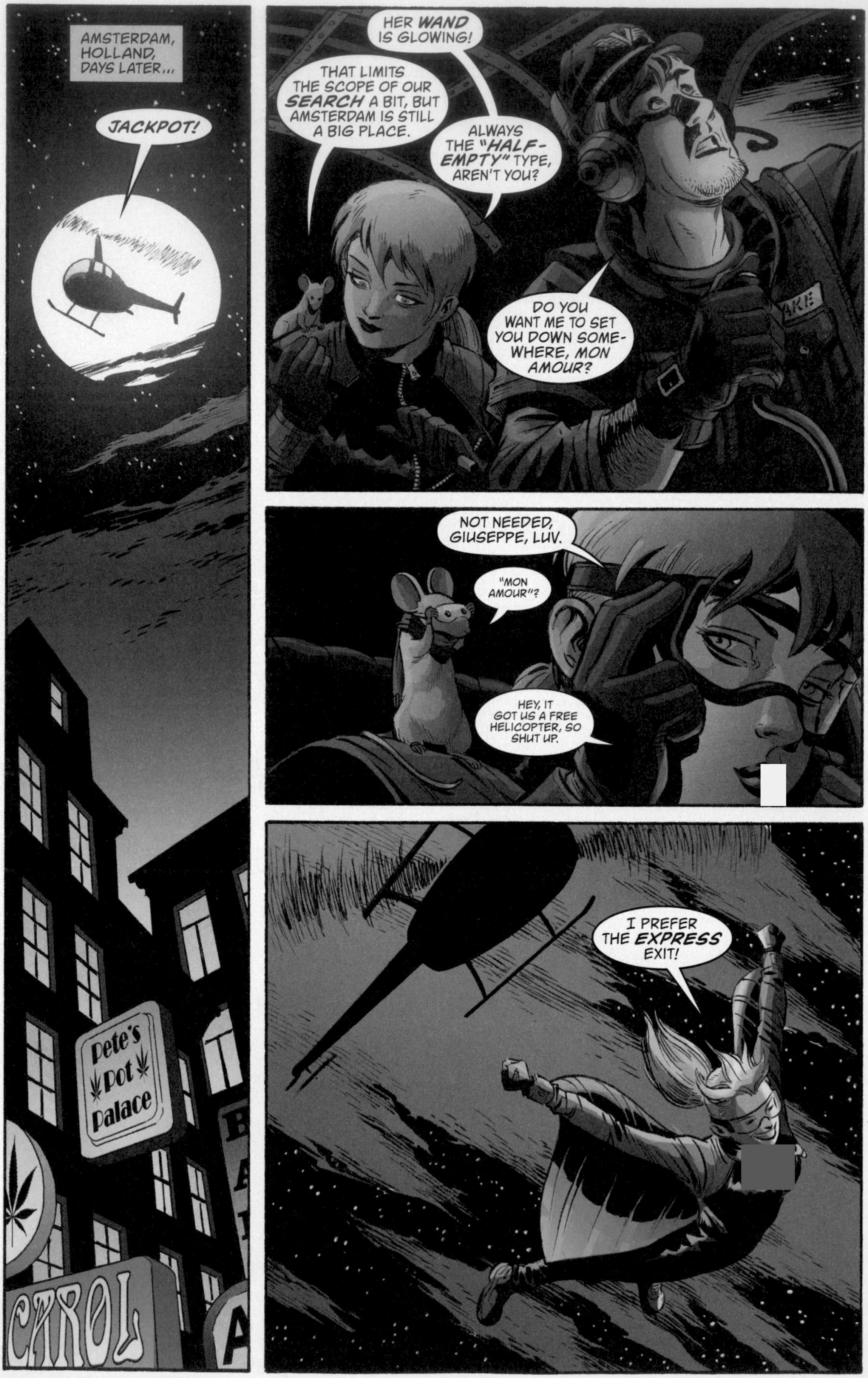
AMSTERDAM, HOLLAND, DAYS LATER...
JACKPOT!
Pete's Pot Palace
CAROL
HER WAND IS GLOWING!
THAT LIMITS THE SCOPE OF OUR SEARCH A BIT, BUT AMSTERDAM IS STILL A BIG PLACE.
ALWAYS THE "HALF-EMPTY" TYPE, AREN'T YOU?
DO YOU WANT ME TO SET YOU DOWN SOME-WHERE, MON AMOUR?
NOT NEEDED, GIUSEPPE, LUV.
"MON AMOUR"?
HEY, IT GOT US A FREE HELICOPTER, SO SHUT UP.
I PREFER THE EXPRESS EXIT!

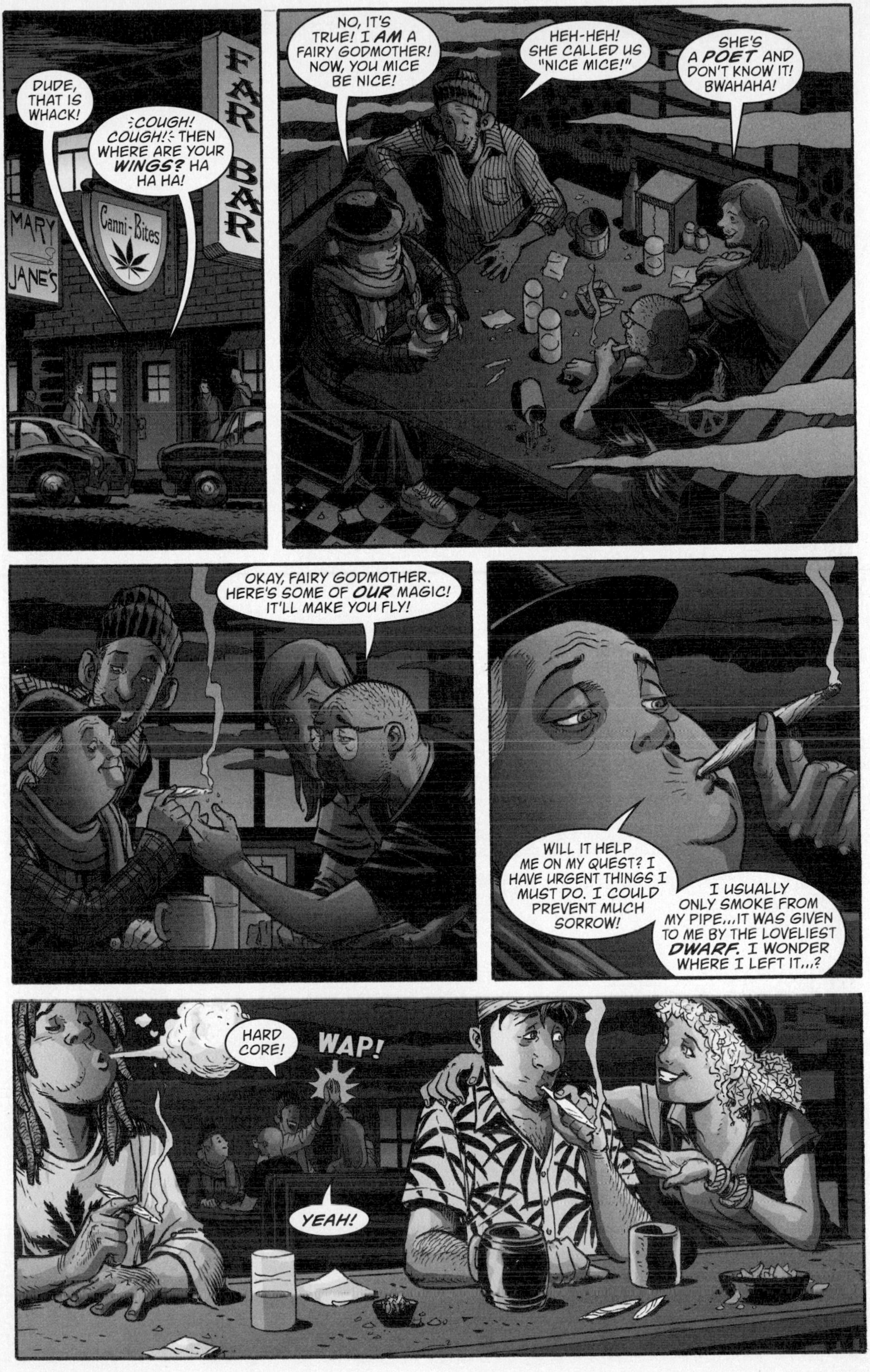
FAR BAR
MARY JANE'S
Canni-Bites
DUDE, THAT IS WHACK!
COUGH! COUGH! THEN WHERE ARE YOUR WINGS? HA HA HA!
NO, IT'S TRUE! I AM A FAIRY GODMOTHER! NOW, YOU MICE BE NICE!
HEH-HEH! SHE CALLED US "NICE MICE!"
SHE'S A POET AND DON'T KNOW IT! BWAHAHA!
OKAY, FAIRY GODMOTHER. HERE'S SOME OF OUR MAGIC! IT'LL MAKE YOU FLY!
WILL IT HELP ME ON MY QUEST? I HAVE URGENT THINGS I MUST DO. I COULD PREVENT MUCH SORROW!
I USUALLY ONLY SMOKE FROM MY PIPE...IT WAS GIVEN TO ME BY THE LOVELIEST DWARF. I WONDER WHERE I LEFT IT...?
HARD CORE!
WAP!
YEAH!

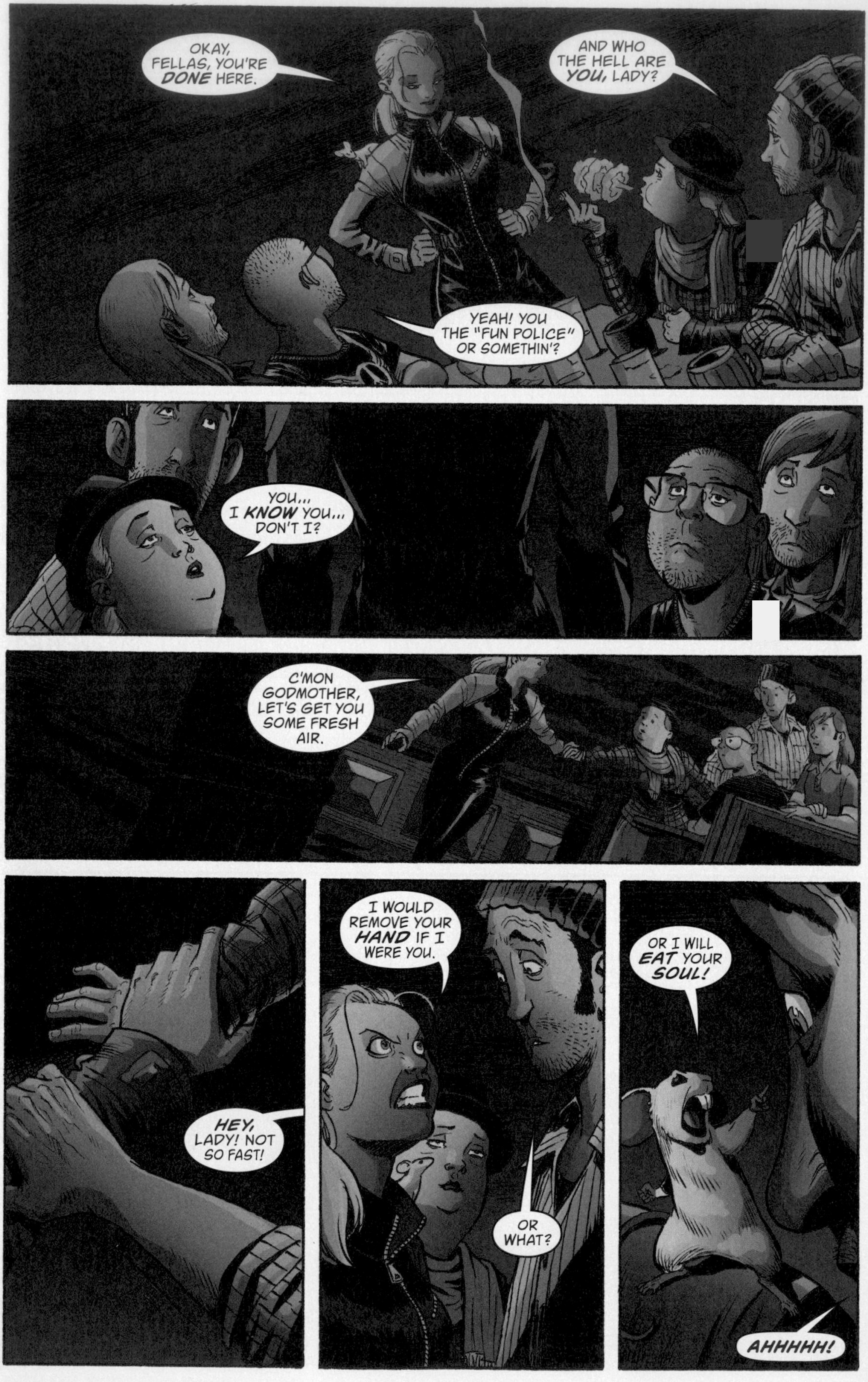
OKAY, FELLAS, YOU'RE DONE HERE.
AND WHO THE HELL ARE YOU, LADY?
YEAH! YOU THE "FUN POLICE" OR SOMETHIN'?
YOU... I KNOW YOU... DON'T I?
C'MON GODMOTHER, LET'S GET YOU SOME FRESH AIR.
HEY, LADY! NOT SO FAST!
I WOULD REMOVE YOUR HAND IF I WERE YOU.
OR WHAT?
OR I WILL EAT YOUR SOUL!
AHHHHH!

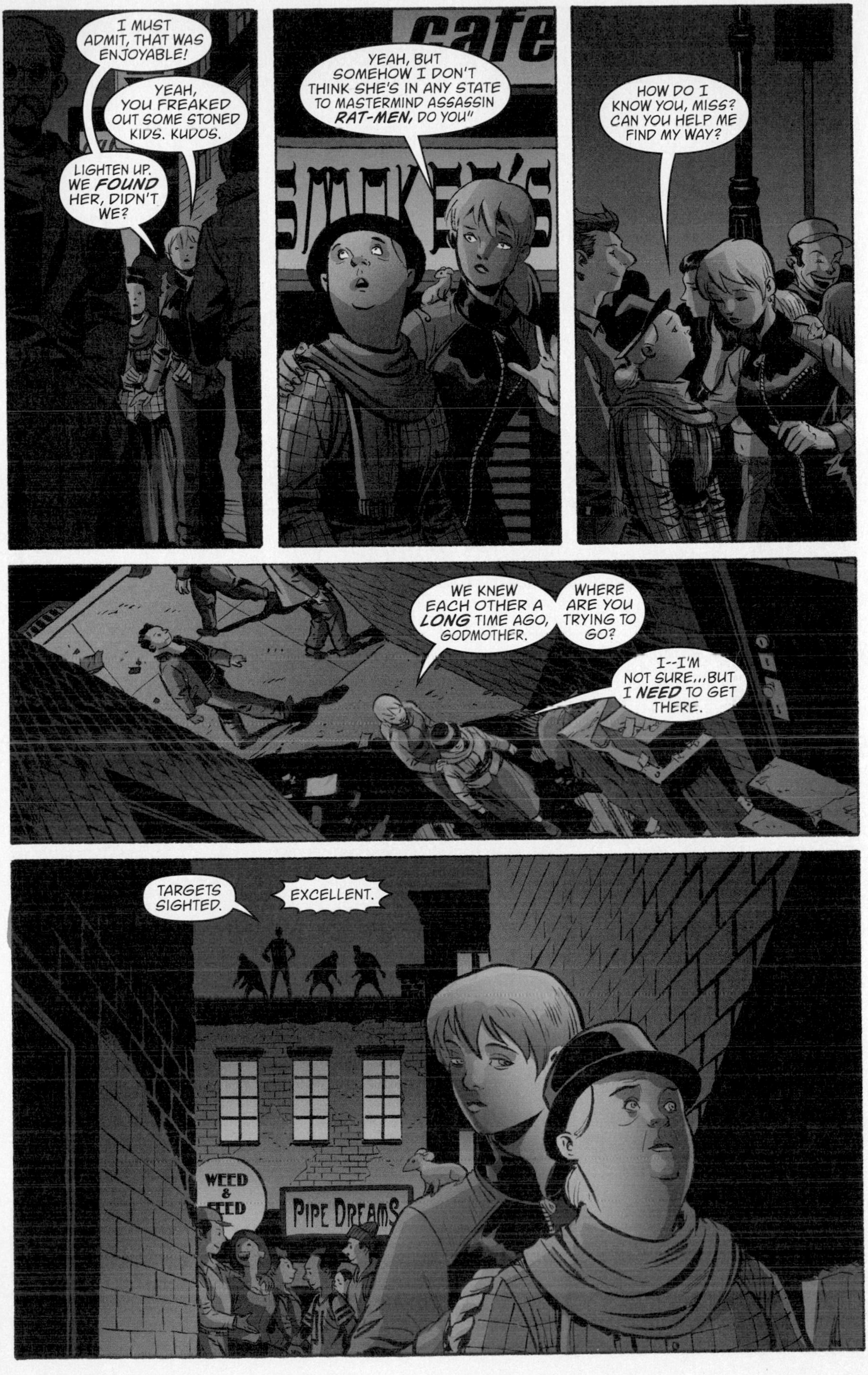
I MUST ADMIT, THAT WAS ENJOYABLE!
YEAH, YOU FREAKED OUT SOME STONED KIDS. KUDOS.
LIGHTEN UP. WE FOUND HER, DIDN'T WE?
cafe
YEAH, BUT SOMEHOW I DON'T THINK SHE'S IN ANY STATE TO MASTERMIND ASSASSIN RAT-MEN, DO YOU"
HOW DO I KNOW YOU, MISS? CAN YOU HELP ME FIND MY WAY?
WE KNEW EACH OTHER A LONG TIME AGO, GODMOTHER.
WHERE ARE YOU TRYING TO GO?
I--I'M NOT SURE...BUT I NEED TO GET THERE.
TARGETS SIGHTED.
EXCELLENT.
WEED & FEED
PIPE DREAMS

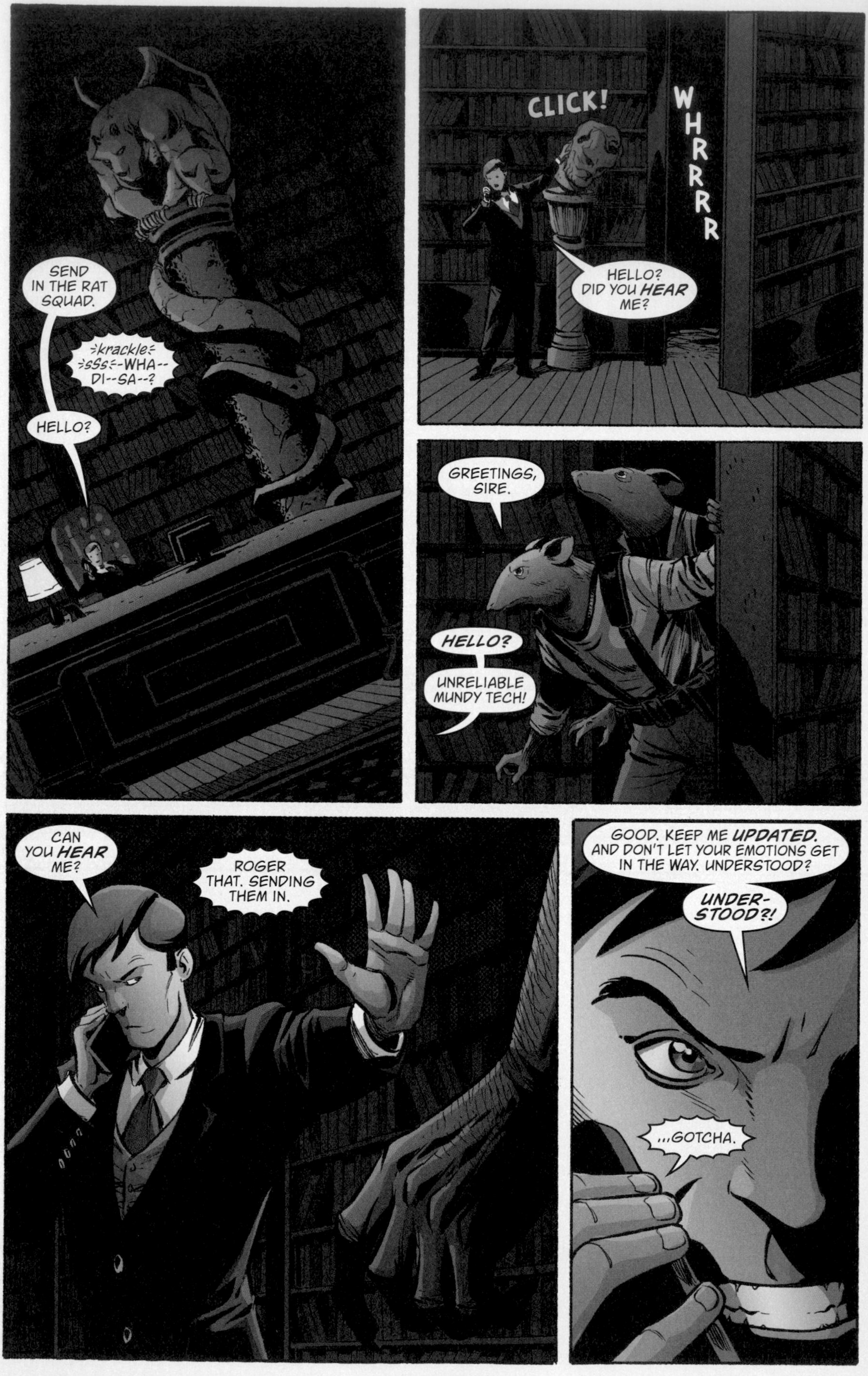
SEND IN THE RAT SQUAD.
krackle sSs-WHA--DI--SA--?
HELLO?
CLICK!
WHRRRR
HELLO? DID YOU HEAR ME?
GREETINGS, SIRE.
HELLO?
UNRELIABLE MUNDY TECH!
CAN YOU HEAR ME?
ROGER THAT. SENDING THEM IN.
GOOD. KEEP ME UPDATED. AND DON'T LET YOUR EMOTIONS GET IN THE WAY. UNDERSTOOD?
UNDER-STOOD?!
...GOTCHA.

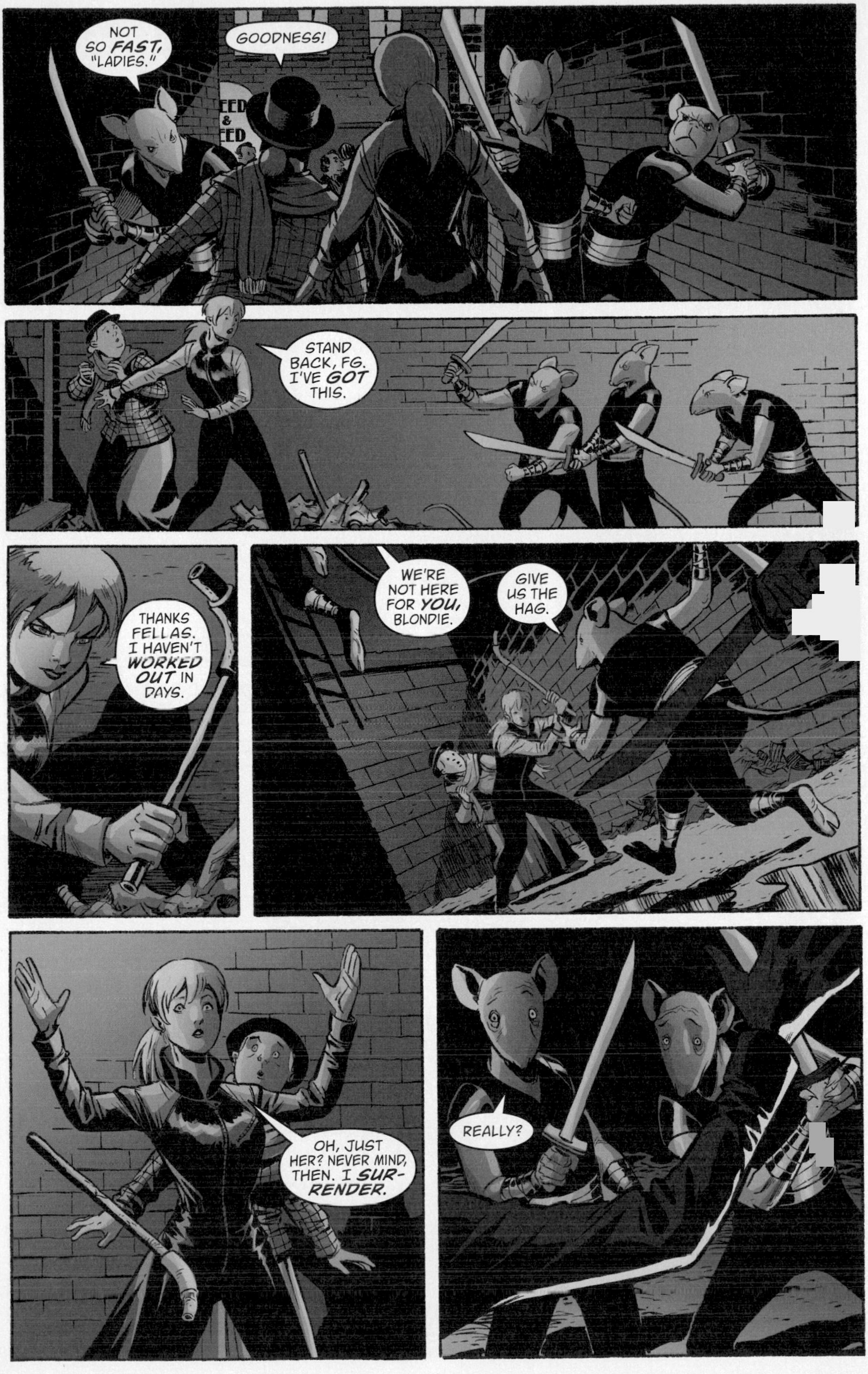
NOT SO FAST, "LADIES."
GOODNESS!
STAND BACK, FG. I'VE GOT THIS.
THANKS FELLAS. I HAVEN'T WORKED OUT IN DAYS.
WE'RE NOT HERE FOR YOU, BLONDIE.
GIVE US THE HAG.
OH, JUST HER? NEVER MIND, THEN. I SURRENDER.
REALLY?

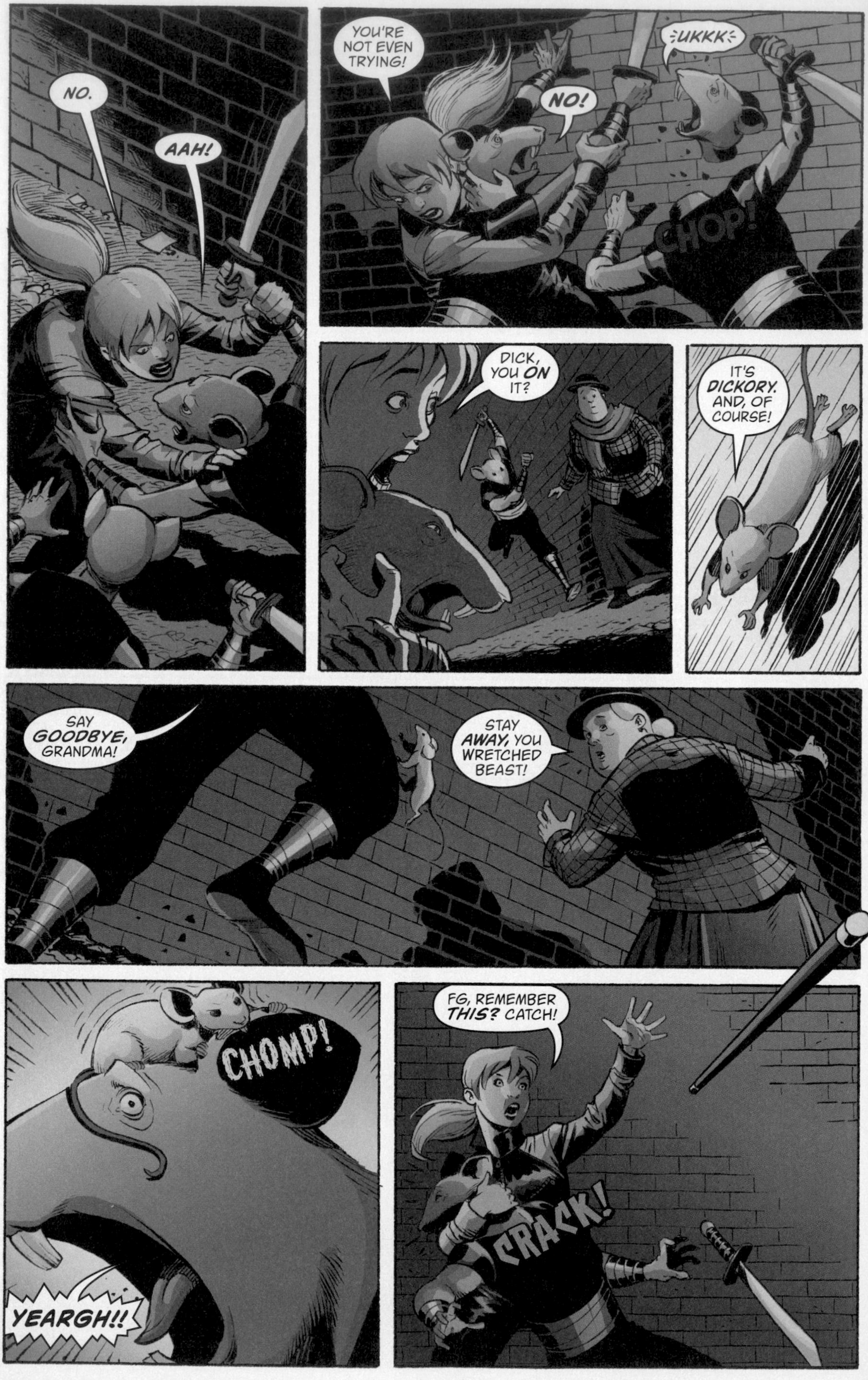
NO.
AAH!
YOU'RE NOT EVEN TRYING!
NO!
UKKK
CHOP!
DICK, YOU ON IT?
IT'S DICKORY. AND, OF COURSE!
SAY GOODBYE, GRANDMA!
STAY AWAY, YOU WRETCHED BEAST!
CHOMP!
YEARGH!!
FG, REMEMBER THIS? CATCH!
CRACK!

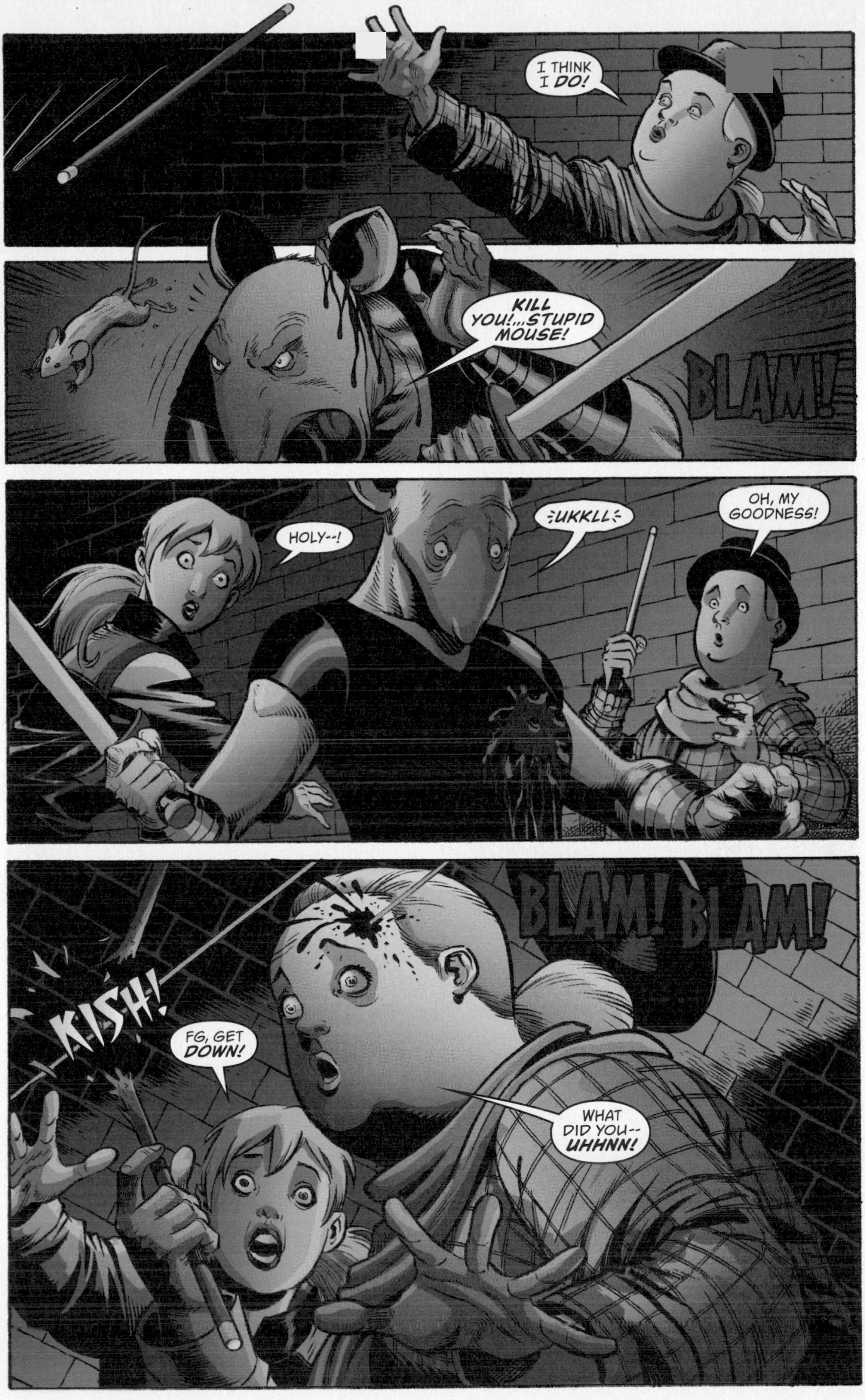

I THINK I DO!
KILL YOU!...STUPID MOUSE!
BLAM!
HOLY--!
UKKLL
OH, MY GOODNESS!
BLAM! BLAM!
KISH!
FG, GET DOWN!
WHAT DID YOU-- UHHNN!

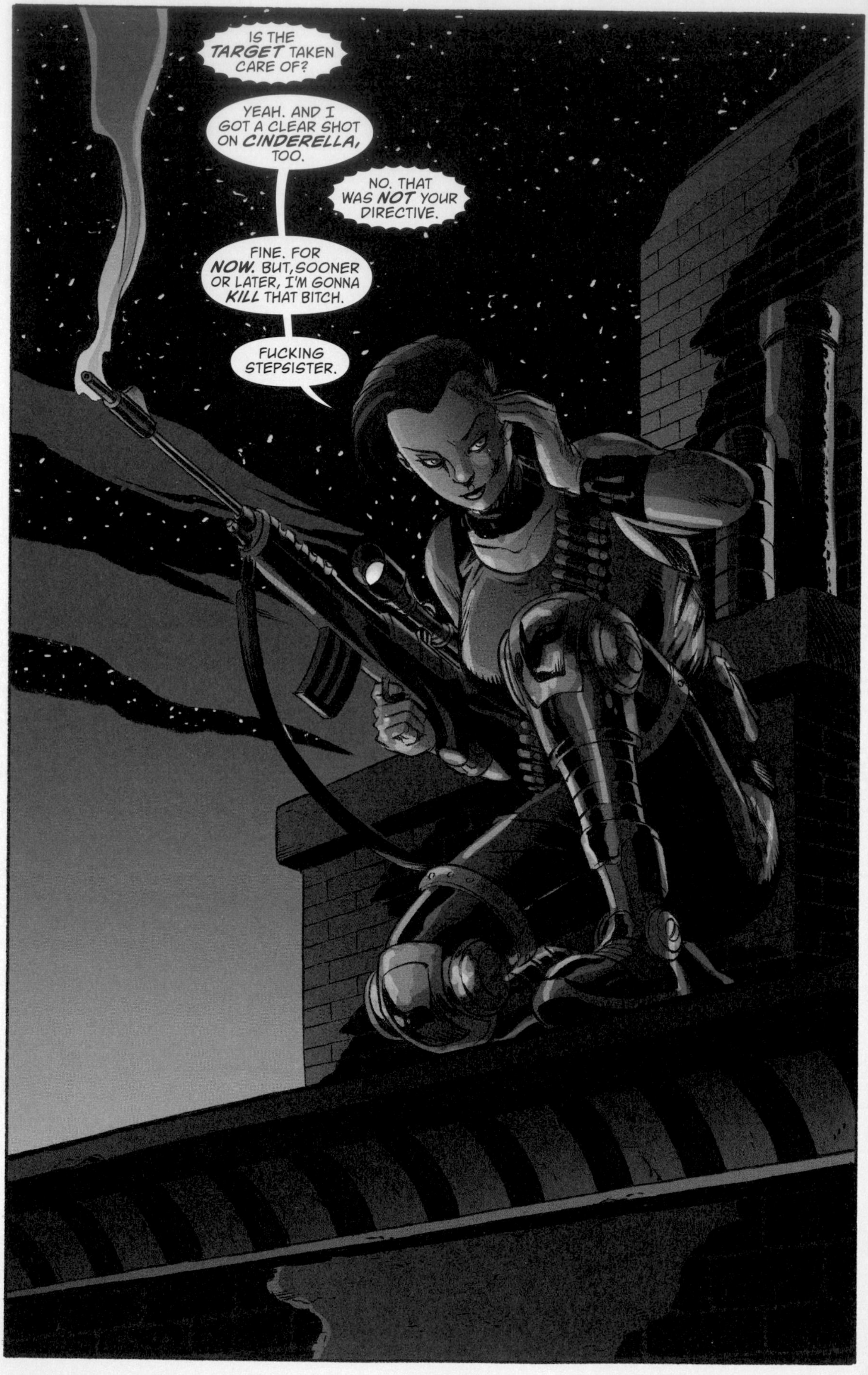
IS THE TARGET TAKEN CARE OF?
YEAH. AND I GOT A CLEAR SHOT ON CINDERELLA, TOO.
NO. THAT WAS NOT YOUR DIRECTIVE.
FINE. FOR NOW. BUT, SOONER OR LATER, I'M GONNA KILL THAT BITCH.
FUCKING STEPSISTER.

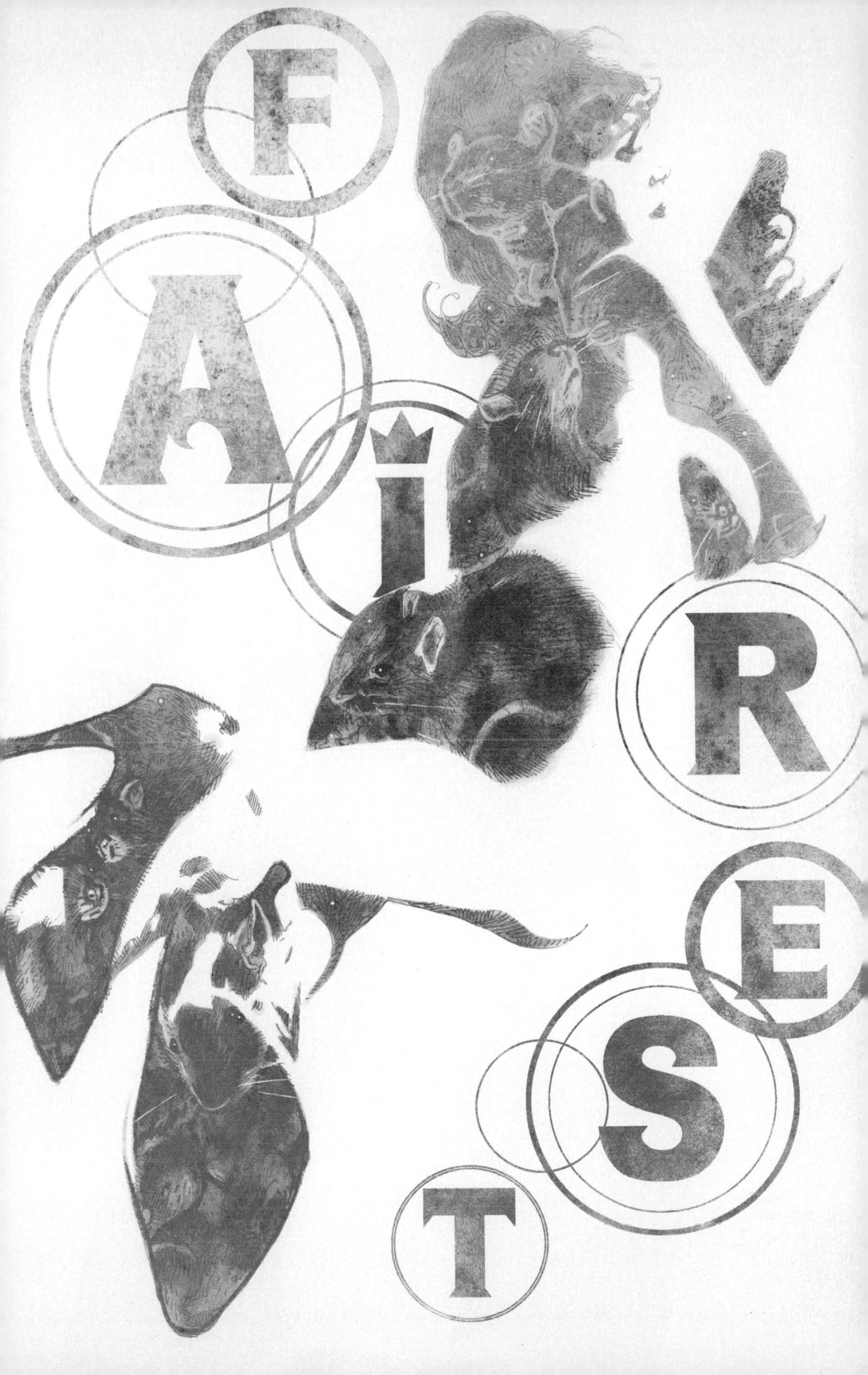
F
A
i
R
E
S
T

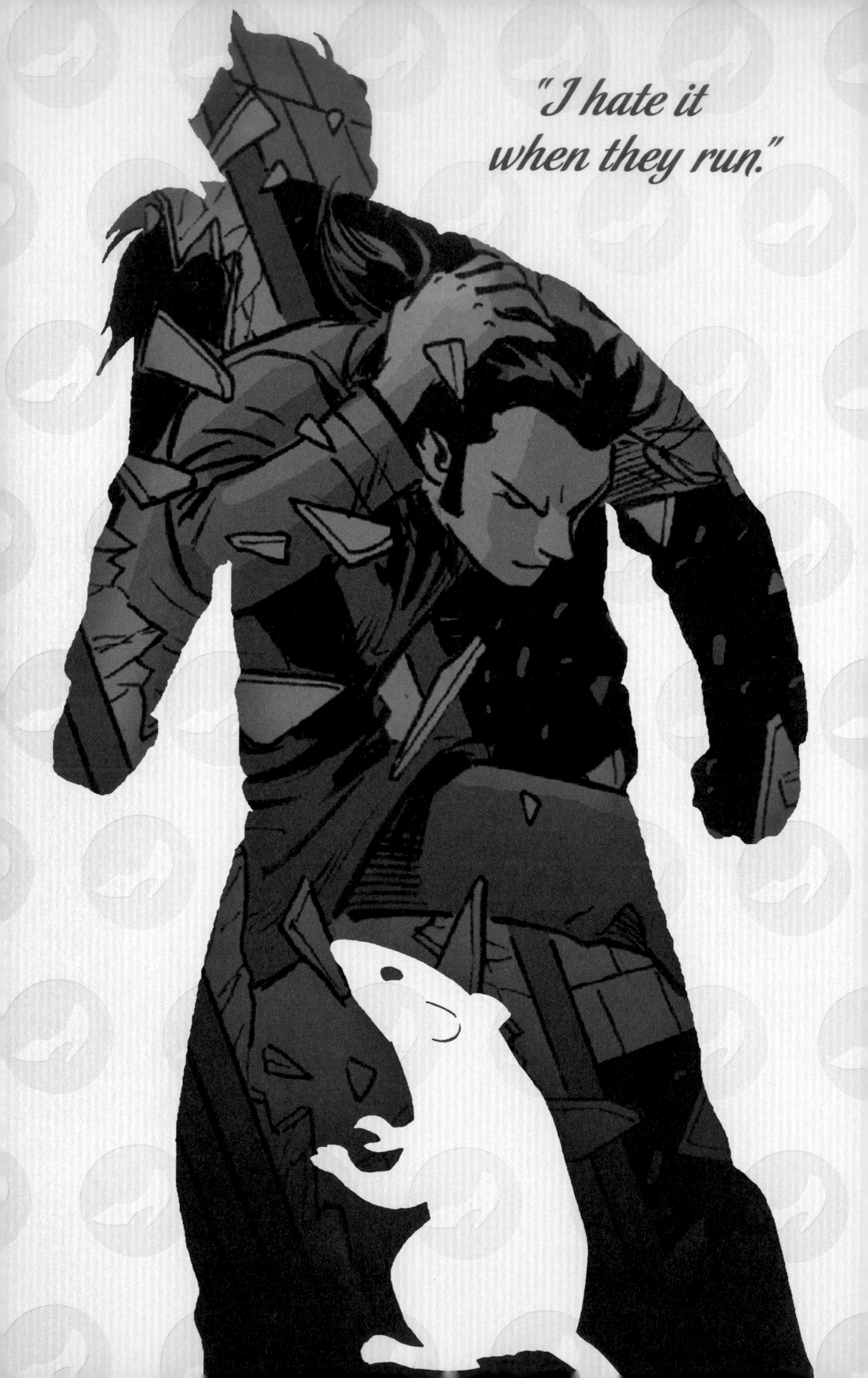
"I hate it
when they run."

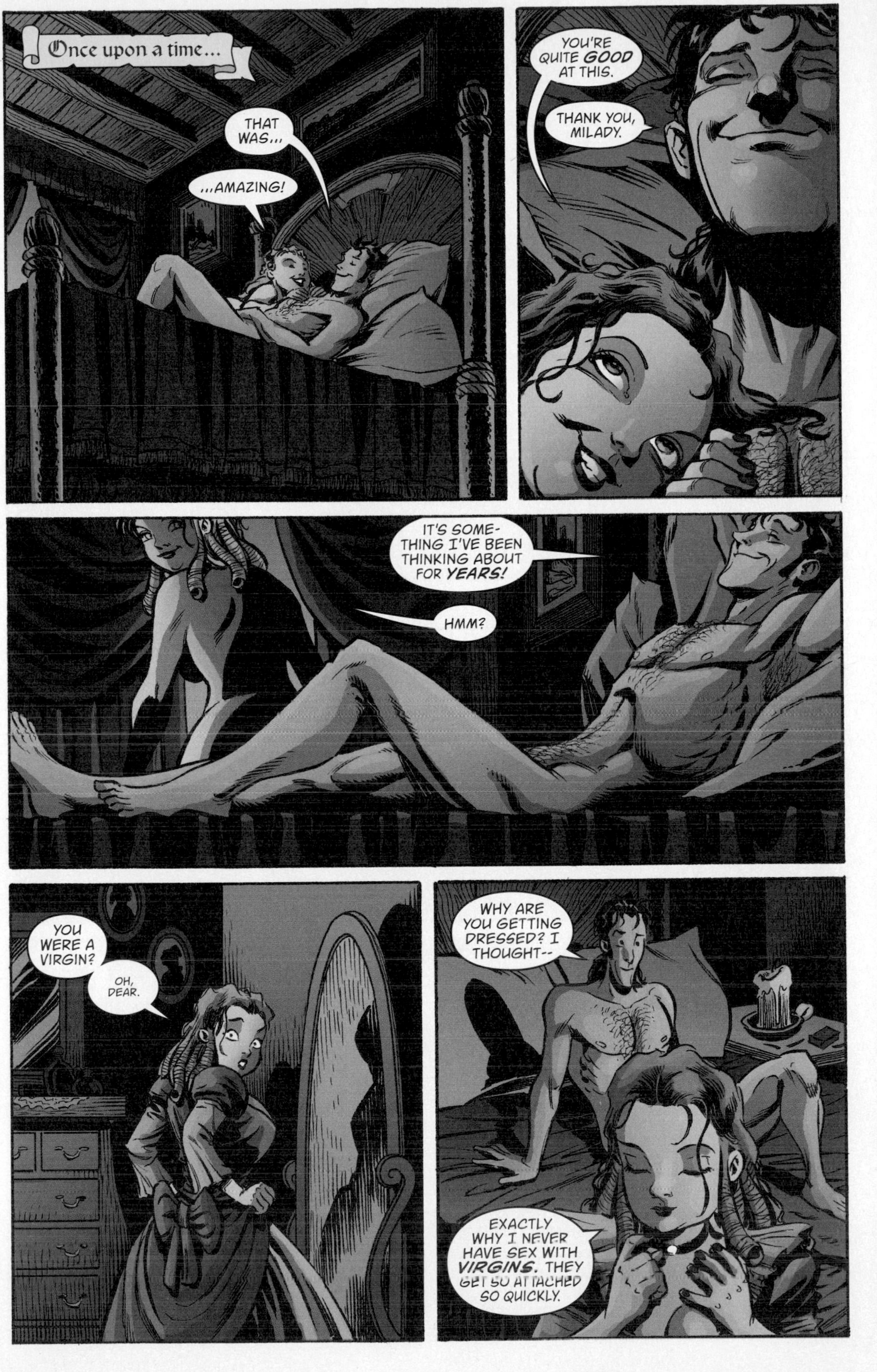
Once upon a time...
THAT WAS...
...AMAZING!
YOU'RE QUITE GOOD AT THIS.
THANK YOU, MILADY.
IT'S SOME-THING I'VE BEEN THINKING ABOUT FOR YEARS!
HMM?
YOU WERE A VIRGIN?
OH, DEAR.
WHY ARE YOU GETTING DRESSED? I THOUGHT--
EXACTLY WHY I NEVER HAVE SEX WITH VIRGINS. THEY GET SO ATTACHED SO QUICKLY.

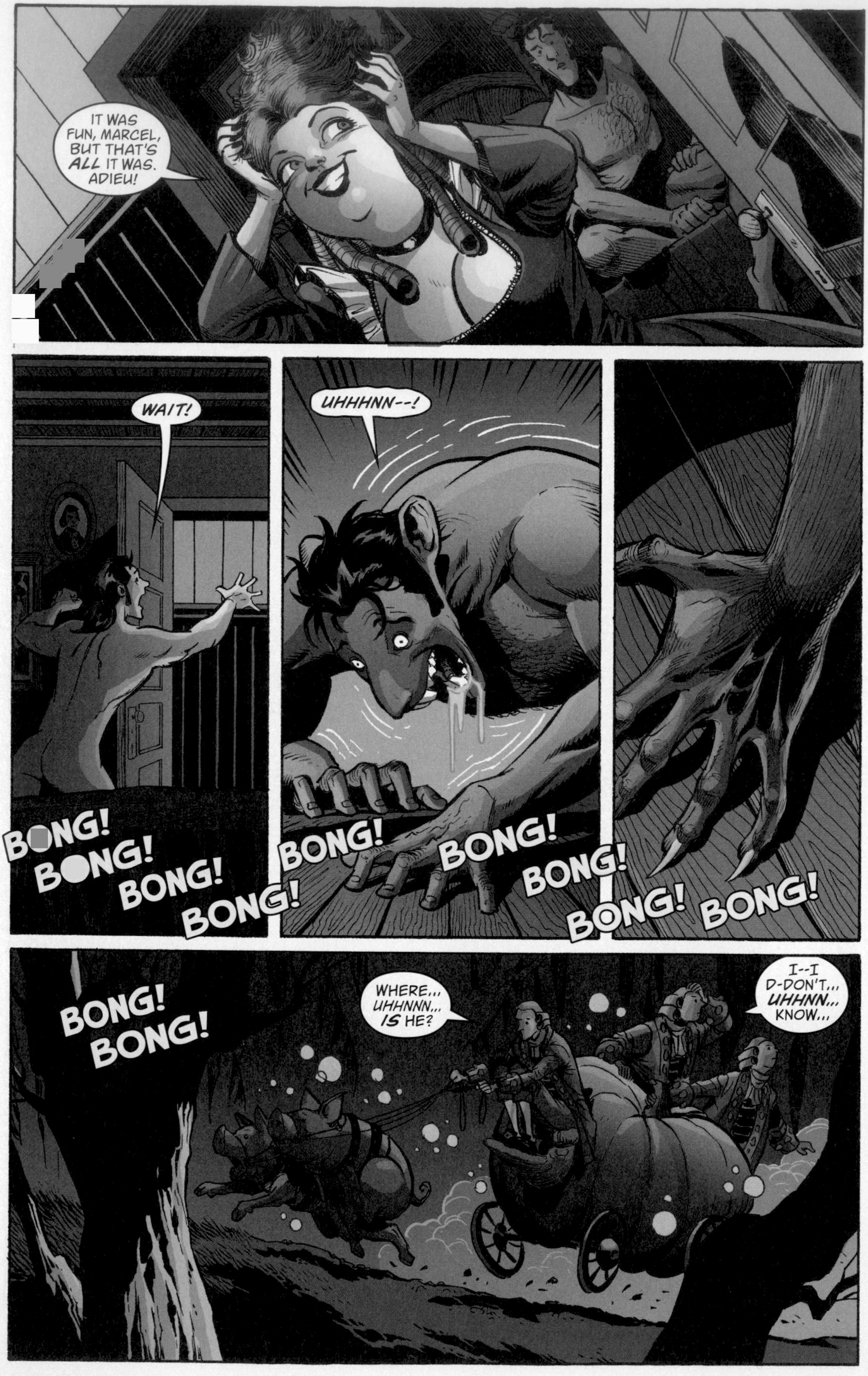
IT WAS FUN, MARCEL, BUT THAT'S ALL IT WAS. ADIEU!
WAIT!
BONG!
BONG!
BONG!
BONG!
UHHHNN--!
BONG!
BONG!
BONG!
BONG!
BONG!
BONG!
BONG!
WHERE... UHHNNN... IS HE?
I--I D-DON'T... UHHNN... KNOW...

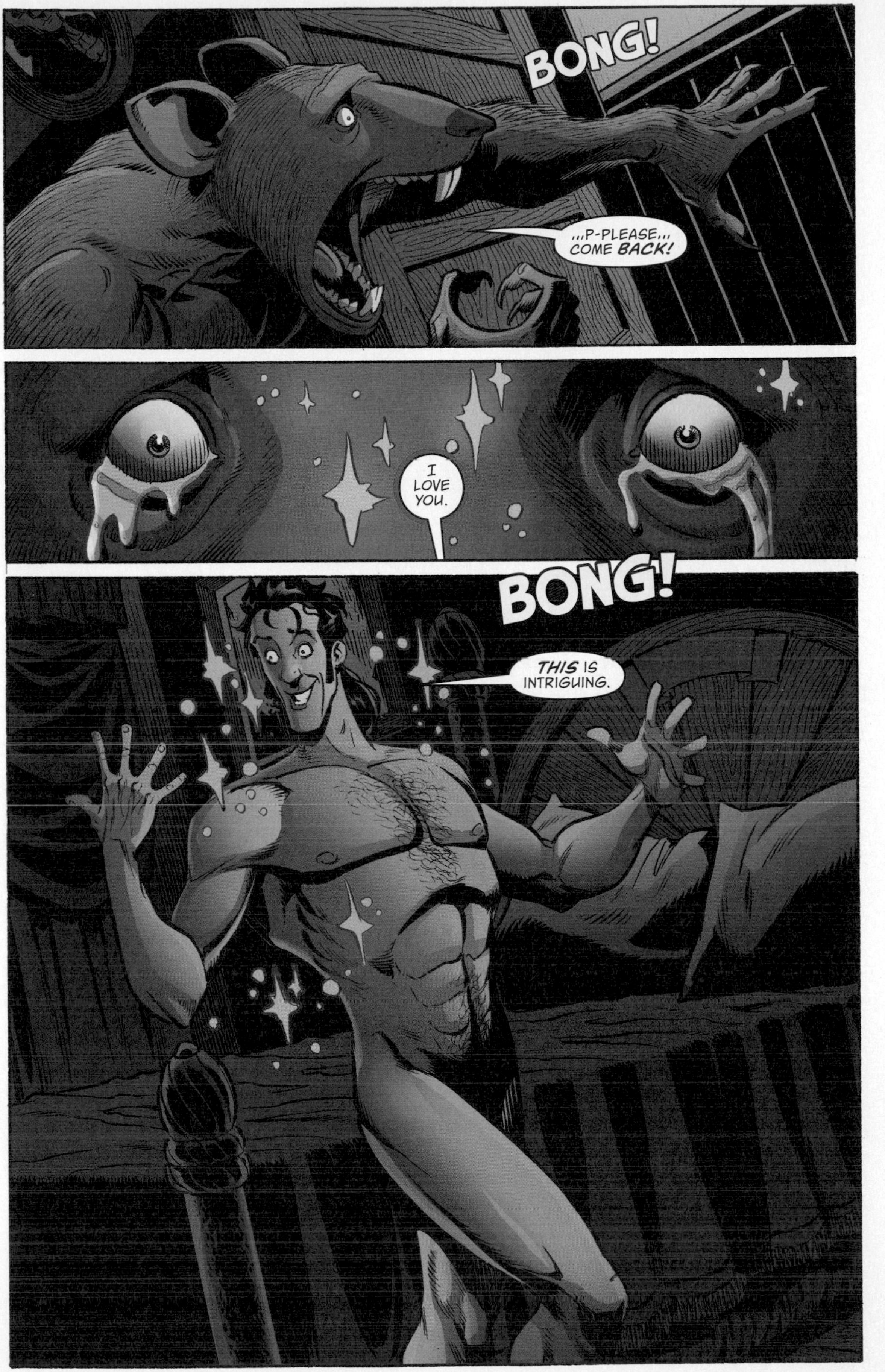
BONG!
...P-PLEASE... COME BACK!
I LOVE YOU.
BONG!
THIS IS INTRIGUING.

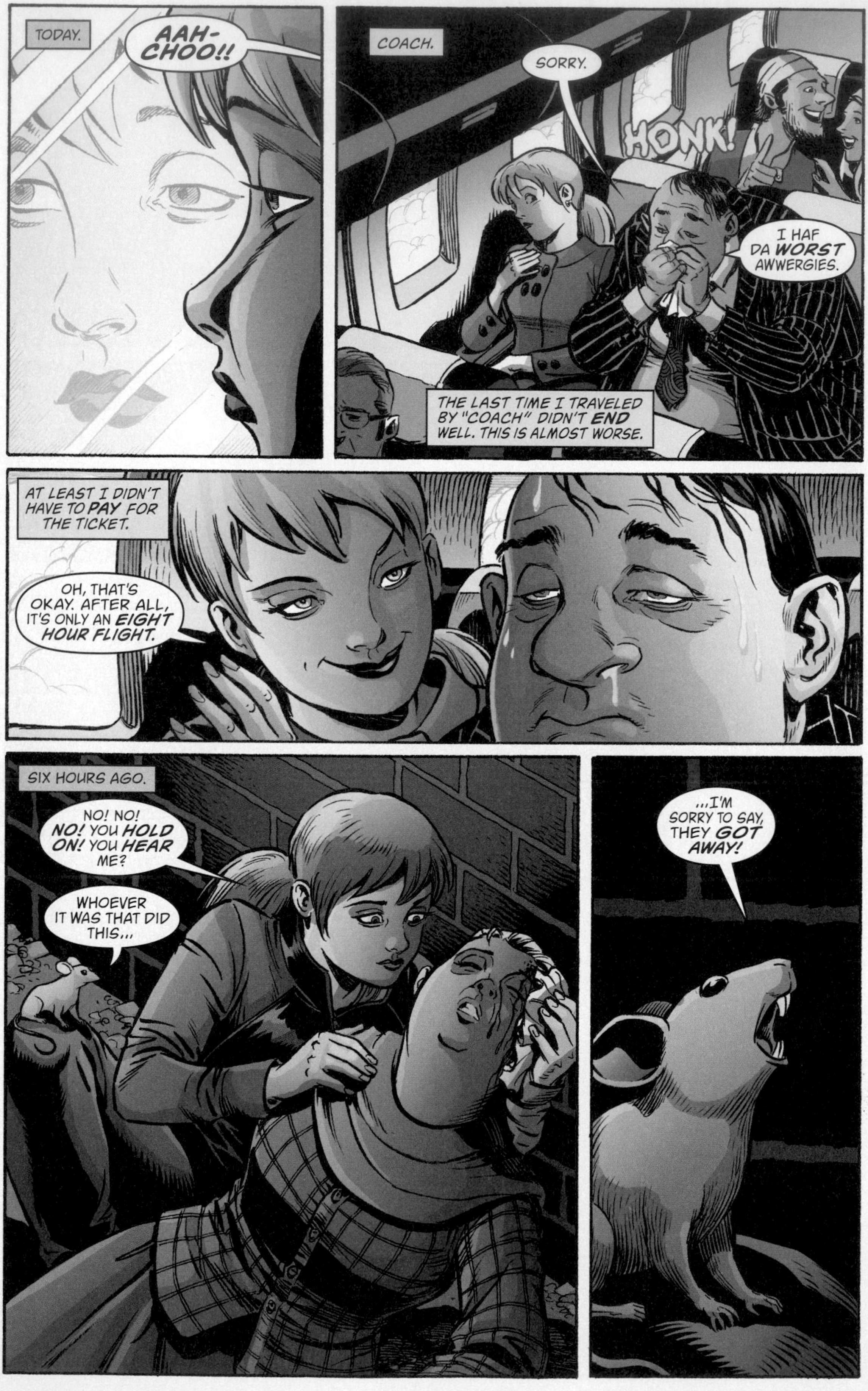
TODAY.
AAH-CHOO!!
COACH.
SORRY.
HONK!
I HAF DA WORST AWWERGIES.
THE LAST TIME I TRAVELED BY "COACH" DIDN'T END WELL. THIS IS ALMOST WORSE.
AT LEAST I DIDN'T HAVE TO PAY FOR THE TICKET.
OH, THAT'S OKAY. AFTER ALL, IT'S ONLY AN EIGHT HOUR FLIGHT.
SIX HOURS AGO.
NO! NO! NO! YOU HOLD ON! YOU HEAR ME?
WHOEVER IT WAS THAT DID THIS...
...I'M SORRY TO SAY, THEY GOT AWAY!

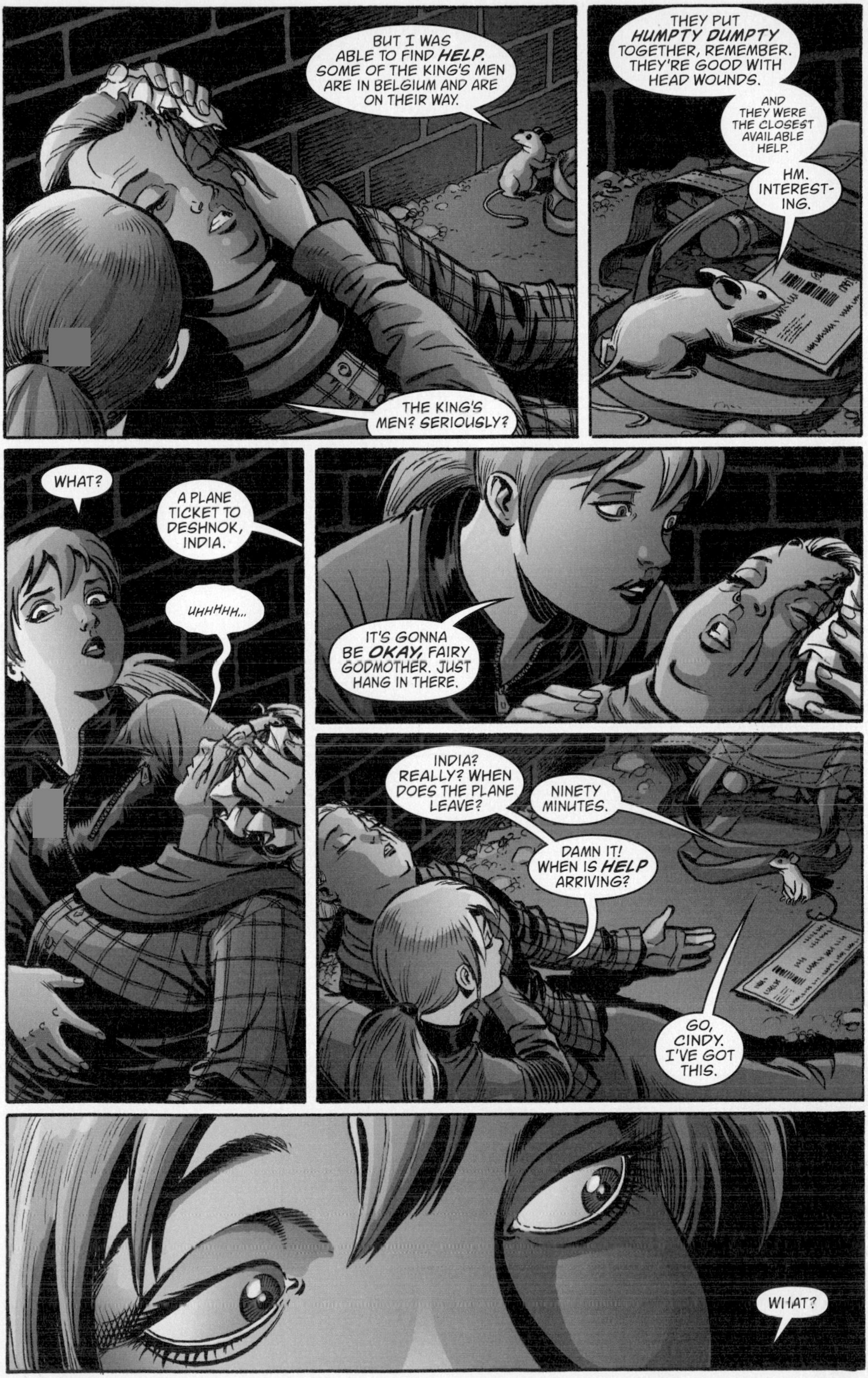
BUT I WAS ABLE TO FIND HELP. SOME OF THE KING'S MEN ARE IN BELGIUM AND ARE ON THEIR WAY.
THE KING'S MEN? SERIOUSLY?
THEY PUT HUMPTY DUMPTY TOGETHER, REMEMBER. THEY'RE GOOD WITH HEAD WOUNDS.
AND THEY WERE THE CLOSEST AVAILABLE HELP.
HM. INTEREST-ING.
WHAT?
A PLANE TICKET TO DESHNOK, INDIA.
UHHHHH...
IT'S GONNA BE OKAY, FAIRY GODMOTHER. JUST HANG IN THERE.
INDIA? REALLY? WHEN DOES THE PLANE LEAVE?
NINETY MINUTES.
DAMN IT! WHEN IS HELP ARRIVING?
GO, CINDY. I'VE GOT THIS.
WHAT?

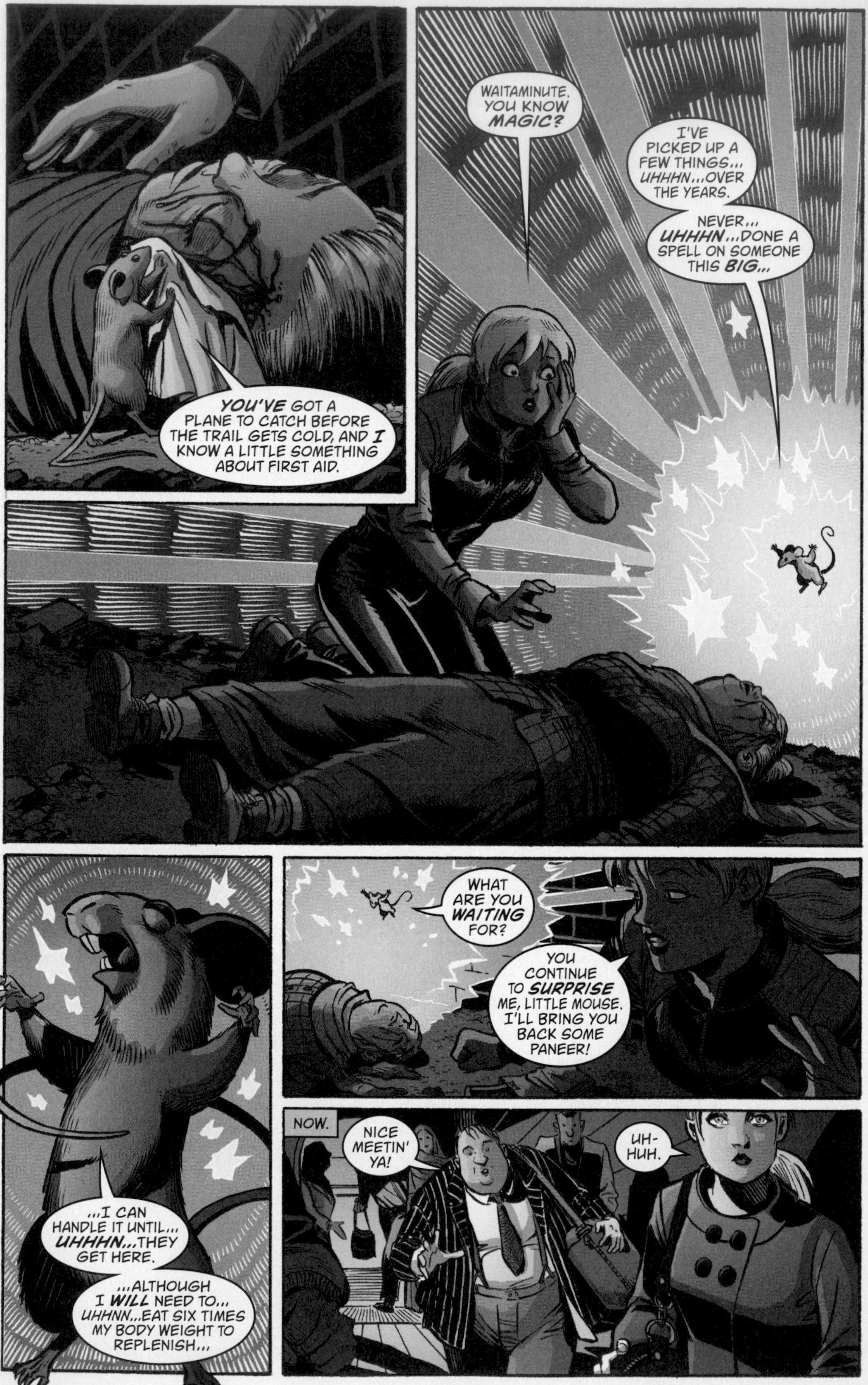
YOU'VE GOT A PLANE TO CATCH BEFORE THE TRAIL GETS COLD, AND I KNOW A LITTLE SOMETHING ABOUT FIRST AID.
WAITAMINUTE. YOU KNOW MAGIC?
I'VE PICKED UP A FEW THINGS... UHHHN...OVER THE YEARS.
NEVER... UHHHN...DONE A SPELL ON SOMEONE THIS BIG...
...I CAN HANDLE IT UNTIL... UHHHN...THEY GET HERE.
...ALTHOUGH I WILL NEED TO... UHHNN...EAT SIX TIMES MY BODY WEIGHT TO REPLENISH...
WHAT ARE YOU WAITING FOR?
YOU CONTINUE TO SURPRISE ME, LITTLE MOUSE. I'LL BRING YOU BACK SOME PANEER!
NOW.
NICE MEETIN' YA!
UH-HUH.

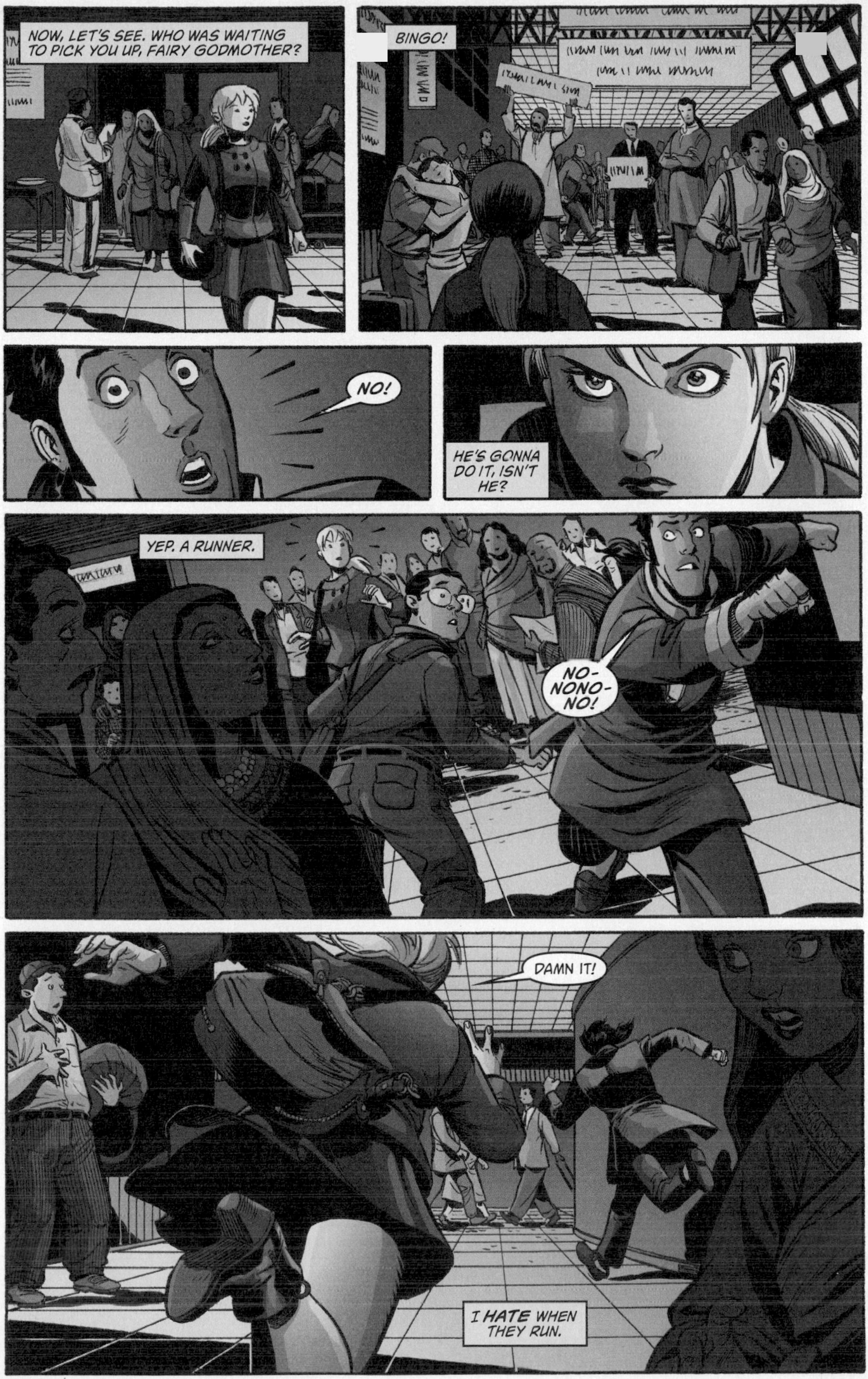
NOW, LET'S SEE. WHO WAS WAITING TO PICK YOU UP, FAIRY GODMOTHER?
BINGO!
NO!
HE'S GONNA DO IT, ISN'T HE?
YEP. A RUNNER.
NO-NONO-NO!
DAMN IT!
I HATE WHEN THEY RUN.

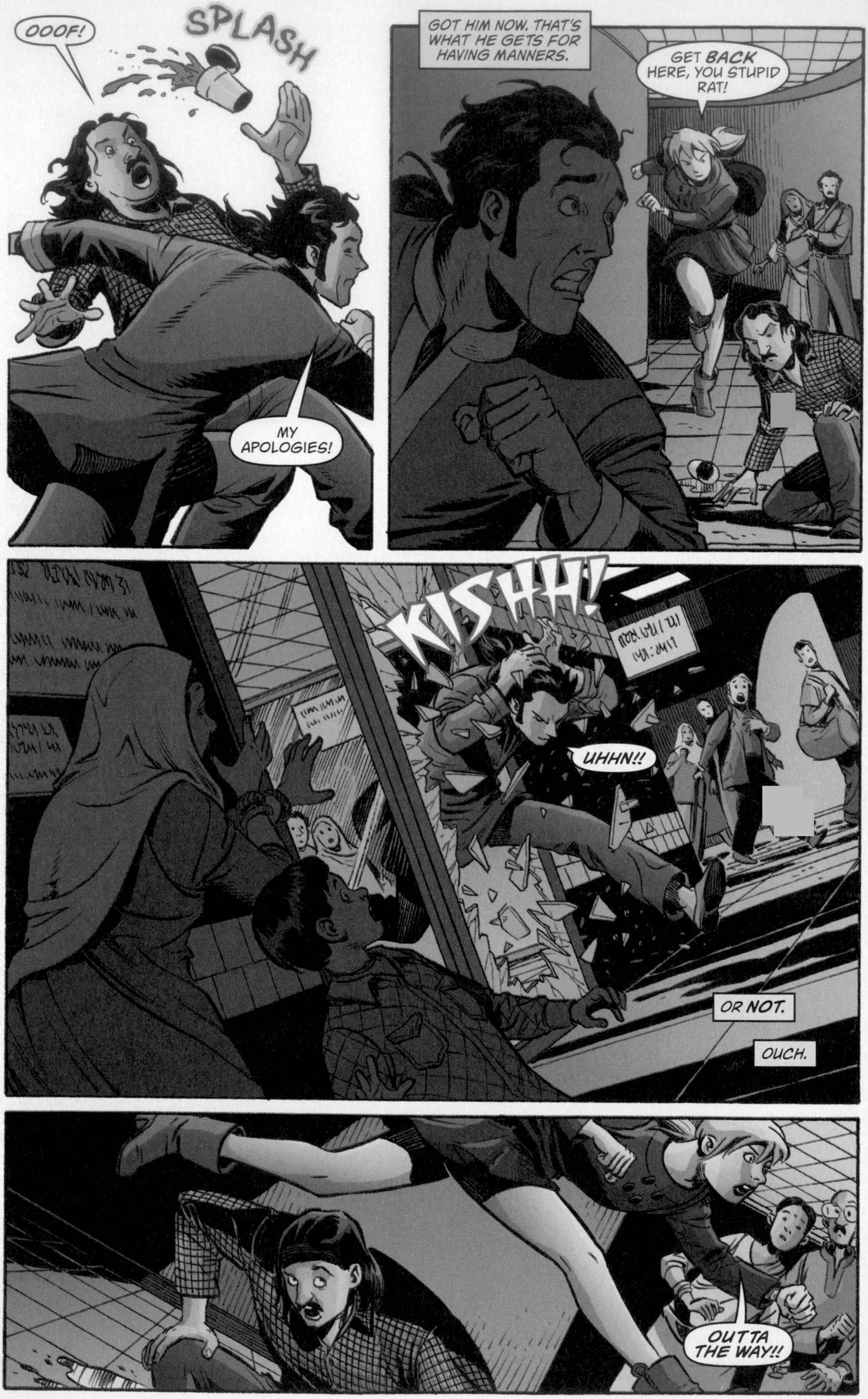
OOOF!
SPLASH
MY APOLOGIES!
GOT HIM NOW. THAT'S WHAT HE GETS FOR HAVING MANNERS.
GET BACK HERE, YOU STUPID RAT!
KISHH!
UHHN!!
OR NOT.
OUCH.
OUTTA THE WAY!!

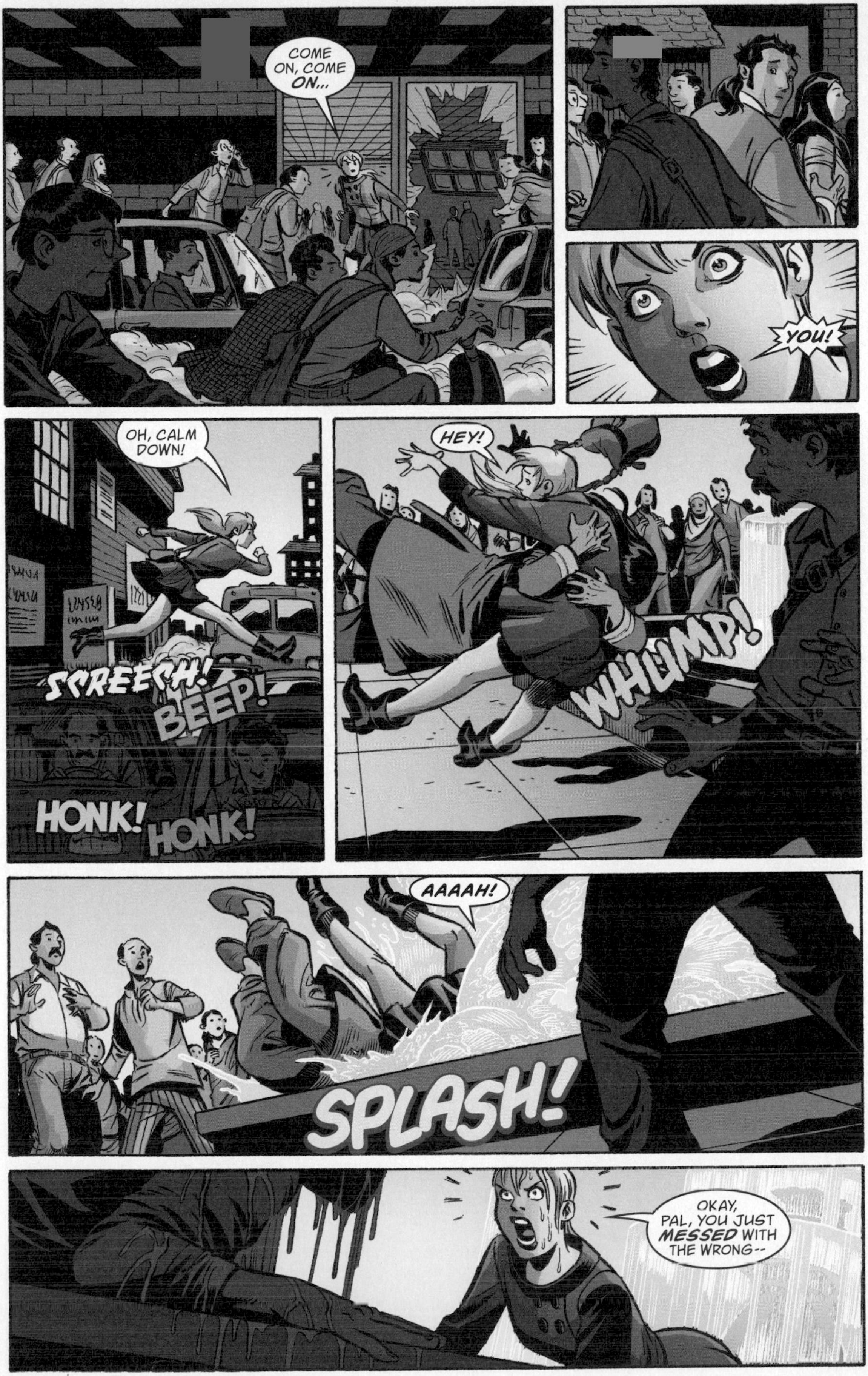
COME ON, COME ON...
YOU!
OH, CALM DOWN!
SCREECH!
BEEP!
HONK! HONK!
HEY!
WHUMP!
AAAAH!
SPLASH!
OKAY, PAL, YOU JUST MESSED WITH THE WRONG--

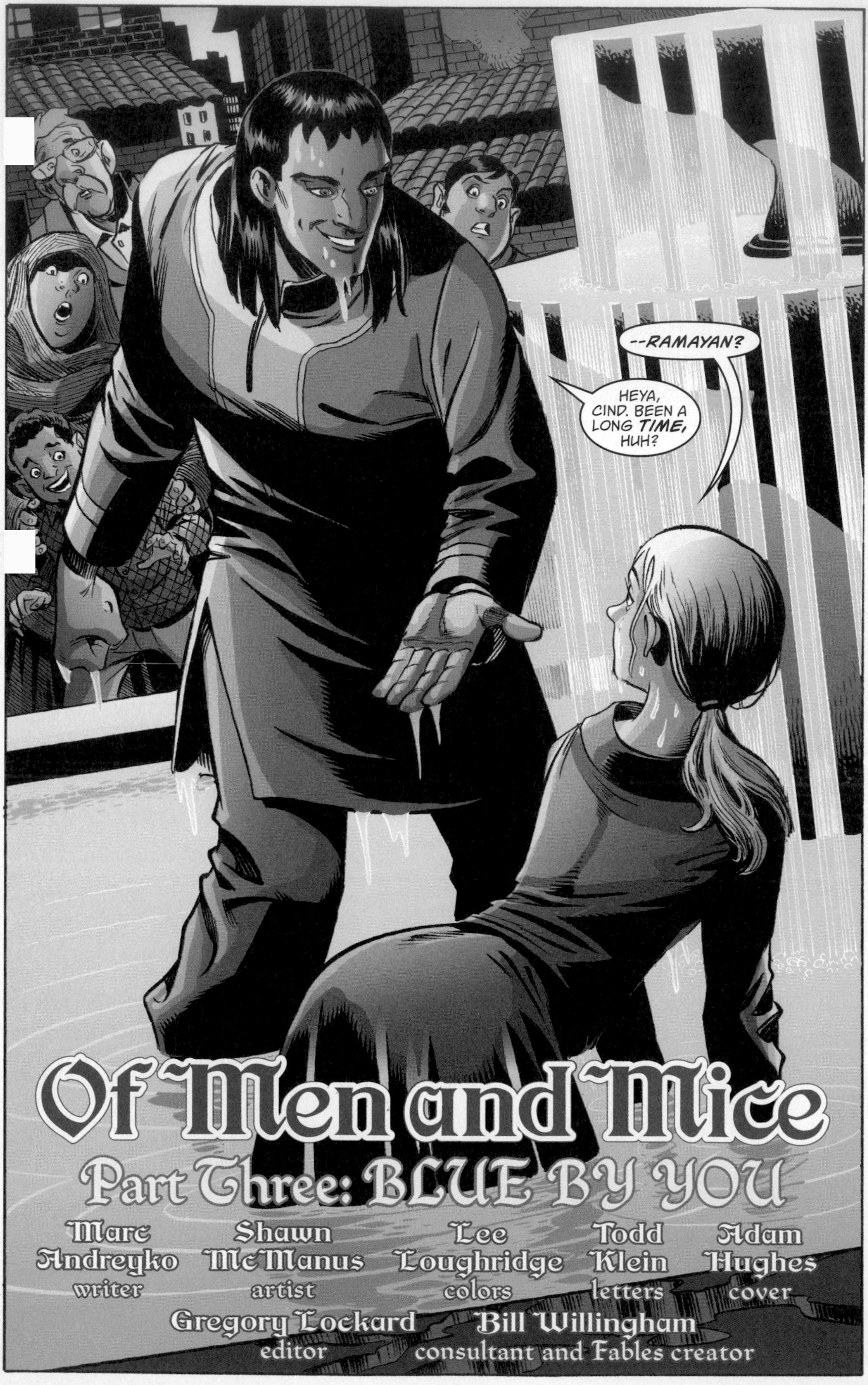
--RAMAYAN?
HEYA, CIND. BEEN A LONG TIME, HUH?
Of Men and Mice
Part Three: BLUE BY YOU
Marc Andreyko writer
Shawn McManus artist
Lee Loughridge colors
Todd Klein letters
Adam Hughes cover
Gregory Lockard editor
Bill Willingham consultant and Fables creator

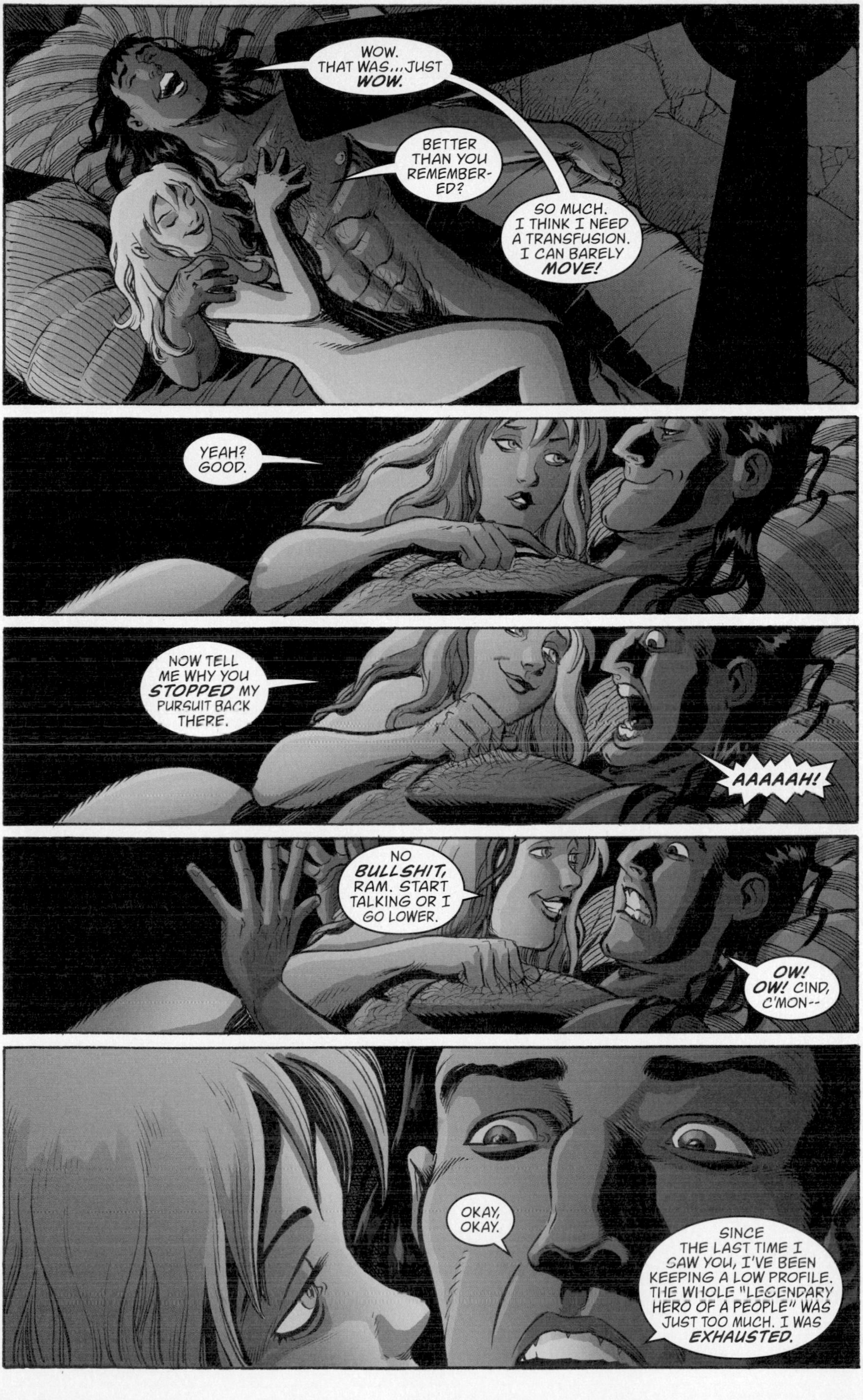
WOW. THAT WAS...JUST WOW.
BETTER THAN YOU REMEMBERED?
SO MUCH. I THINK I NEED A TRANSFUSION. I CAN BARELY MOVE!
YEAH? GOOD.
NOW TELL ME WHY YOU STOPPED MY PURSUIT BACK THERE.
AAAAAH!
NO BULLSHIT, RAM. START TALKING OR I GO LOWER.
OW! OW! CIND, C'MON--
OKAY, OKAY.
SINCE THE LAST TIME I SAW YOU, I'VE BEEN KEEPING A LOW PROFILE. THE WHOLE "LEGENDARY HERO OF A PEOPLE" WAS JUST TOO MUCH. I WAS EXHAUSTED.

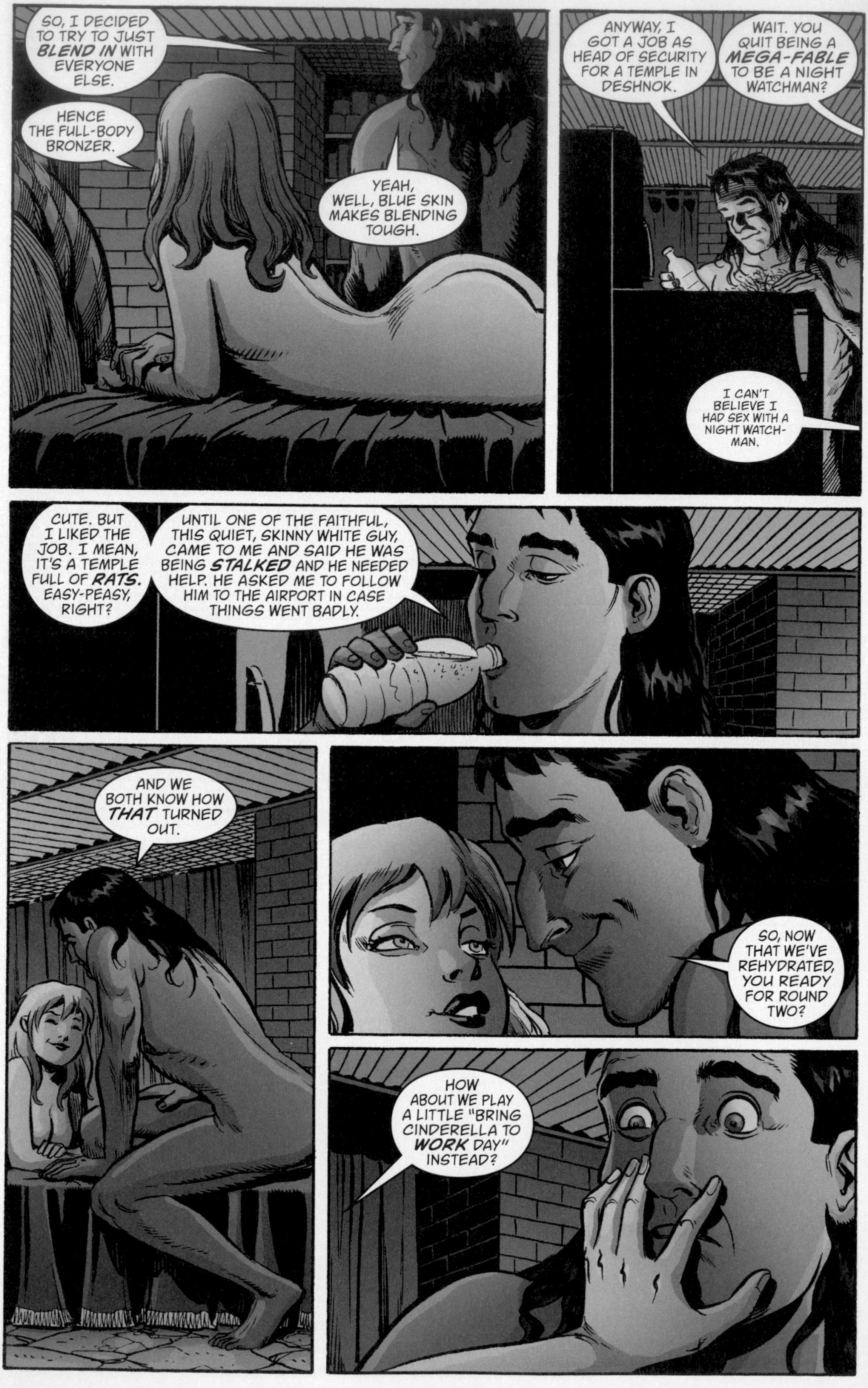
SO, I DECIDED TO TRY TO JUST BLEND IN WITH EVERYONE ELSE.
HENCE THE FULL-BODY BRONZER.
YEAH, WELL, BLUE SKIN MAKES BLENDING TOUGH.
ANYWAY, I GOT A JOB AS HEAD OF SECURITY FOR A TEMPLE IN DESHNOK.
WAIT. YOU QUIT BEING A MEGA-FABLE TO BE A NIGHT WATCHMAN?
I CAN'T BELIEVE I HAD SEX WITH A NIGHT WATCH-MAN.
CUTE. BUT I LIKED THE JOB. I MEAN, IT'S A TEMPLE FULL OF RATS. EASY-PEASY, RIGHT?
UNTIL ONE OF THE FAITHFUL, THIS QUIET, SKINNY WHITE GUY, CAME TO ME AND SAID HE WAS BEING STALKED AND HE NEEDED HELP. HE ASKED ME TO FOLLOW HIM TO THE AIRPORT IN CASE THINGS WENT BADLY.
AND WE BOTH KNOW HOW THAT TURNED OUT.
SO, NOW THAT WE'VE REHYDRATED, YOU READY FOR ROUND TWO?
HOW ABOUT WE PLAY A LITTLE "BRING CINDERELLA TO WORK DAY" INSTEAD?

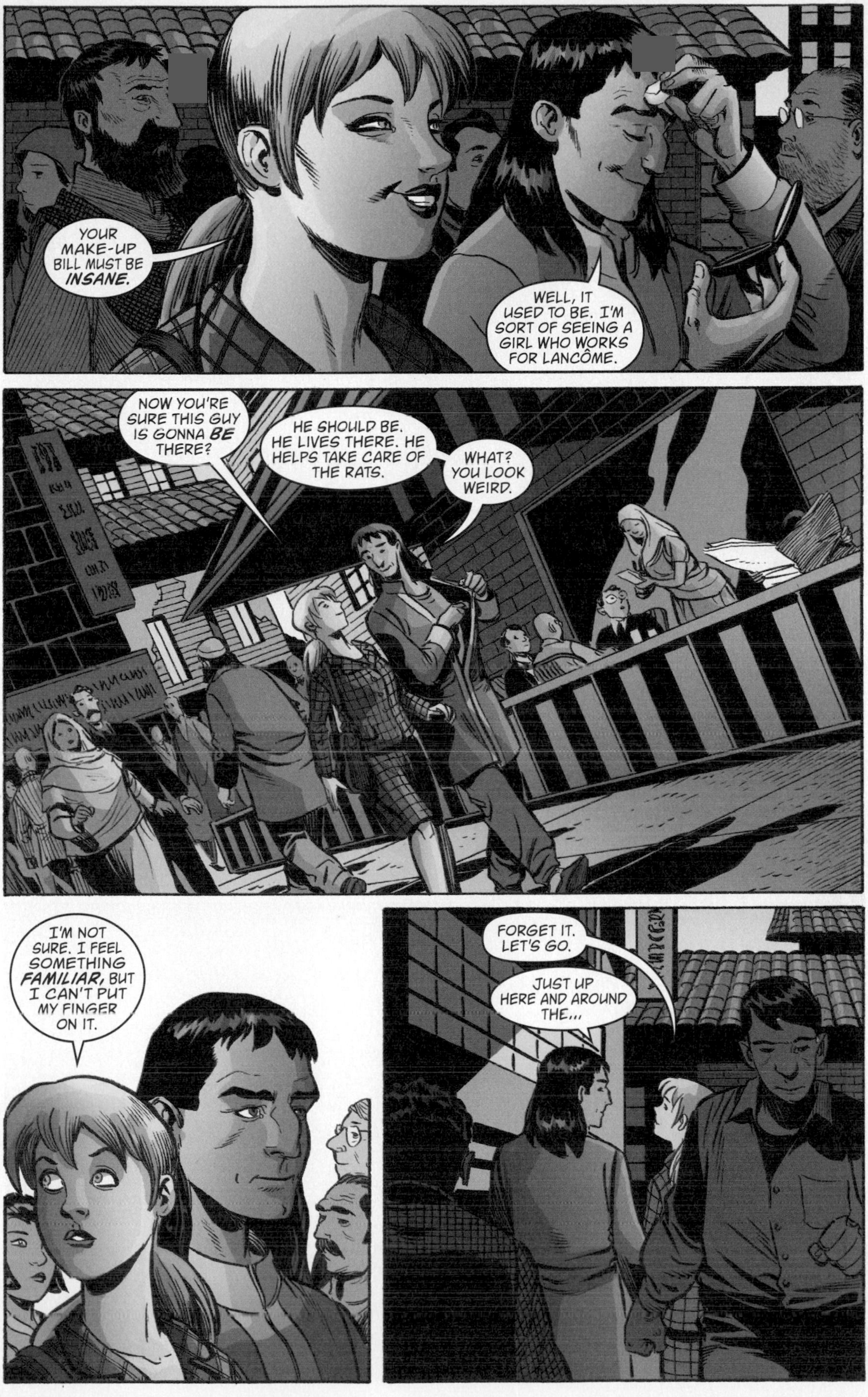
YOUR MAKE-UP BILL MUST BE ***INSANE.***
WELL, IT USED TO BE. I'M SORT OF SEEING A GIRL WHO WORKS FOR LANCÔME.
NOW YOU'RE SURE THIS GUY IS GONNA ***BE*** THERE?
HE SHOULD BE. HE LIVES THERE. HE HELPS TAKE CARE OF THE RATS.
WHAT? YOU LOOK WEIRD.
I'M NOT SURE. I FEEL SOMETHING ***FAMILIAR,*** BUT I CAN'T PUT MY FINGER ON IT.
FORGET IT. LET'S GO.
JUST UP HERE AND AROUND THE...

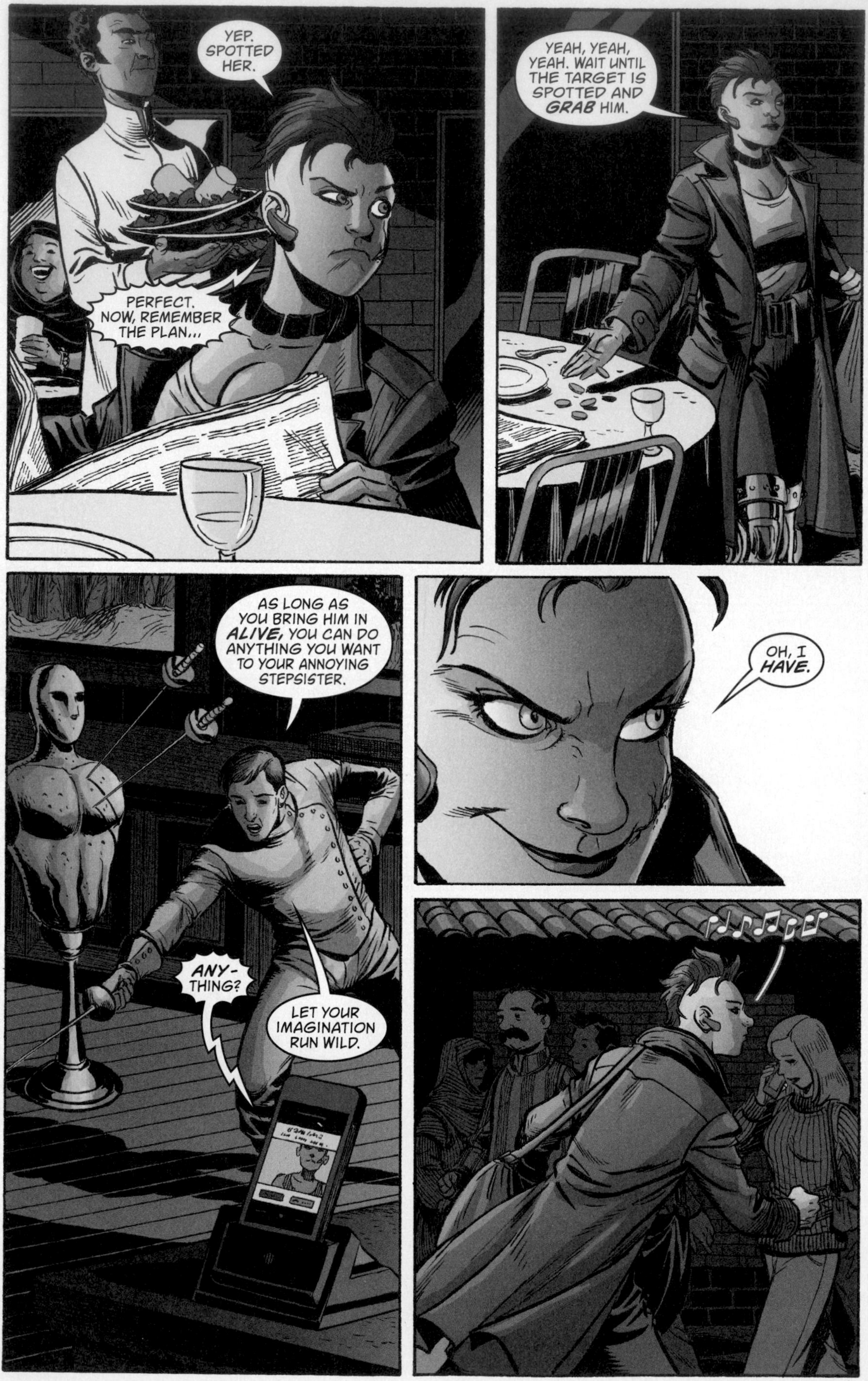
YEP. SPOTTED HER.
PERFECT. NOW, REMEMBER THE PLAN...
YEAH, YEAH, YEAH. WAIT UNTIL THE TARGET IS SPOTTED AND GRAB HIM.
AS LONG AS YOU BRING HIM IN ALIVE, YOU CAN DO ANYTHING YOU WANT TO YOUR ANNOYING STEPSISTER.
ANY-THING?
LET YOUR IMAGINATION RUN WILD.
OH, I HAVE.

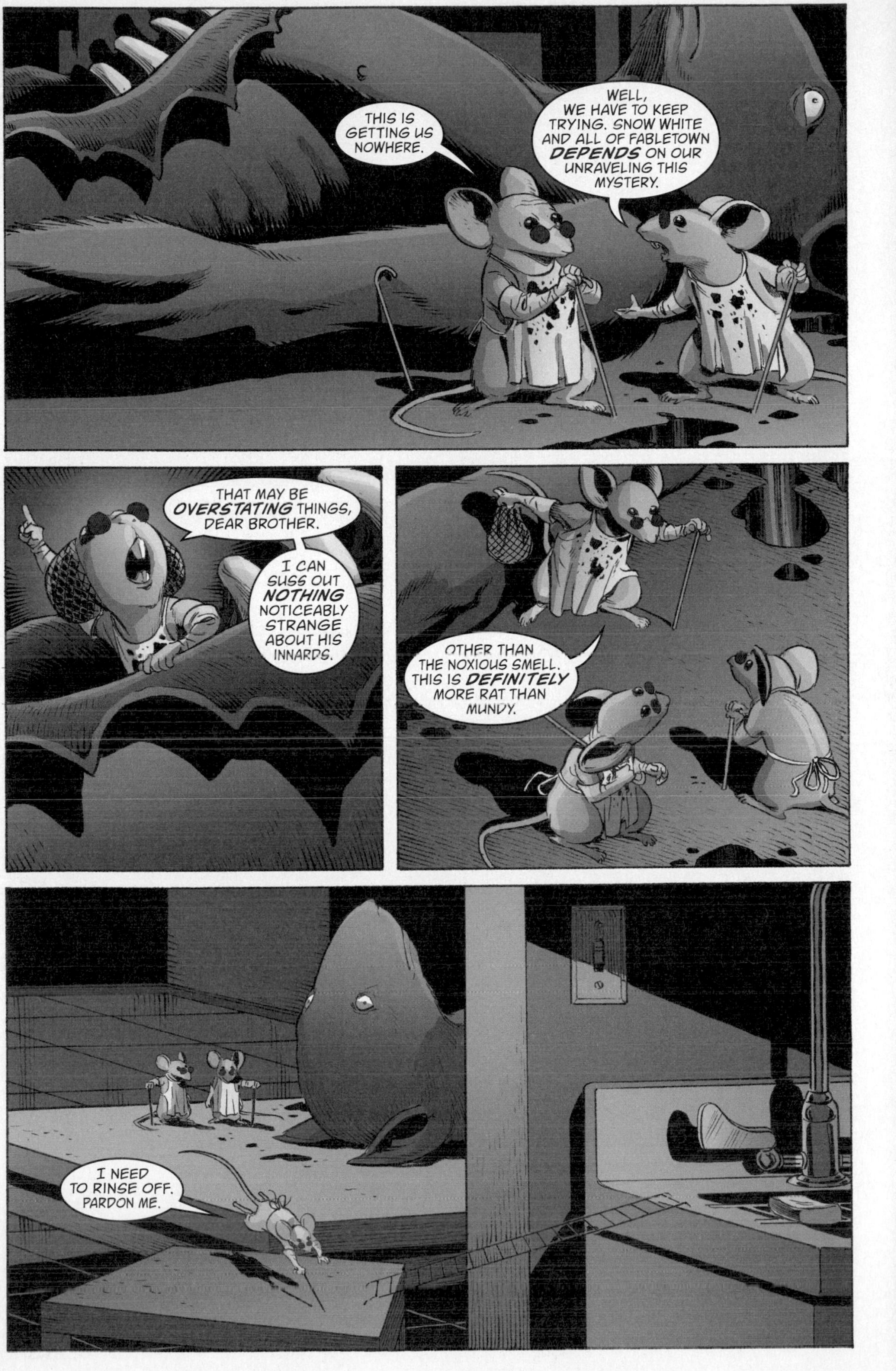

THIS IS GETTING US NOWHERE.
WELL, WE HAVE TO KEEP TRYING. SNOW WHITE AND ALL OF FABLETOWN *DEPENDS* ON OUR UNRAVELING THIS MYSTERY.
THAT MAY BE *OVERSTATING* THINGS, DEAR BROTHER.
I CAN SUSS OUT *NOTHING* NOTICEABLY STRANGE ABOUT HIS INNARDS.
OTHER THAN THE NOXIOUS SMELL. THIS IS *DEFINITELY* MORE RAT THAN MUNDY.
I NEED TO RINSE OFF. PARDON ME.

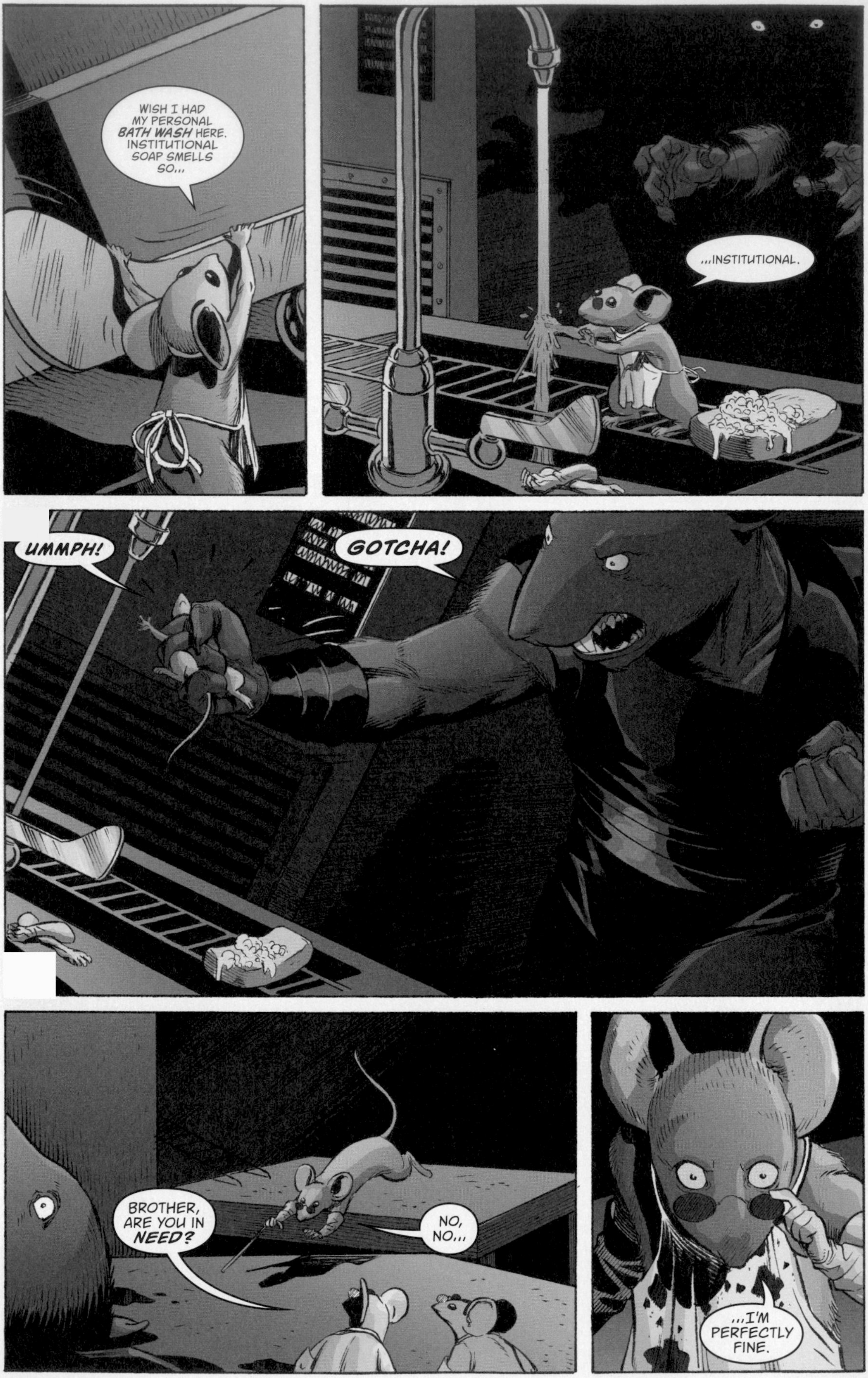
WISH I HAD MY PERSONAL BATH WASH HERE. INSTITUTIONAL SOAP SMELLS SO...
...INSTITUTIONAL.
UMMPH!
GOTCHA!
BROTHER, ARE YOU IN NEED?
NO, NO...
...I'M PERFECTLY FINE.

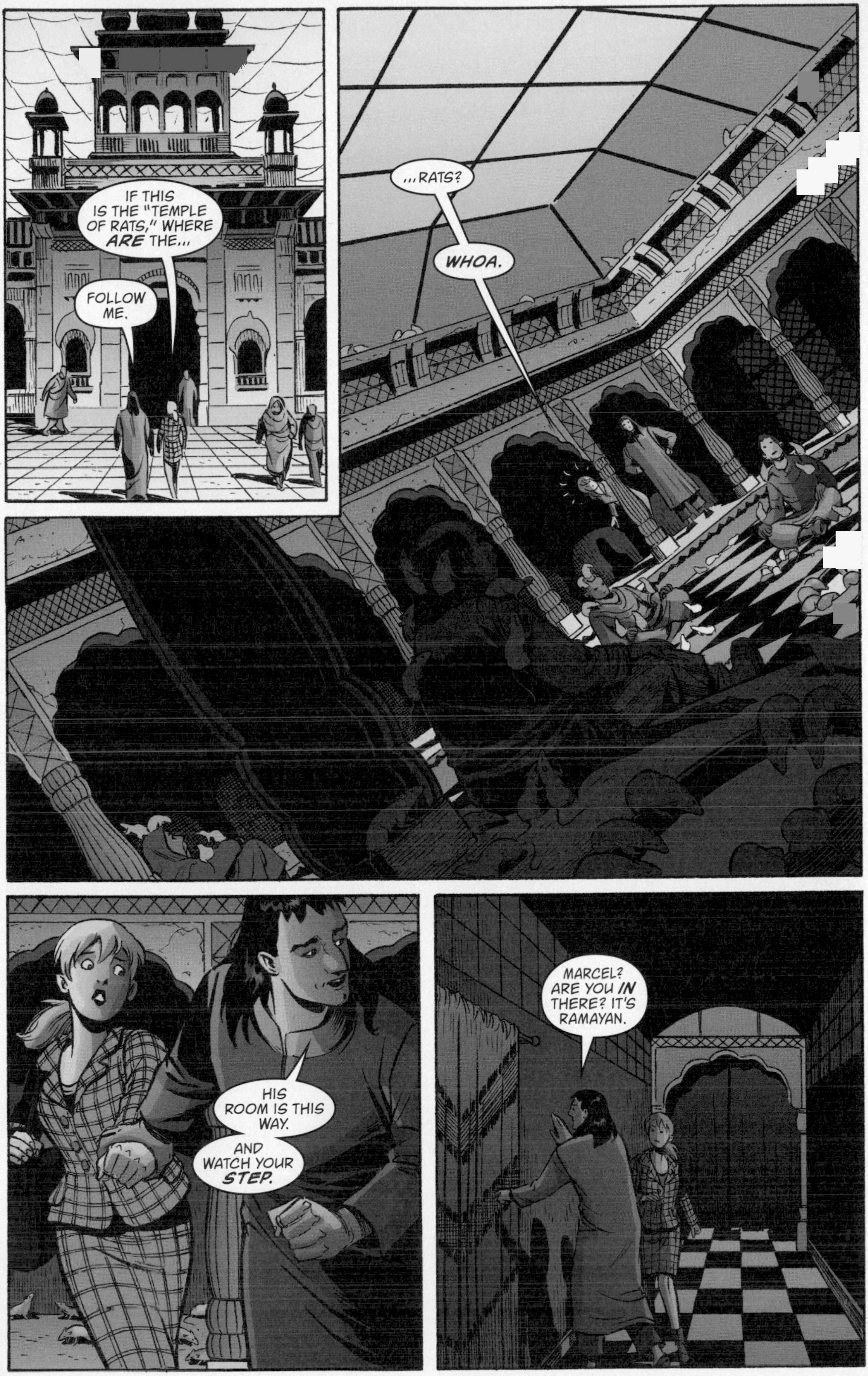

IF THIS IS THE "TEMPLE OF RATS," WHERE ARE THE...
FOLLOW ME.
...RATS?
WHOA.
HIS ROOM IS THIS WAY.
AND WATCH YOUR STEP.
MARCEL? ARE YOU IN THERE? IT'S RAMAYAN.

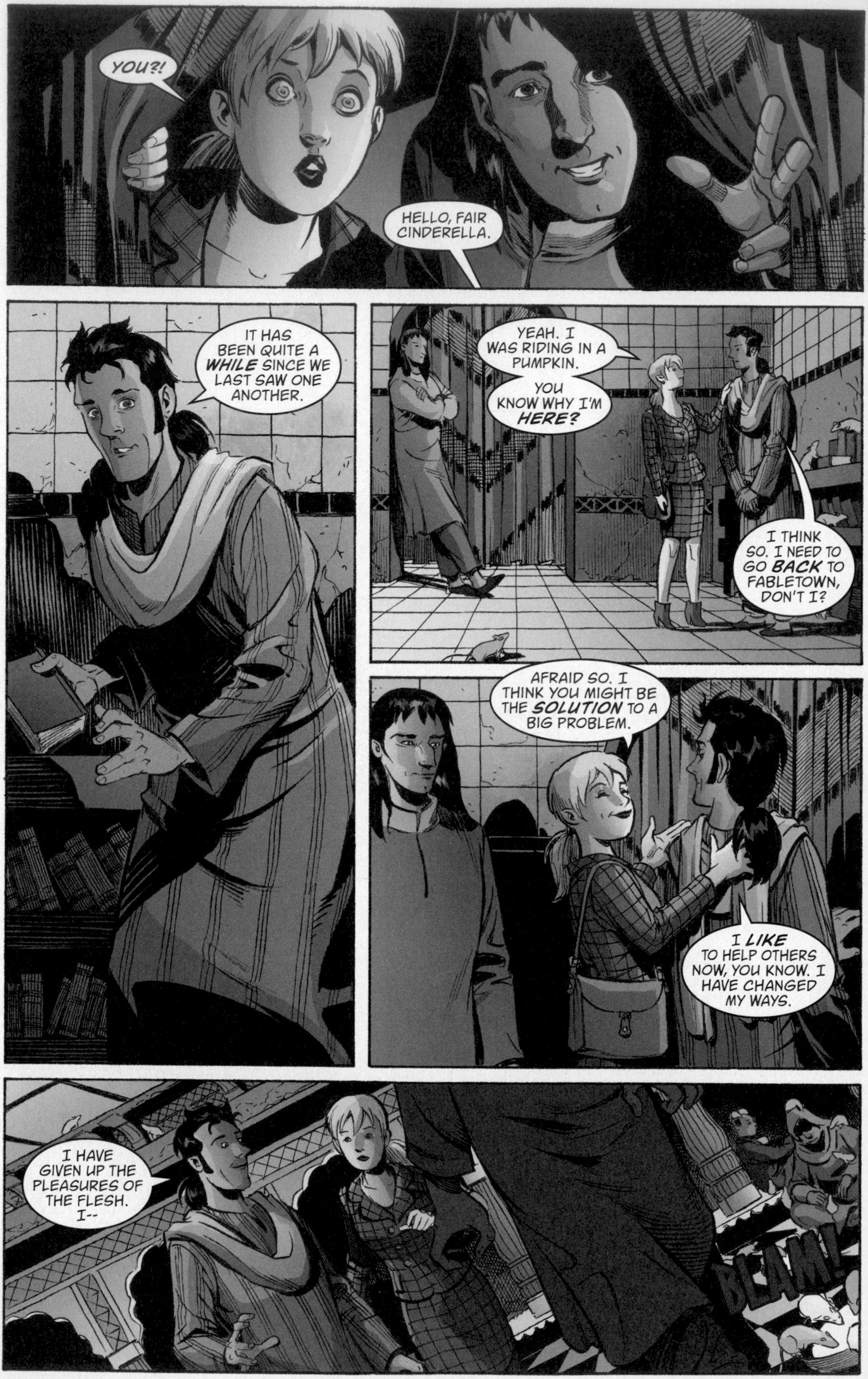
YOU?!
HELLO, FAIR CINDERELLA.
IT HAS BEEN QUITE A WHILE SINCE WE LAST SAW ONE ANOTHER.
YEAH. I WAS RIDING IN A PUMPKIN.
YOU KNOW WHY I'M HERE?
I THINK SO. I NEED TO GO BACK TO FABLETOWN, DON'T I?
AFRAID SO. I THINK YOU MIGHT BE THE SOLUTION TO A BIG PROBLEM.
I LIKE TO HELP OTHERS NOW, YOU KNOW. I HAVE CHANGED MY WAYS.
I HAVE GIVEN UP THE PLEASURES OF THE FLESH. I--
BLAM!

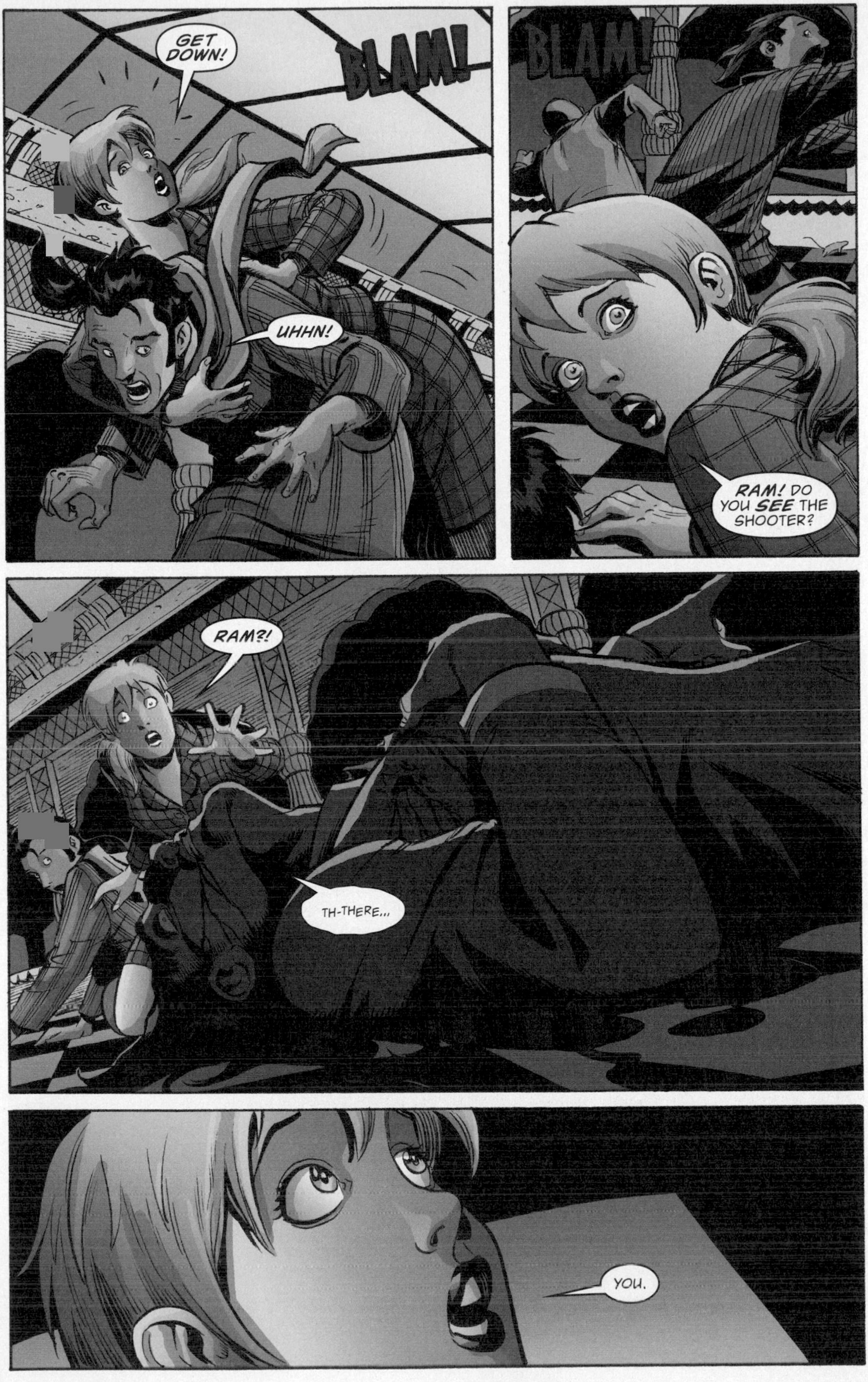
GET DOWN!
BLAM!
UHHN!
BLAM!
RAM! DO YOU SEE THE SHOOTER?
RAM?!
TH-THERE...
YOU.

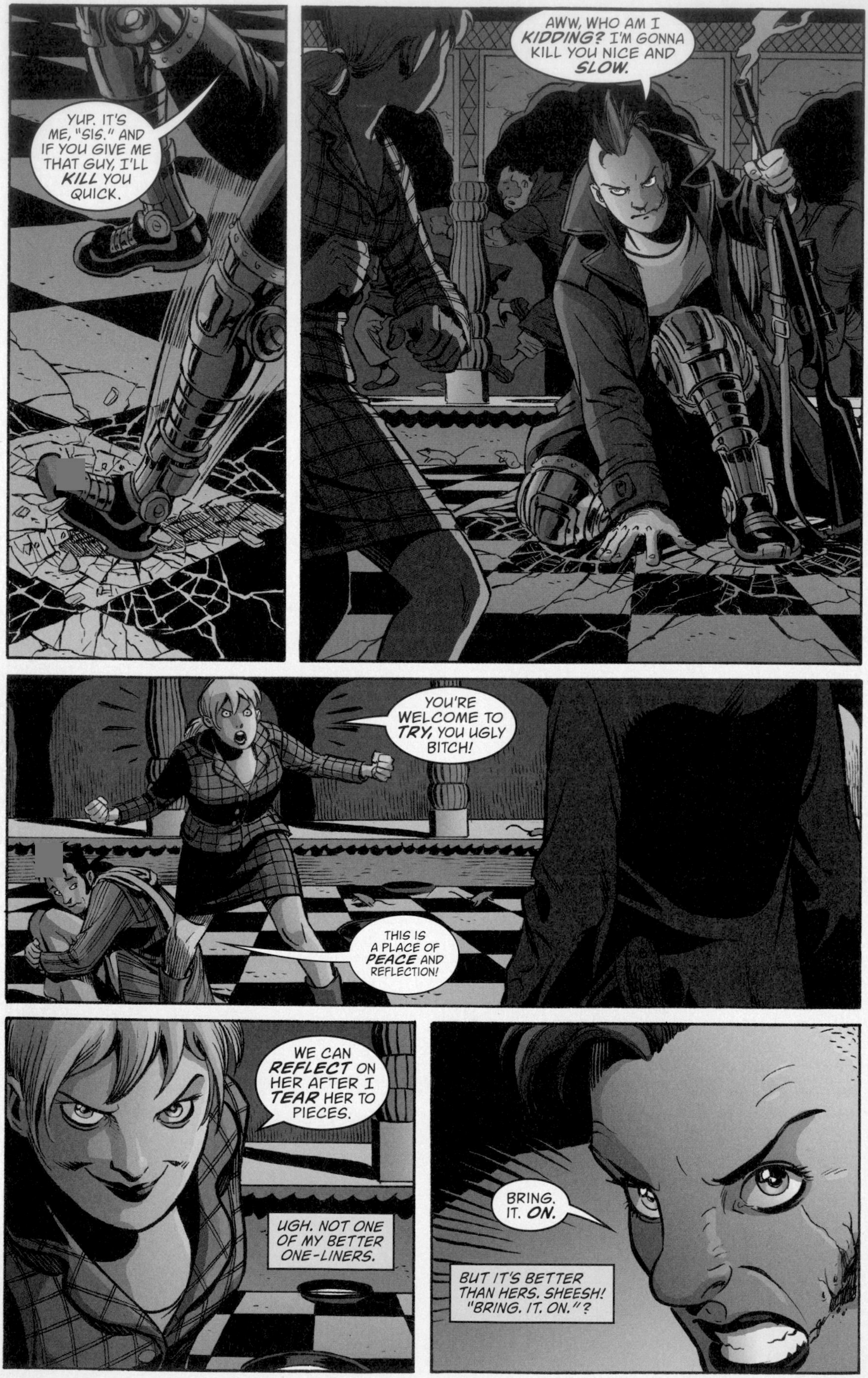
YUP. IT'S ME, "SIS." AND IF YOU GIVE ME THAT GUY, I'LL KILL YOU QUICK.
AWW, WHO AM I KIDDING? I'M GONNA KILL YOU NICE AND SLOW.
YOU'RE WELCOME TO TRY, YOU UGLY BITCH!
THIS IS A PLACE OF PEACE AND REFLECTION!
WE CAN REFLECT ON HER AFTER I TEAR HER TO PIECES.
UGH. NOT ONE OF MY BETTER ONE-LINERS.
BRING. IT. ON.
BUT IT'S BETTER THAN HERS. SHEESH! "BRING. IT. ON."?

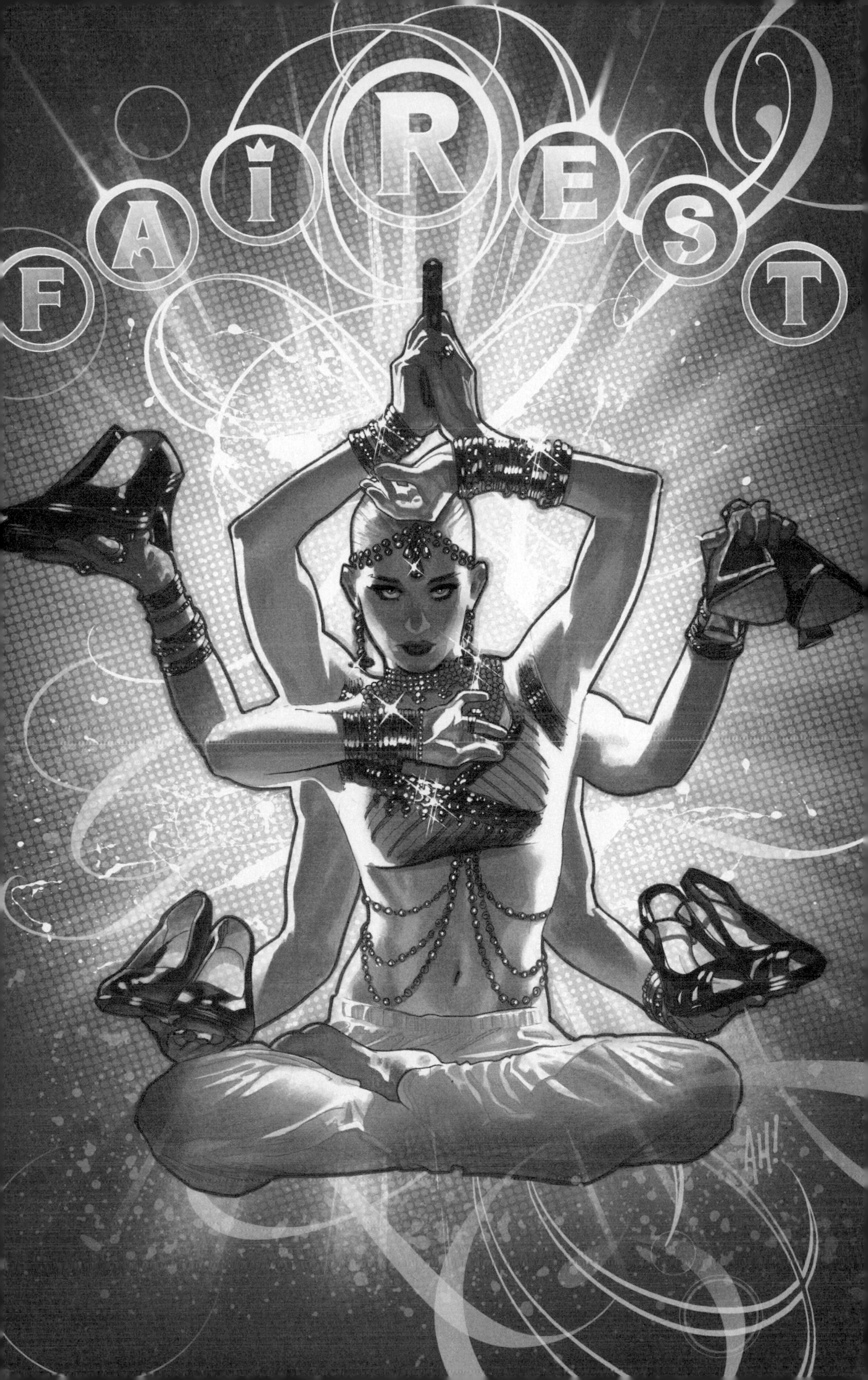
FAIREST
AH!

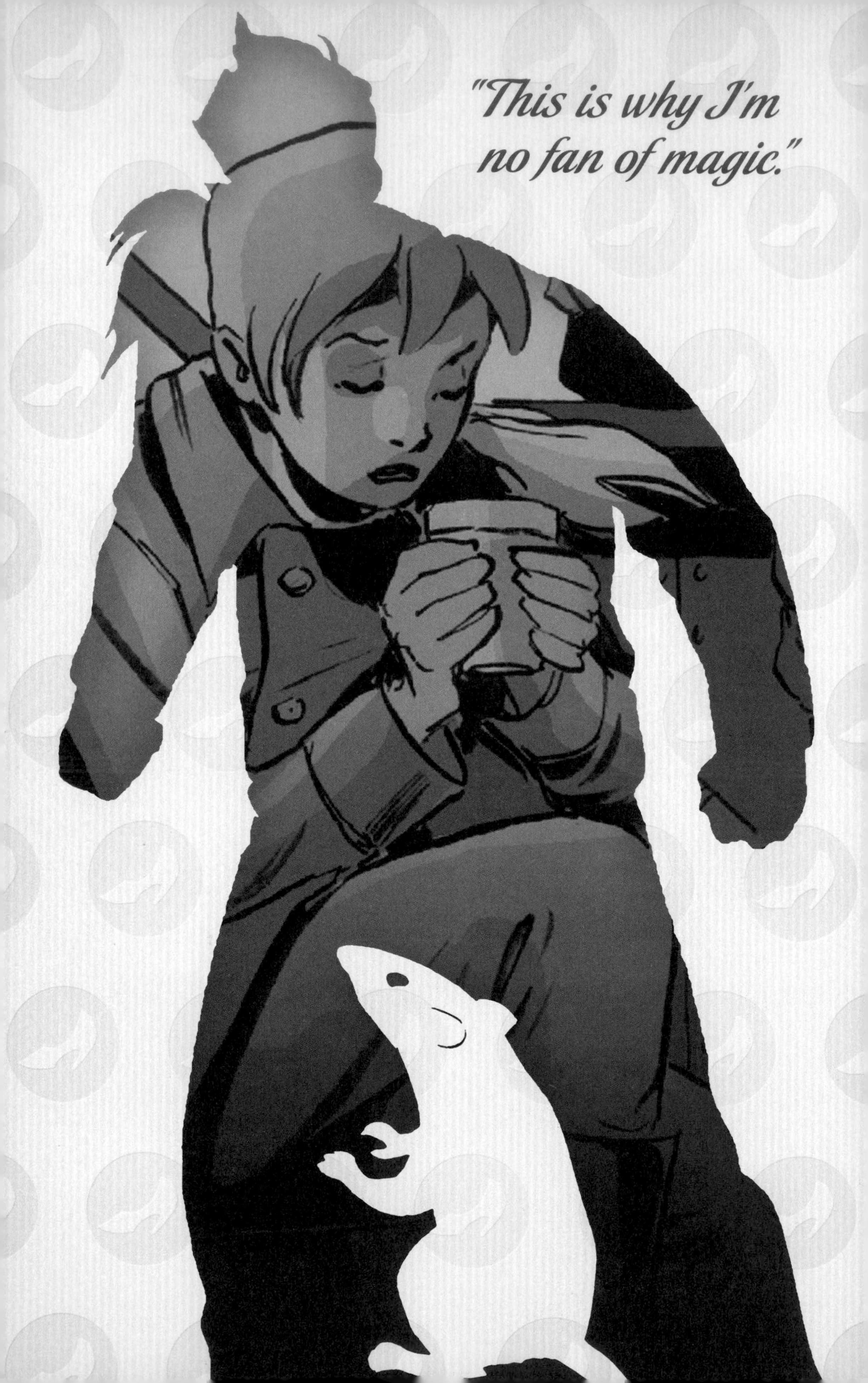
"This is why I'm no fan of magic."

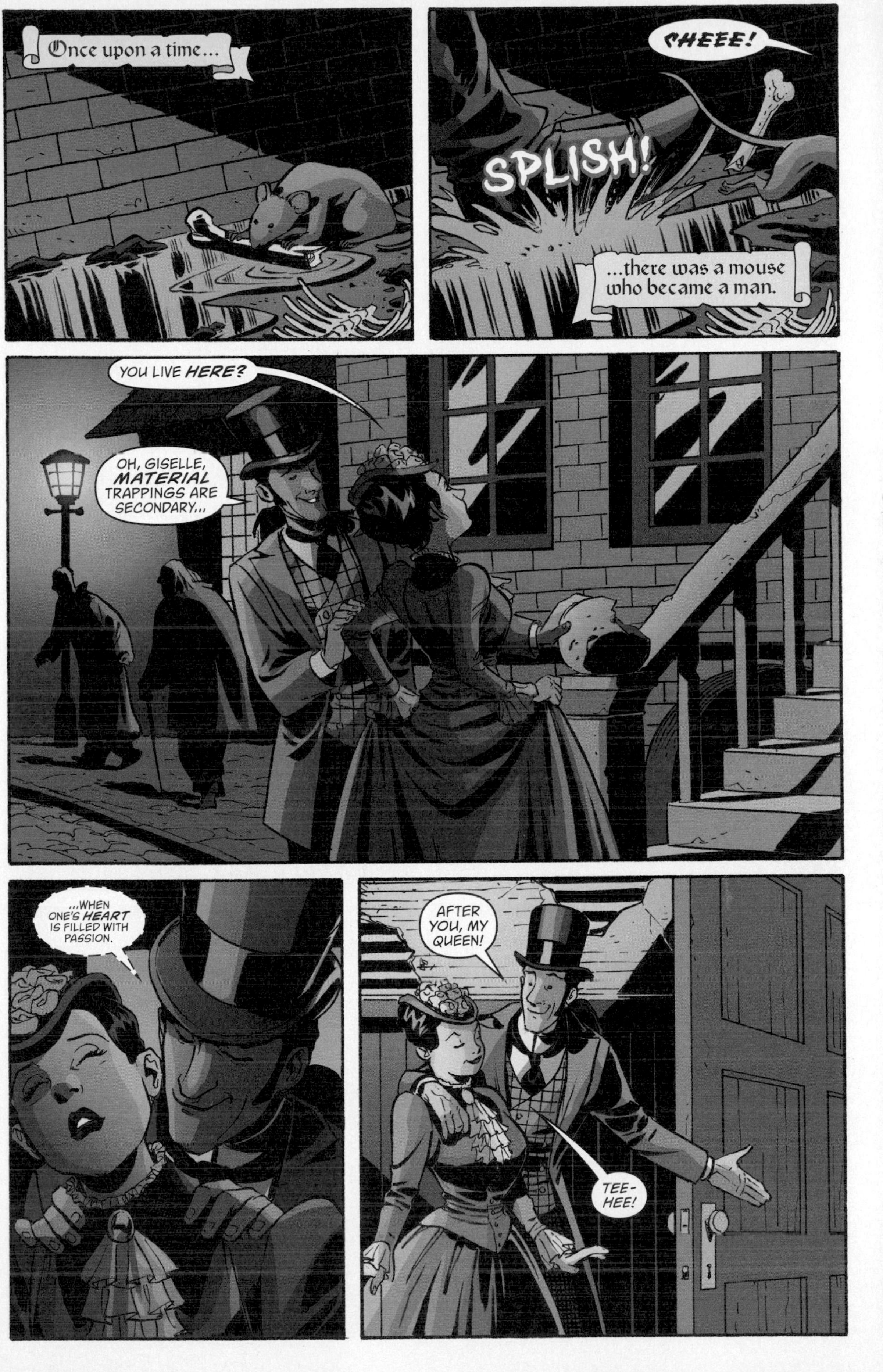
Once upon a time...
CHEEE!
SPLISH!
...there was a mouse who became a man.
YOU LIVE HERE?
OH, GISELLE, MATERIAL TRAPPINGS ARE SECONDARY...
...WHEN ONE'S HEART IS FILLED WITH PASSION.
AFTER YOU, MY QUEEN!
TEE-HEE!

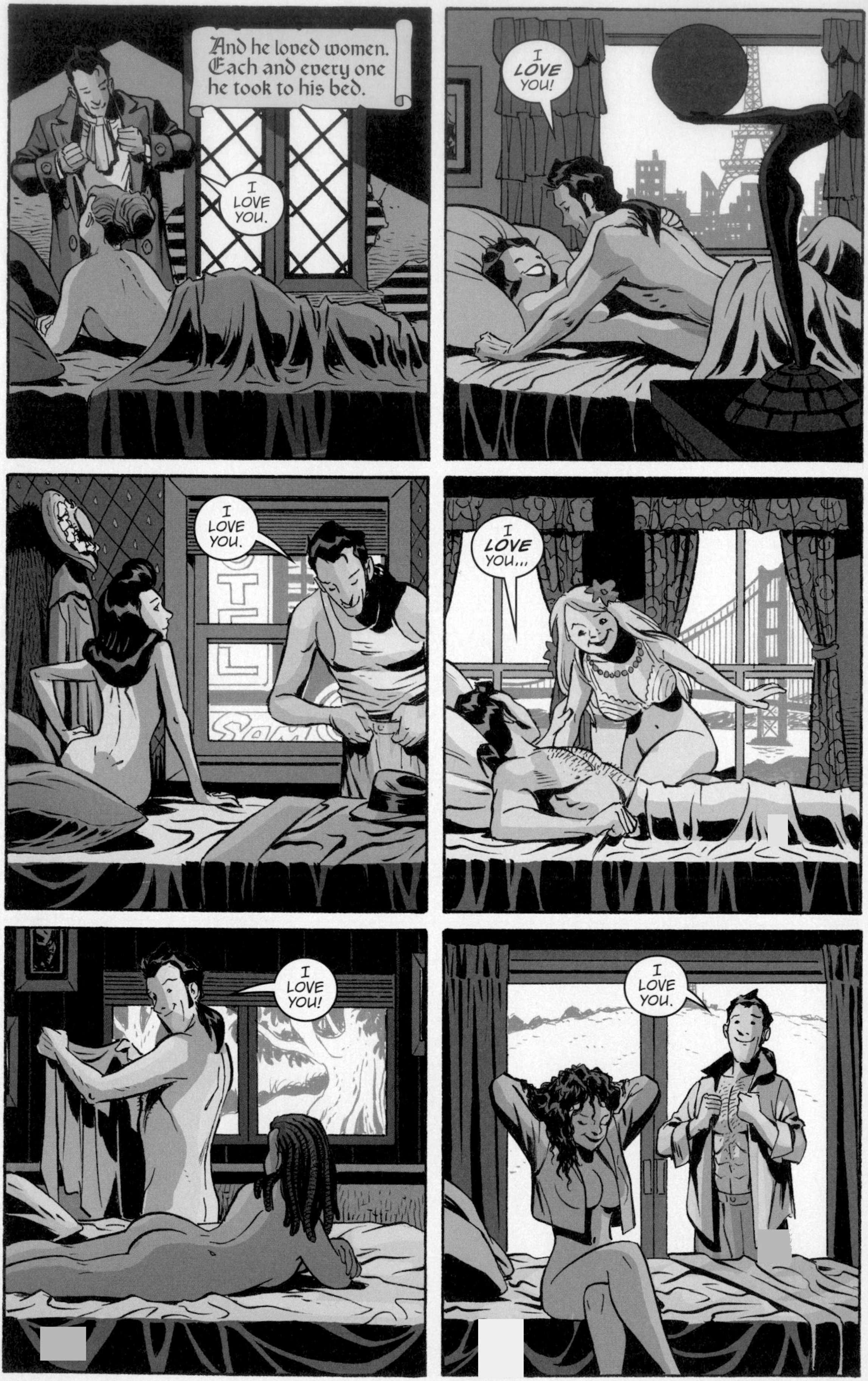
And he loved women. Each and every one he took to his bed.
I LOVE YOU.
I LOVE YOU!
I LOVE YOU.
I LOVE YOU...
I LOVE YOU!
I LOVE YOU.

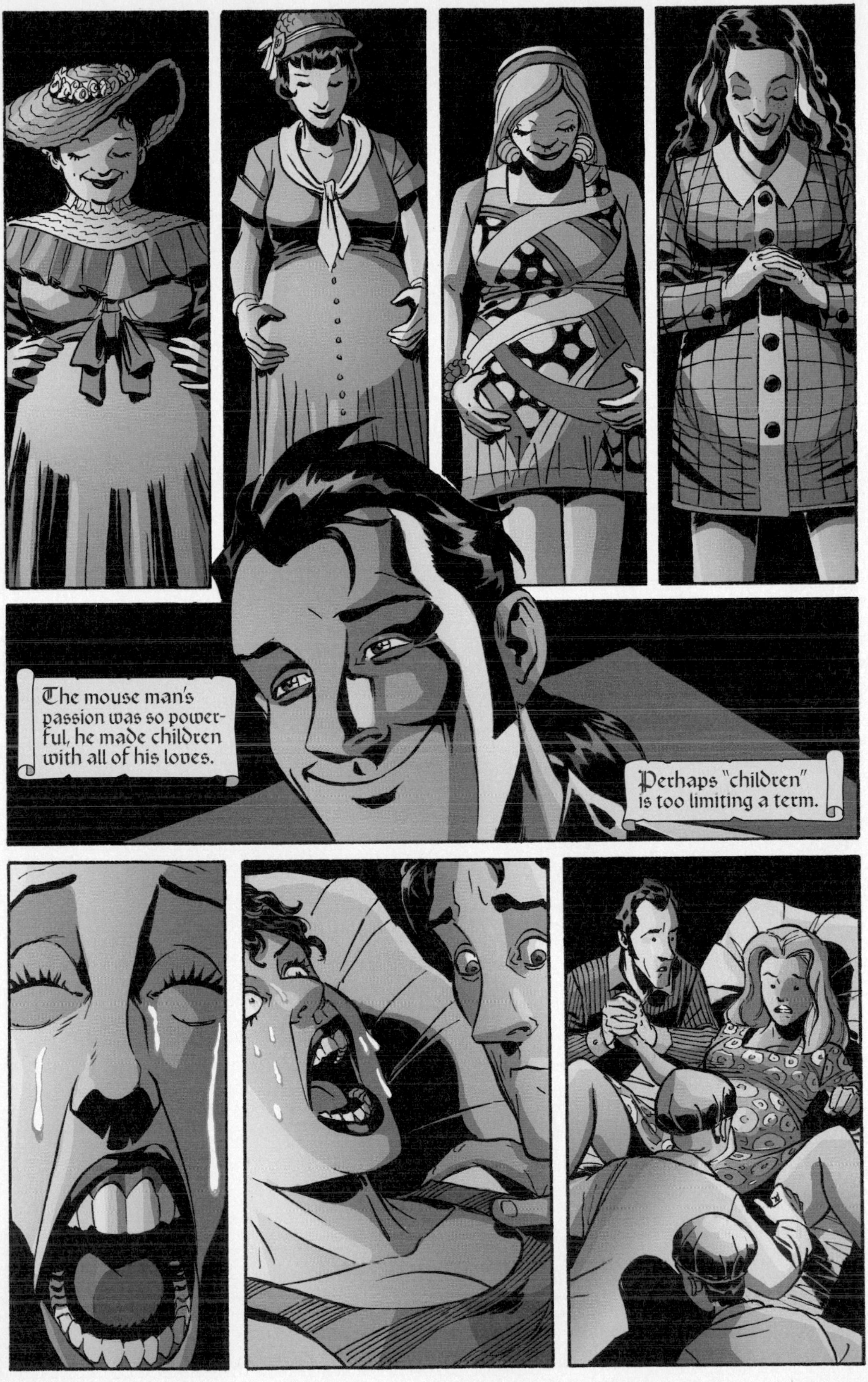
The mouse man's passion was so powerful, he made children with all of his loves.
Perhaps "children" is too limiting a term.

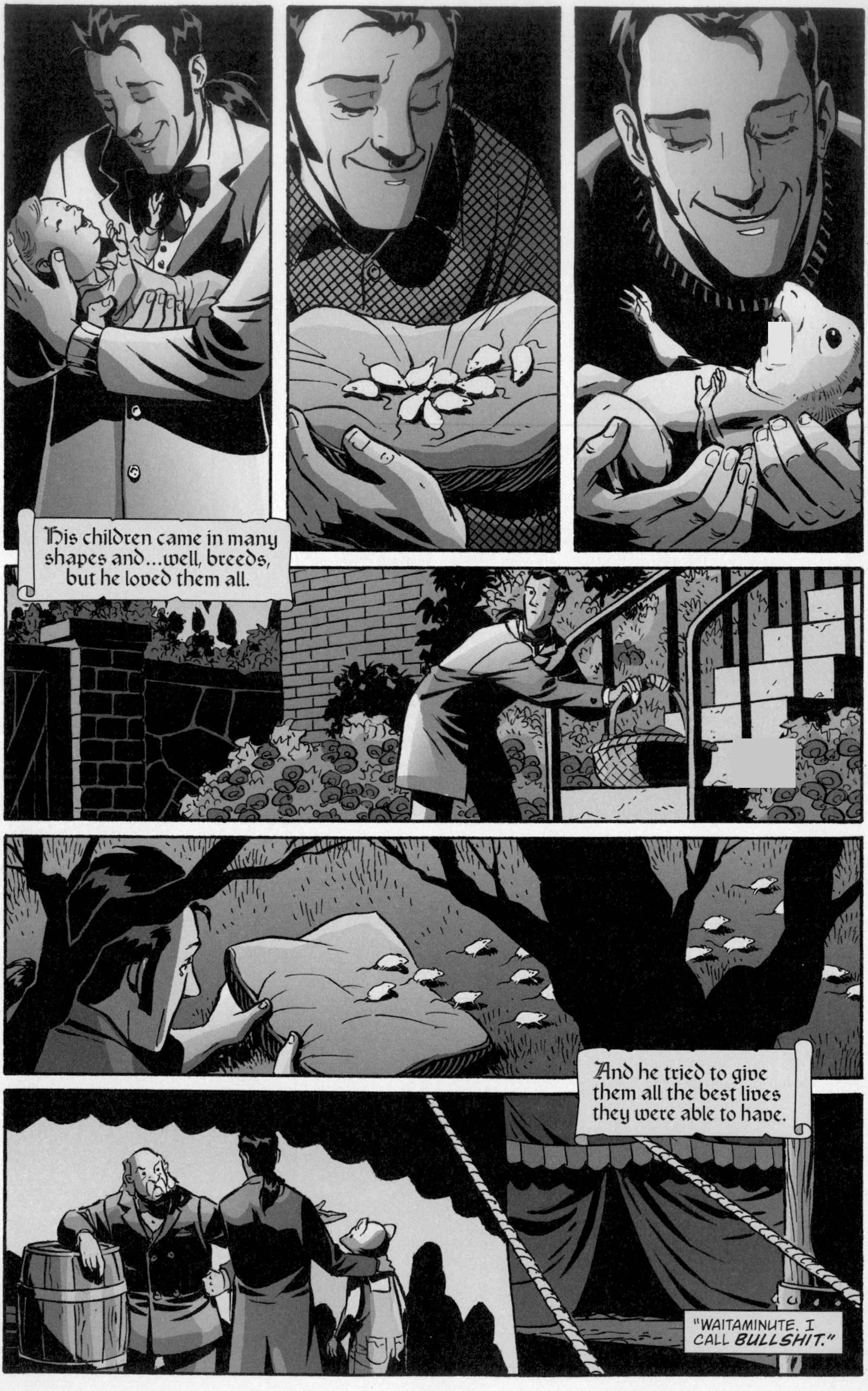
His children came in many shapes and...well, breeds, but he loved them all.
And he tried to give them all the best lives they were able to have.
"WAITAMINUTE. I CALL BULLSHIT."

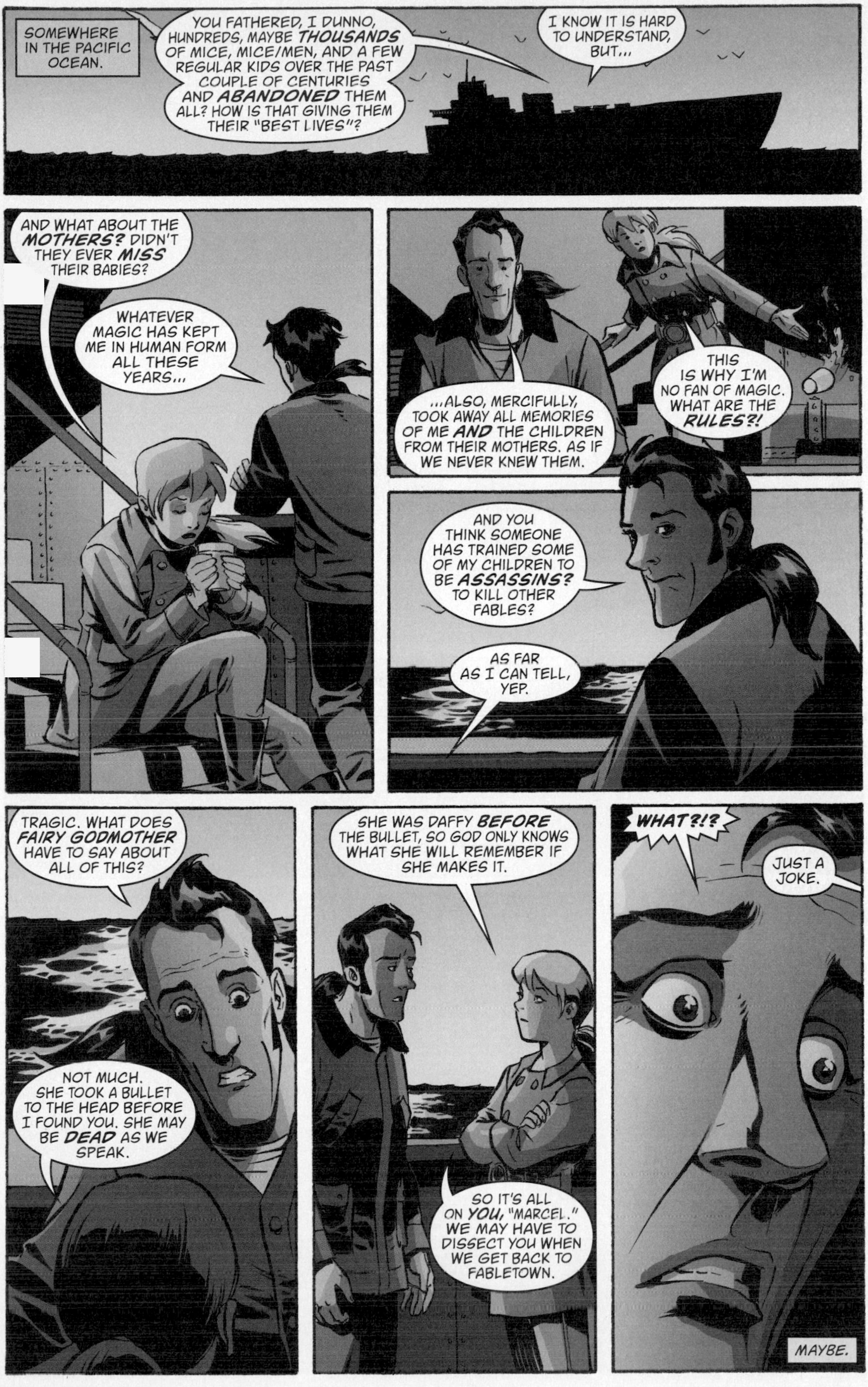
SOMEWHERE IN THE PACIFIC OCEAN.
YOU FATHERED, I DUNNO, HUNDREDS, MAYBE THOUSANDS OF MICE, MICE/MEN, AND A FEW REGULAR KIDS OVER THE PAST COUPLE OF CENTURIES AND ABANDONED THEM ALL? HOW IS THAT GIVING THEM THEIR "BEST LIVES"?
I KNOW IT IS HARD TO UNDERSTAND, BUT...
AND WHAT ABOUT THE MOTHERS? DIDN'T THEY EVER MISS THEIR BABIES?
WHATEVER MAGIC HAS KEPT ME IN HUMAN FORM ALL THESE YEARS...
...ALSO, MERCIFULLY, TOOK AWAY ALL MEMORIES OF ME AND THE CHILDREN FROM THEIR MOTHERS. AS IF WE NEVER KNEW THEM.
THIS IS WHY I'M NO FAN OF MAGIC. WHAT ARE THE RULES?!
AND YOU THINK SOMEONE HAS TRAINED SOME OF MY CHILDREN TO BE ASSASSINS? TO KILL OTHER FABLES?
AS FAR AS I CAN TELL, YEP.
TRAGIC. WHAT DOES FAIRY GODMOTHER HAVE TO SAY ABOUT ALL OF THIS?
NOT MUCH. SHE TOOK A BULLET TO THE HEAD BEFORE I FOUND YOU. SHE MAY BE DEAD AS WE SPEAK.
SHE WAS DAFFY BEFORE THE BULLET, SO GOD ONLY KNOWS WHAT SHE WILL REMEMBER IF SHE MAKES IT.
SO IT'S ALL ON YOU, "MARCEL." WE MAY HAVE TO DISSECT YOU WHEN WE GET BACK TO FABLETOWN.
WHAT?!?
JUST A JOKE.
MAYBE.

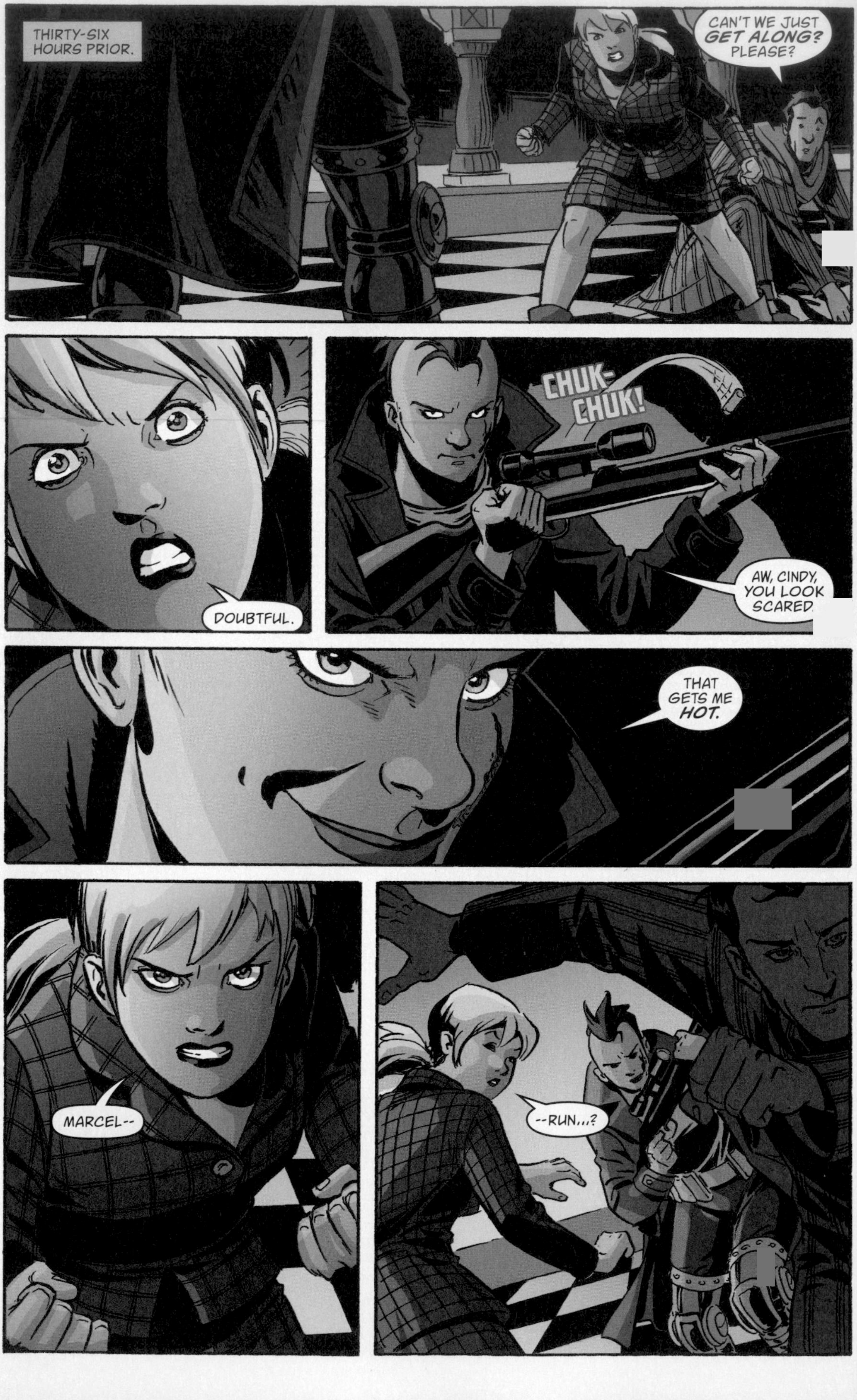
THIRTY-SIX HOURS PRIOR.
CAN'T WE JUST GET ALONG? PLEASE?
DOUBTFUL.
CHUK-CHUK!
AW, CINDY, YOU LOOK SCARED.
THAT GETS ME HOT.
MARCEL--
--RUN...?

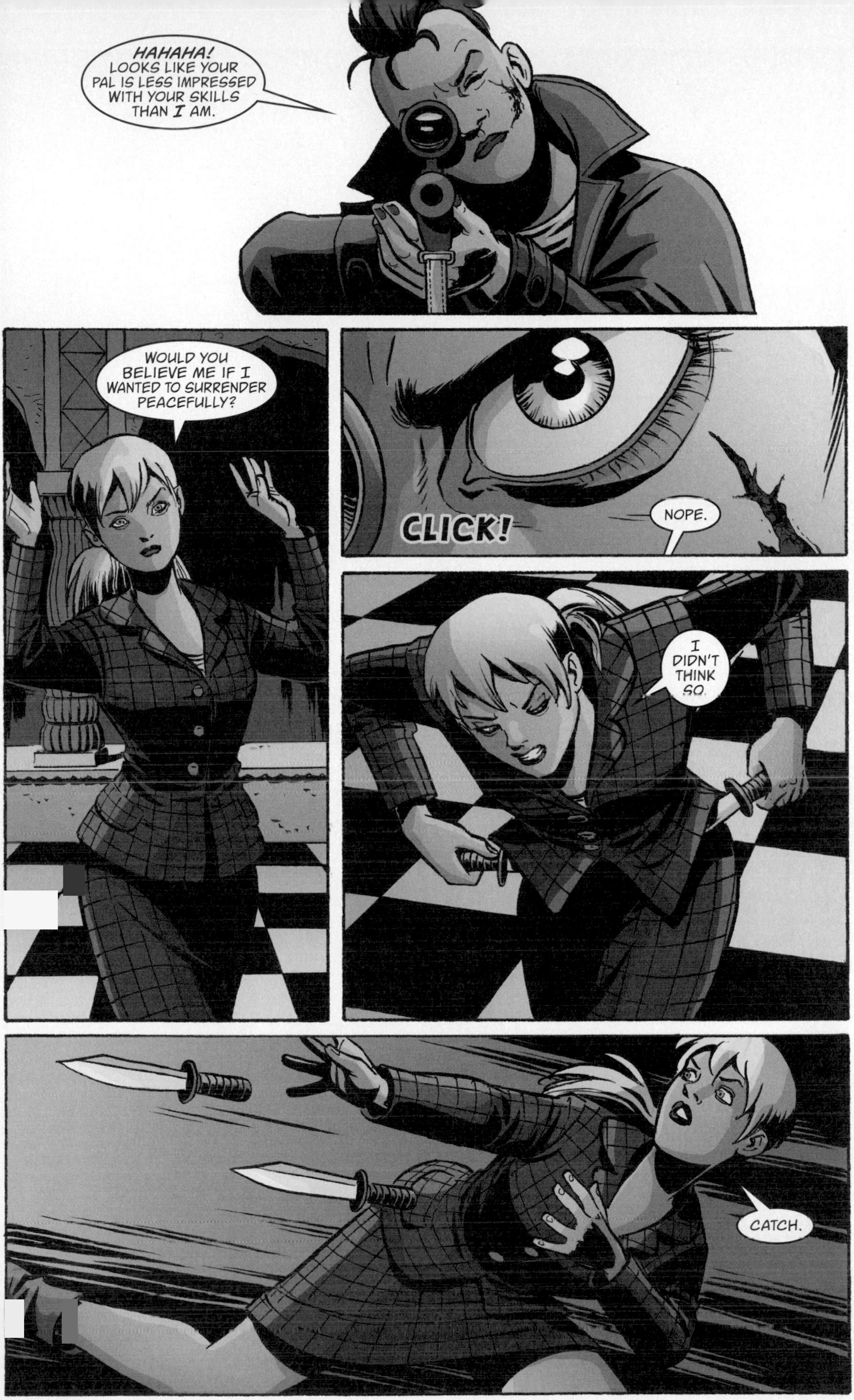
HAHAHA! LOOKS LIKE YOUR PAL IS LESS IMPRESSED WITH YOUR SKILLS THAN I AM.
WOULD YOU BELIEVE ME IF I WANTED TO SURRENDER PEACEFULLY?
CLICK!
NOPE.
I DIDN'T THINK SO.
CATCH.

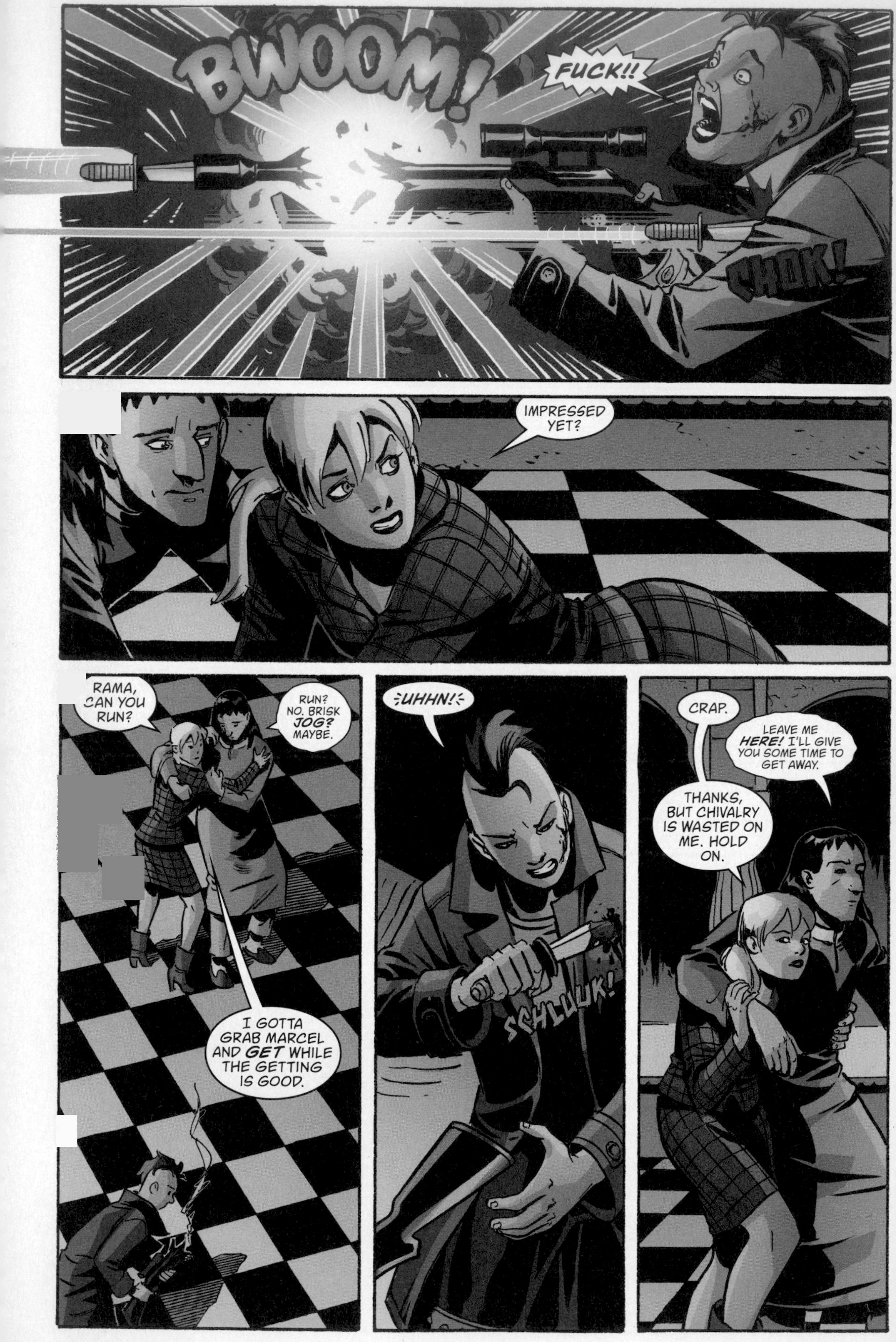
BWOOM!
FUCK!!
CHOK!
IMPRESSED YET?
RAMA, CAN YOU RUN?
RUN? NO. BRISK JOG? MAYBE.
I GOTTA GRAB MARCEL AND GET WHILE THE GETTING IS GOOD.
UHHN!
SCHLUUK!
CRAP.
LEAVE ME HERE! I'LL GIVE YOU SOME TIME TO GET AWAY.
THANKS, BUT CHIVALRY IS WASTED ON ME. HOLD ON.

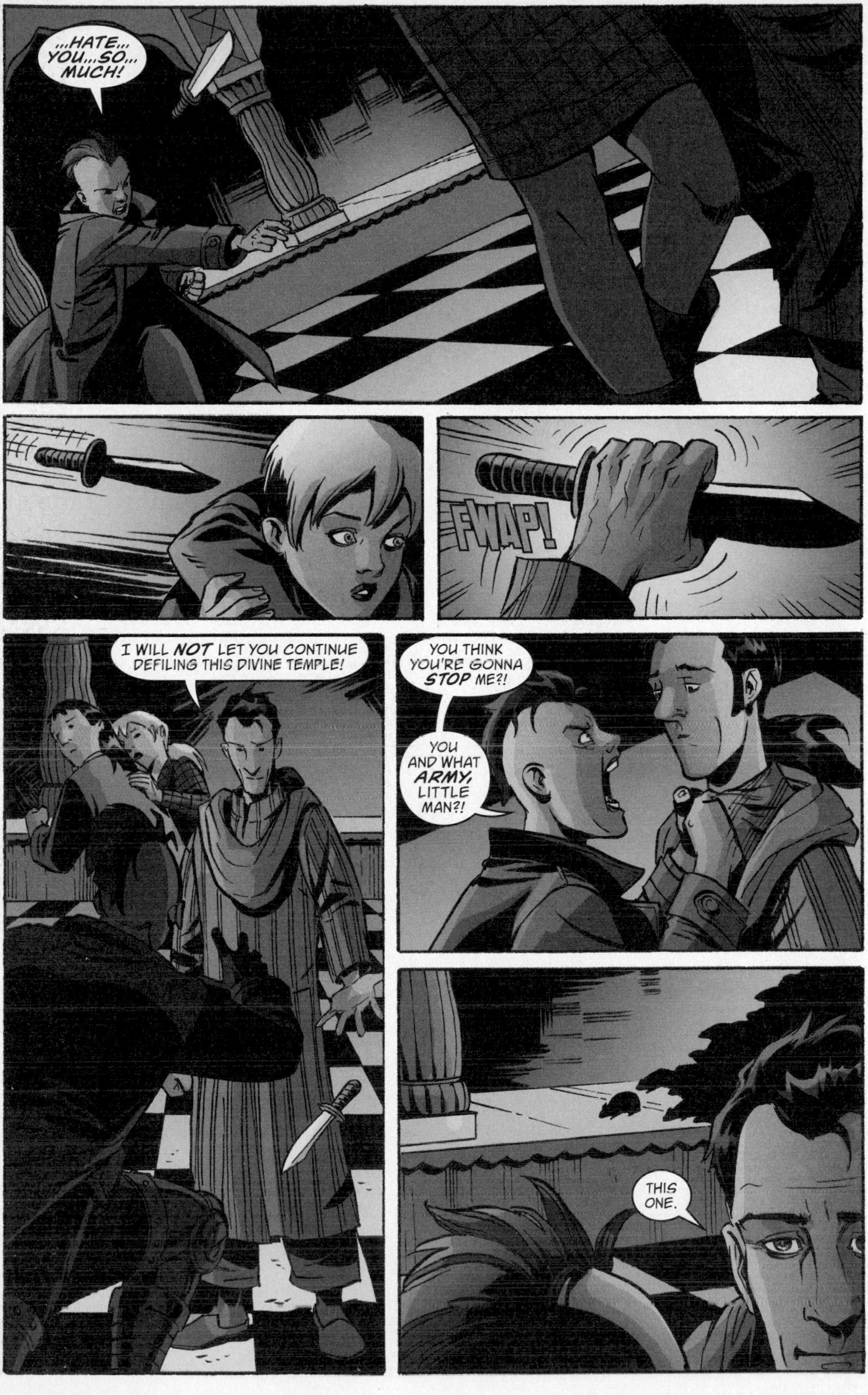
...HATE... YOU...SO... MUCH!
FWAP!
I WILL NOT LET YOU CONTINUE DEFILING THIS DIVINE TEMPLE!
YOU THINK YOU'RE GONNA STOP ME?!
YOU AND WHAT ARMY, LITTLE MAN?!
THIS ONE.

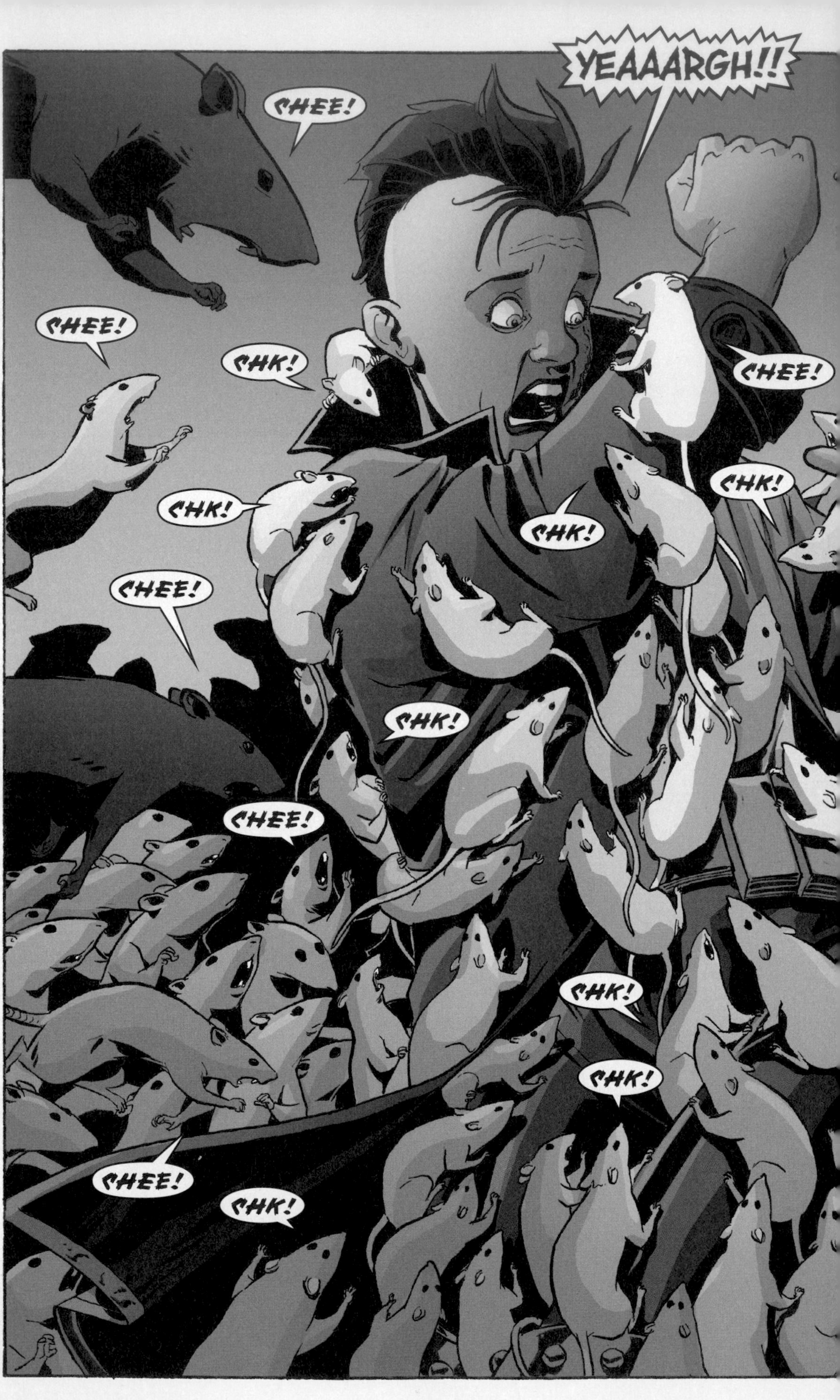
YEAAARGH!!
CHEE!
CHEE!
CHK!
CHEE!
CHK!
CHK!
CHK!
CHEE!
CHK!
CHEE!
CHK!
CHK!
CHEE!
CHK!

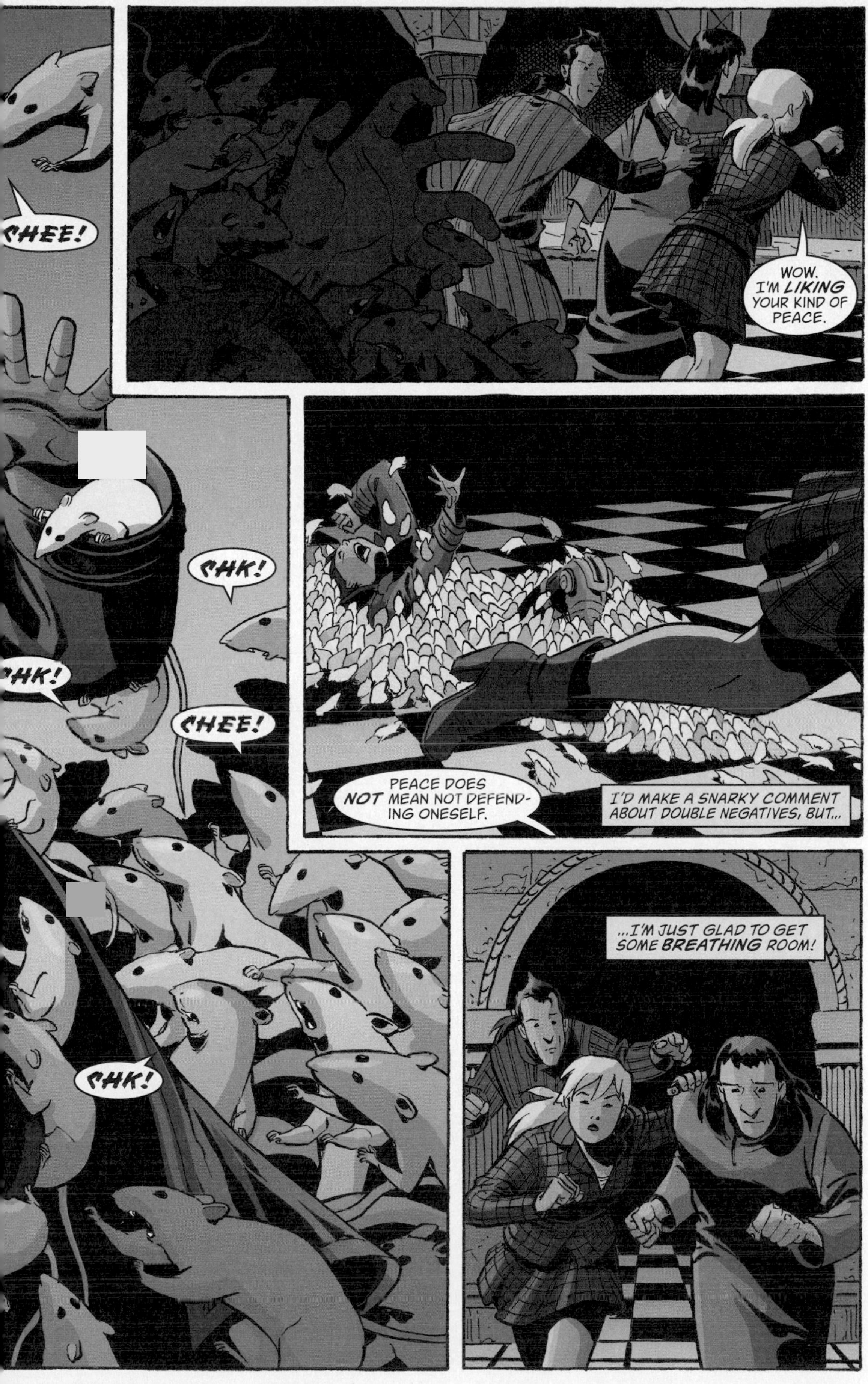
CHEE!
WOW. I'M LIKING YOUR KIND OF PEACE.
CHK!
CHK!
CHEE!
CHK!
PEACE DOES NOT MEAN NOT DEFEND-ING ONESELF.
I'D MAKE A SNARKY COMMENT ABOUT DOUBLE NEGATIVES, BUT...
...I'M JUST GLAD TO GET SOME BREATHING ROOM!

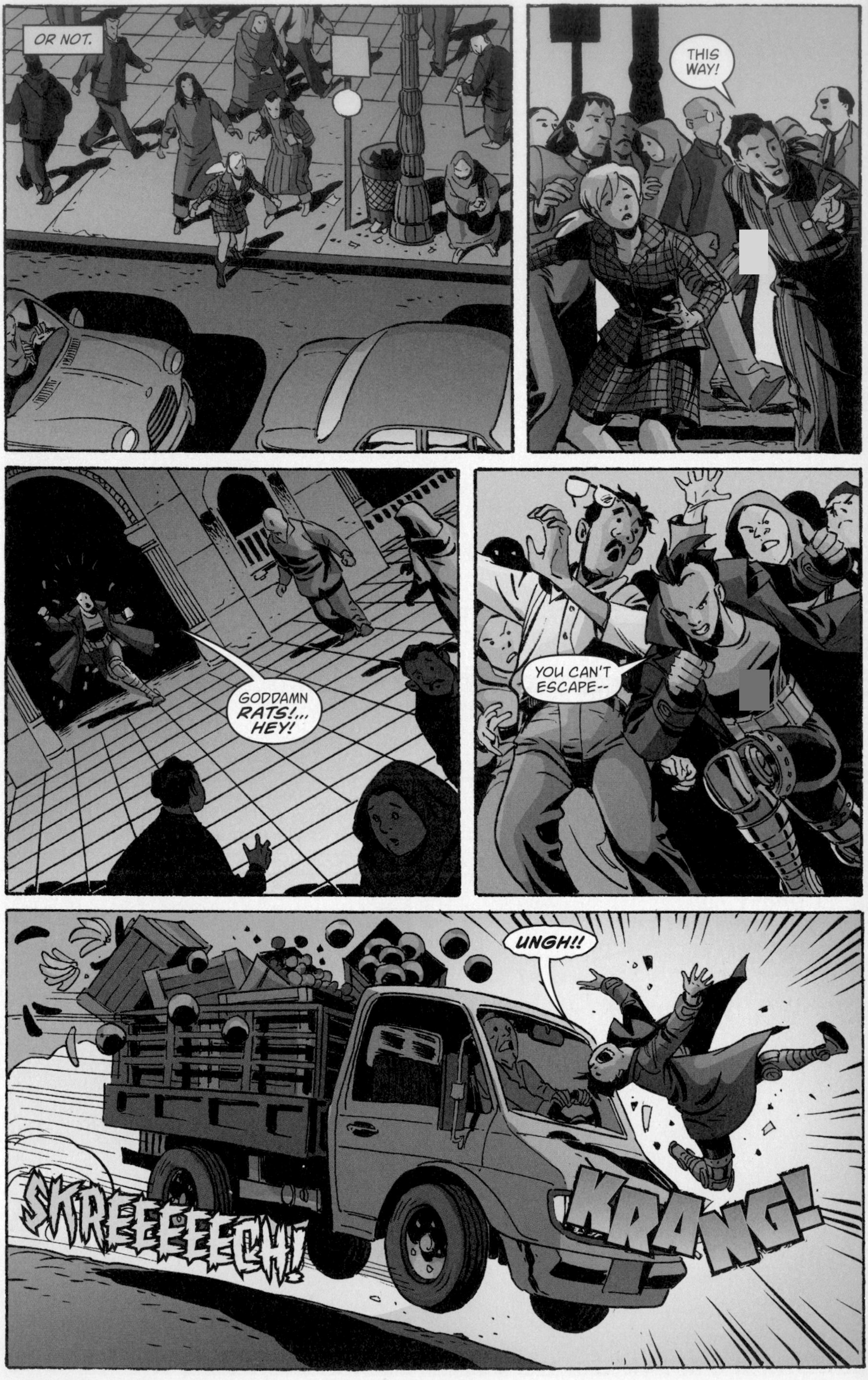
OR NOT.
THIS WAY!
GODDAMN RATS!... HEY!
YOU CAN'T ESCAPE--
UNGH!!
SKREEEEEECH!
KRANG!

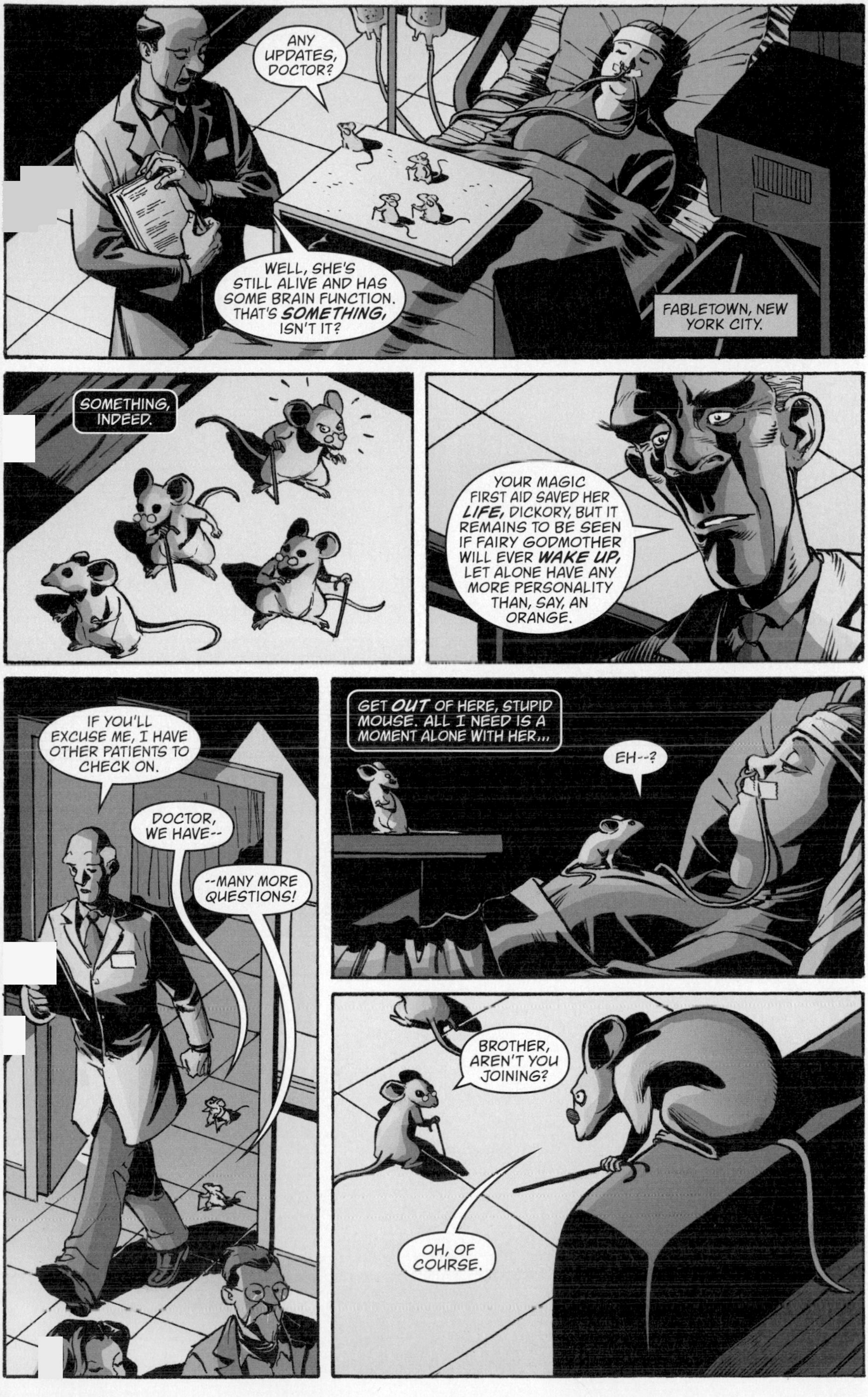
ANY UPDATES, DOCTOR?
WELL, SHE'S STILL ALIVE AND HAS SOME BRAIN FUNCTION. THAT'S SOMETHING, ISN'T IT?
FABLETOWN, NEW YORK CITY.
SOMETHING, INDEED.
YOUR MAGIC FIRST AID SAVED HER LIFE, DICKORY, BUT IT REMAINS TO BE SEEN IF FAIRY GODMOTHER WILL EVER WAKE UP, LET ALONE HAVE ANY MORE PERSONALITY THAN, SAY, AN ORANGE.
IF YOU'LL EXCUSE ME, I HAVE OTHER PATIENTS TO CHECK ON.
DOCTOR, WE HAVE--
--MANY MORE QUESTIONS!
GET OUT OF HERE, STUPID MOUSE. ALL I NEED IS A MOMENT ALONE WITH HER...
EH--?
BROTHER, AREN'T YOU JOINING?
OH, OF COURSE.

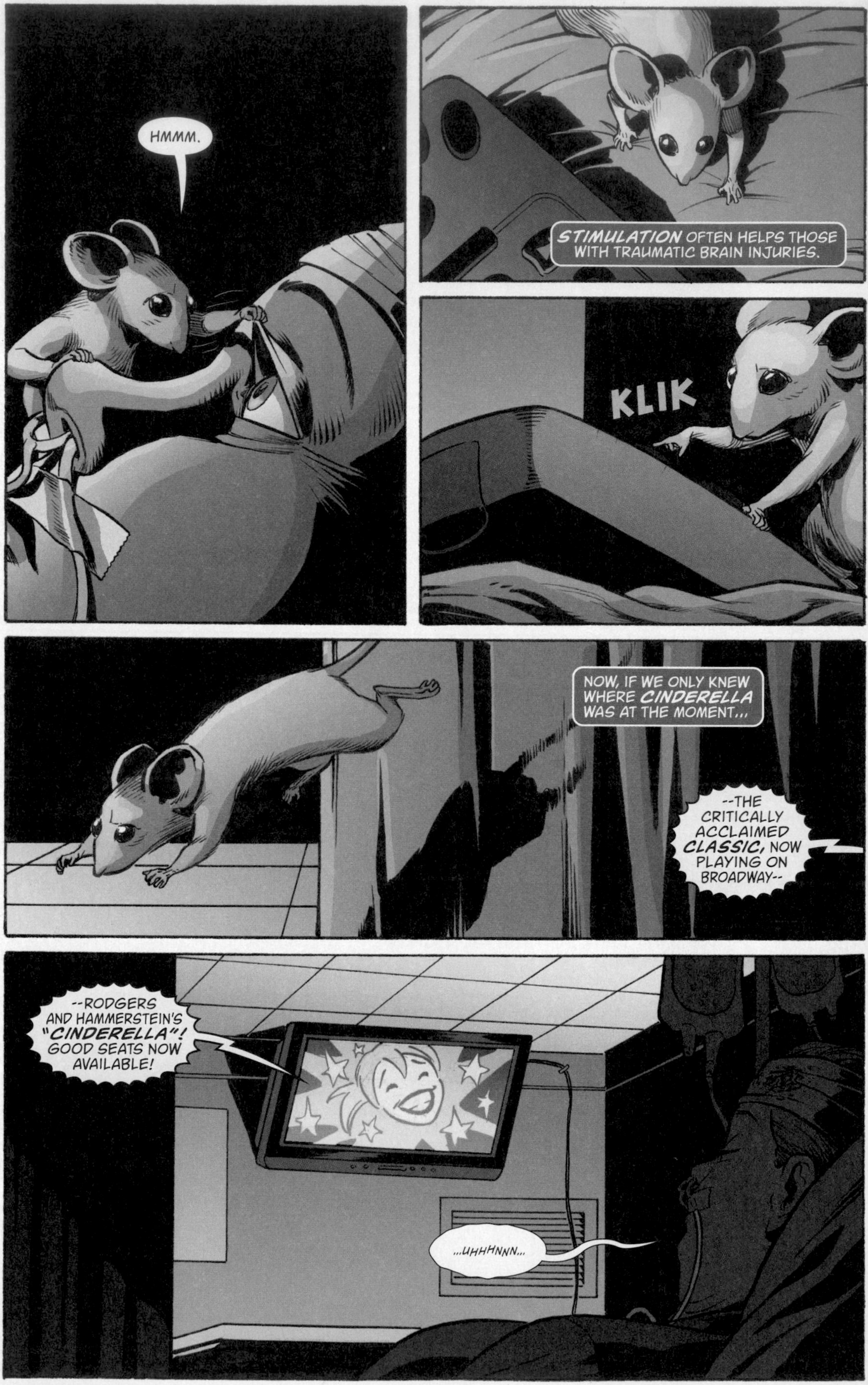
HMMM.
STIMULATION OFTEN HELPS THOSE WITH TRAUMATIC BRAIN INJURIES.
KLIK
NOW, IF WE ONLY KNEW WHERE CINDERELLA WAS AT THE MOMENT...
--THE CRITICALLY ACCLAIMED CLASSIC, NOW PLAYING ON BROADWAY--
--RODGERS AND HAMMERSTEIN'S "CINDERELLA"! GOOD SEATS NOW AVAILABLE!
...UHHHNNN...

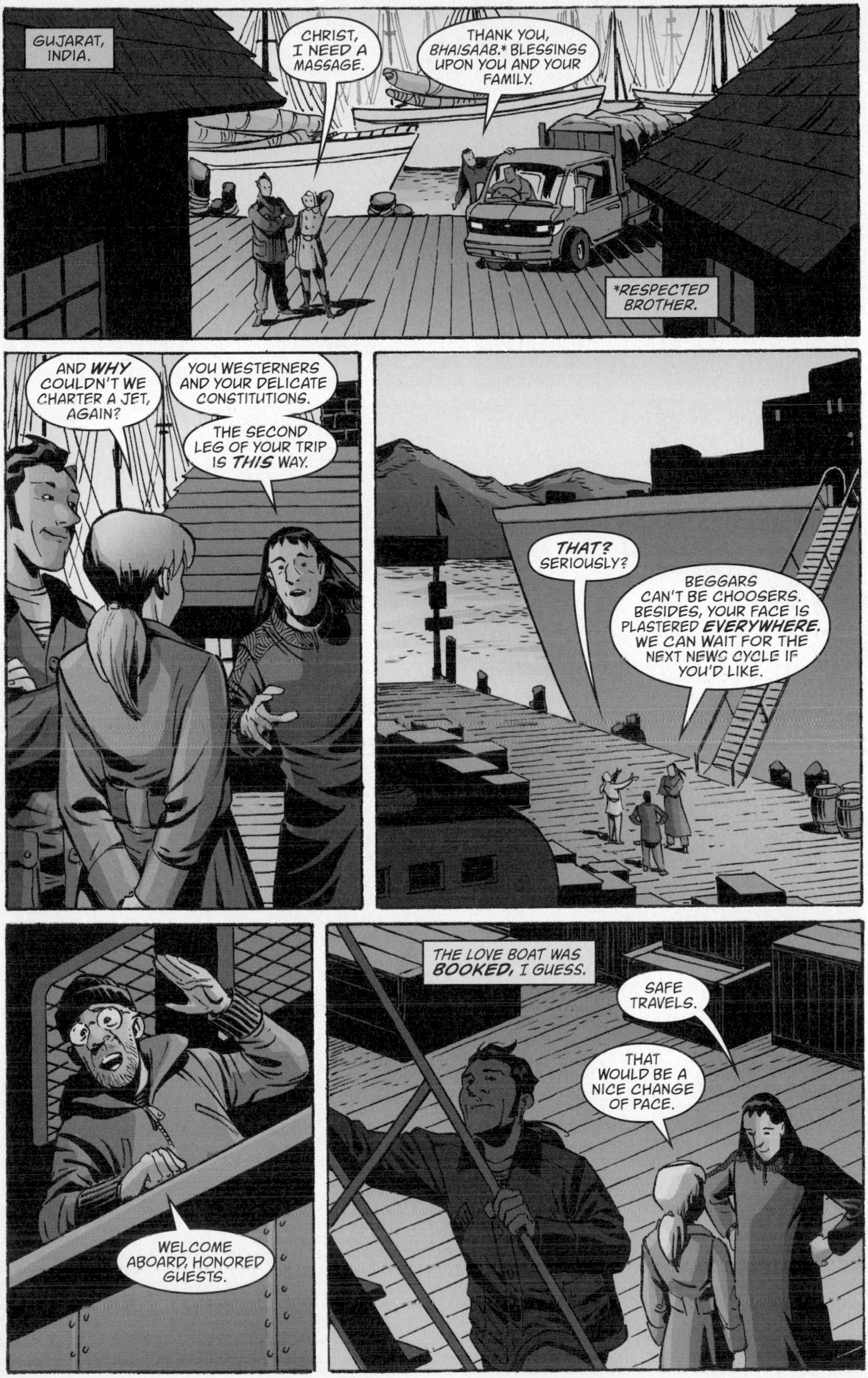
GUJARAT, INDIA.
CHRIST, I NEED A MASSAGE.
THANK YOU, BHAISAAB.* BLESSINGS UPON YOU AND YOUR FAMILY.
*RESPECTED BROTHER.
AND WHY COULDN'T WE CHARTER A JET, AGAIN?
YOU WESTERNERS AND YOUR DELICATE CONSTITUTIONS.
THE SECOND LEG OF YOUR TRIP IS THIS WAY.
THAT? SERIOUSLY?
BEGGARS CAN'T BE CHOOSERS. BESIDES, YOUR FACE IS PLASTERED EVERYWHERE. WE CAN WAIT FOR THE NEXT NEWS CYCLE IF YOU'D LIKE.
WELCOME ABOARD, HONORED GUESTS.
THE LOVE BOAT WAS BOOKED, I GUESS.
SAFE TRAVELS.
THAT WOULD BE A NICE CHANGE OF PACE.

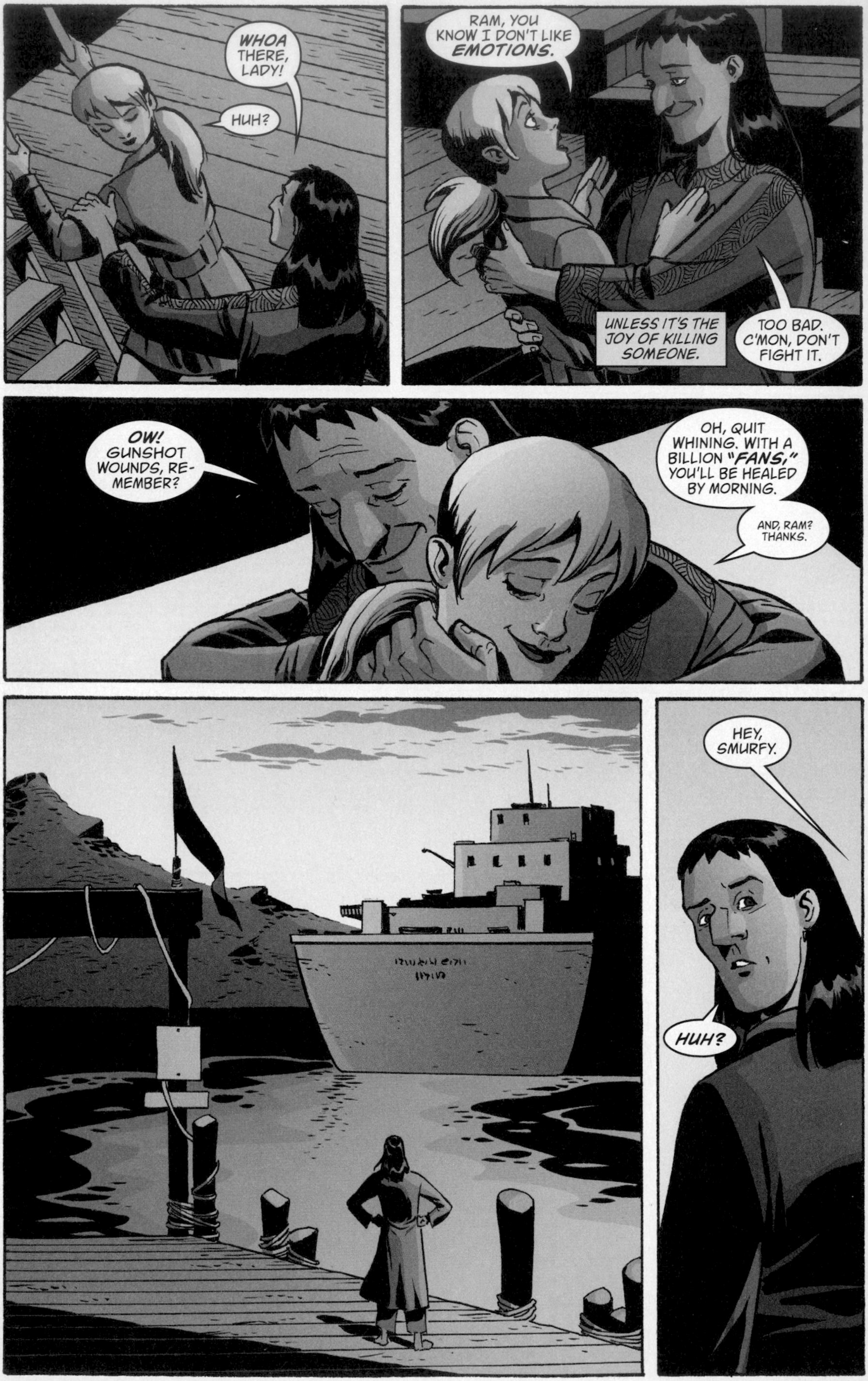
WHOA THERE, LADY!
HUH?
RAM, YOU KNOW I DON'T LIKE EMOTIONS.
UNLESS IT'S THE JOY OF KILLING SOMEONE.
TOO BAD. C'MON, DON'T FIGHT IT.
OW! GUNSHOT WOUNDS, RE-MEMBER?
OH, QUIT WHINING. WITH A BILLION "FANS," YOU'LL BE HEALED BY MORNING.
AND, RAM? THANKS.
HEY, SMURFY.
HUH?

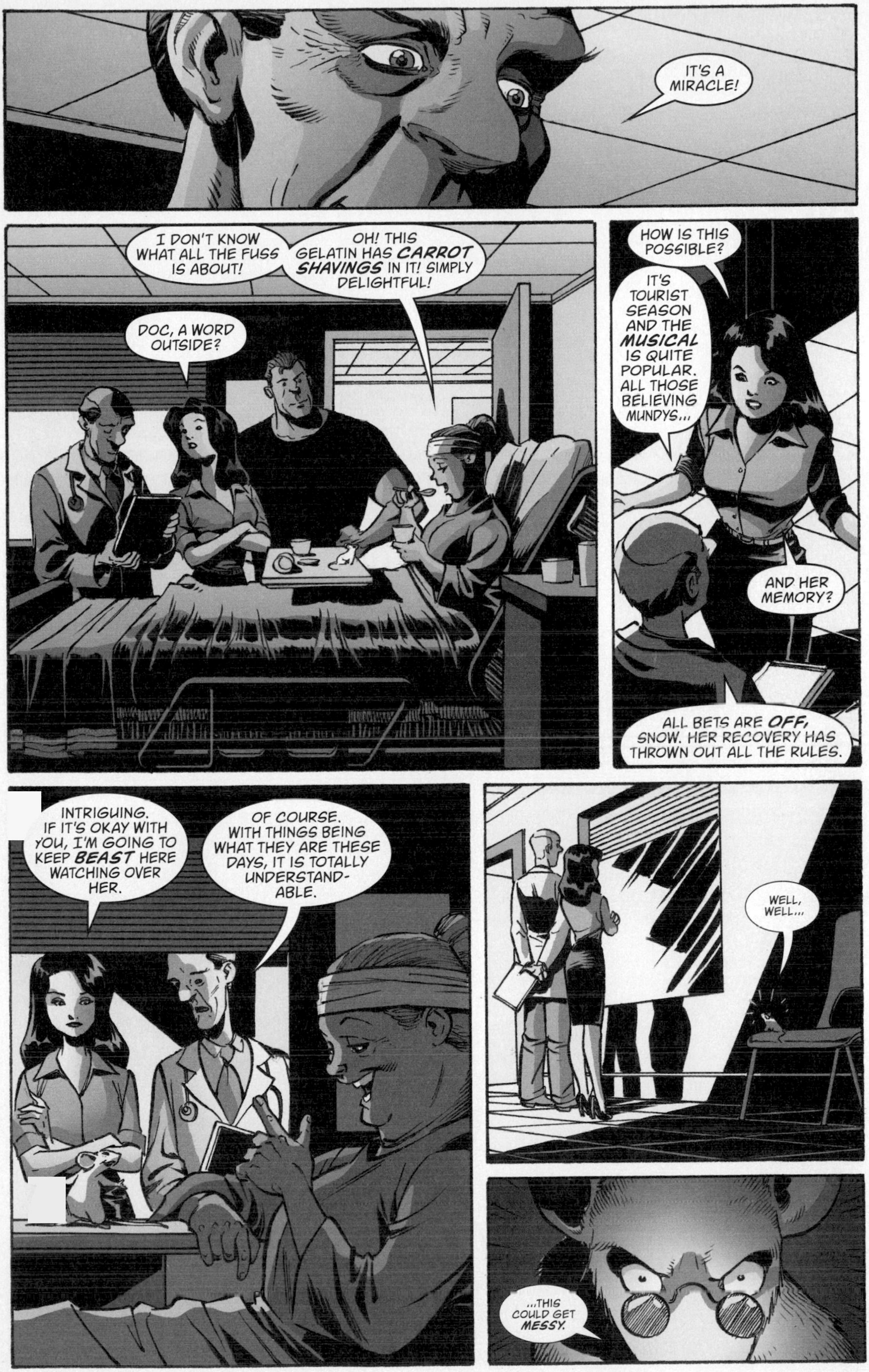
IT'S A MIRACLE!
I DON'T KNOW WHAT ALL THE FUSS IS ABOUT!
OH! THIS GELATIN HAS CARROT SHAVINGS IN IT! SIMPLY DELIGHTFUL!
DOC, A WORD OUTSIDE?
HOW IS THIS POSSIBLE?
IT'S TOURIST SEASON AND THE MUSICAL IS QUITE POPULAR. ALL THOSE BELIEVING MUNDYS...
AND HER MEMORY?
ALL BETS ARE OFF, SNOW. HER RECOVERY HAS THROWN OUT ALL THE RULES.
INTRIGUING. IF IT'S OKAY WITH YOU, I'M GOING TO KEEP BEAST HERE WATCHING OVER HER.
OF COURSE. WITH THINGS BEING WHAT THEY ARE THESE DAYS, IT IS TOTALLY UNDERSTANDABLE.
WELL, WELL...
...THIS COULD GET MESSY.

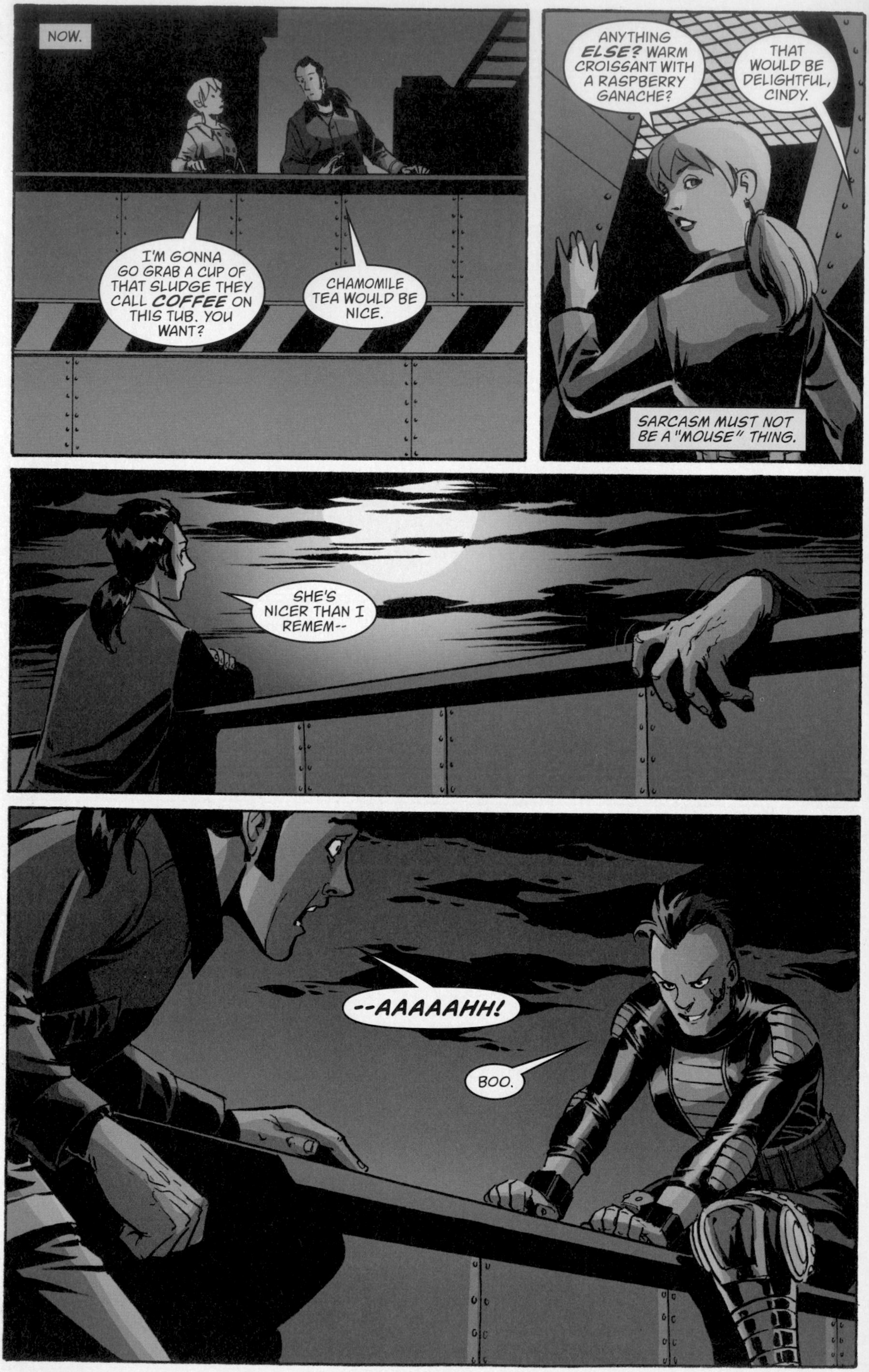
NOW.
I'M GONNA GO GRAB A CUP OF THAT SLUDGE THEY CALL COFFEE ON THIS TUB. YOU WANT?
CHAMOMILE TEA WOULD BE NICE.
ANYTHING ELSE? WARM CROISSANT WITH A RASPBERRY GANACHE?
THAT WOULD BE DELIGHTFUL, CINDY.
SARCASM MUST NOT BE A "MOUSE" THING.
SHE'S NICER THAN I REMEM--
--AAAAAHH!
BOO.

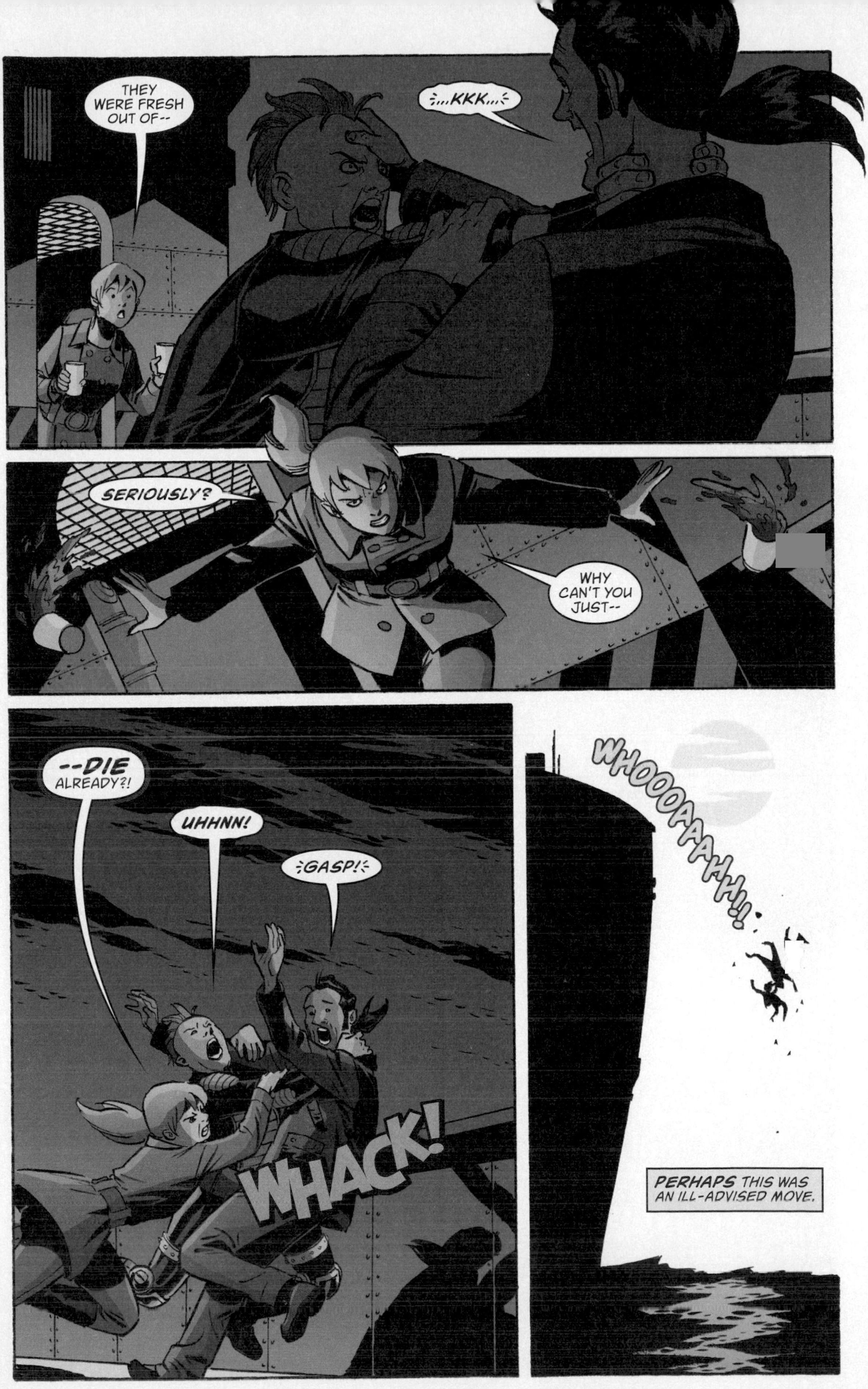
THEY WERE FRESH OUT OF--
...KKK...
SERIOUSLY?
WHY CAN'T YOU JUST--
--DIE ALREADY?!
UHHNN!
GASP!
WHACK!
WHOOOAAAHH!!
PERHAPS THIS WAS AN ILL-ADVISED MOVE.

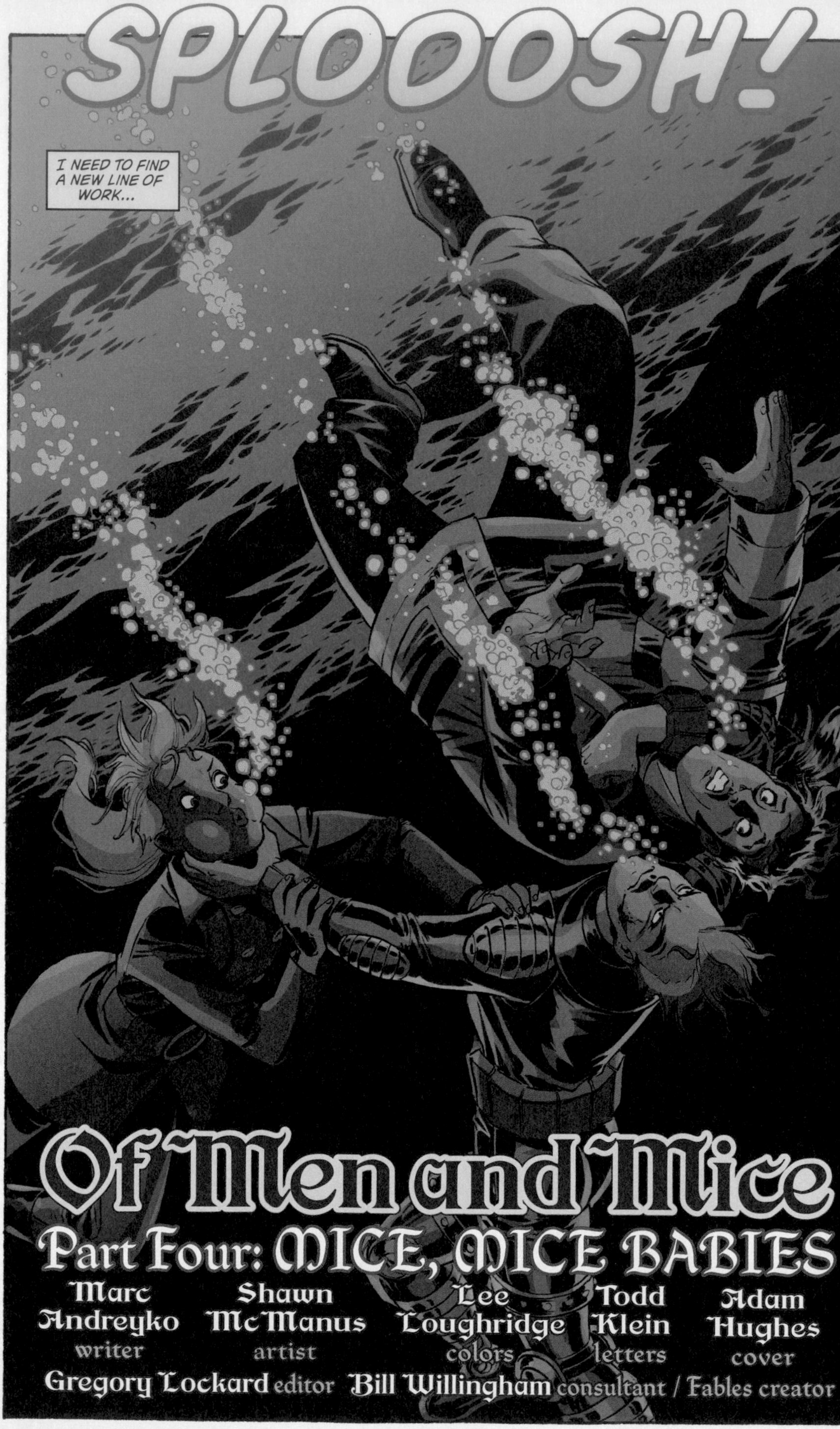
SPLOOOSH!
I NEED TO FIND A NEW LINE OF WORK...
Of Men and Mice
Part Four: MICE, MICE BABIES
Marc Andreyko writer
Shawn McManus artist
Lee Loughridge colors
Todd Klein letters
Adam Hughes cover
Gregory Lockard editor
Bill Willingham consultant / Fables creator

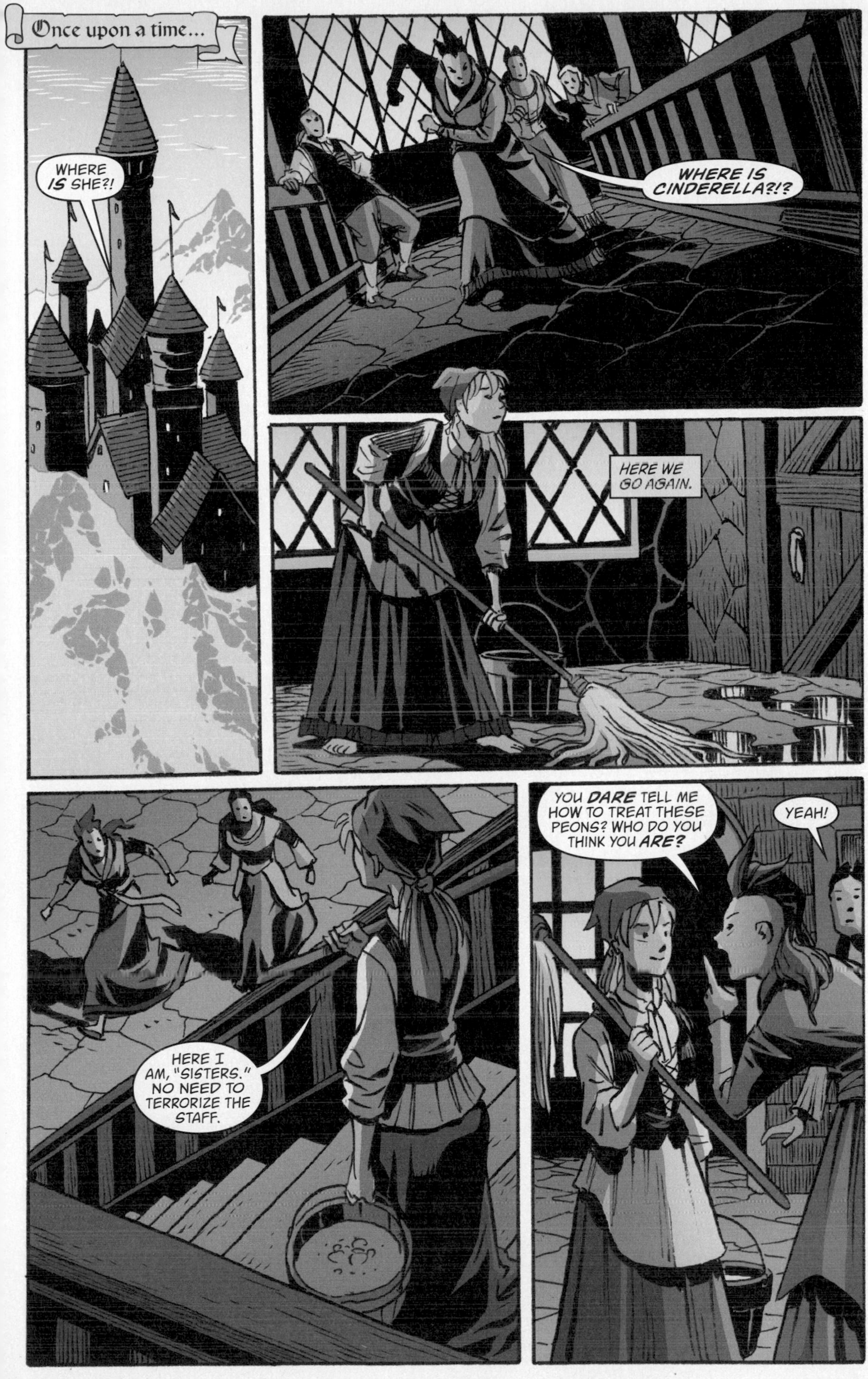

Once upon a time...
WHERE IS SHE?!
WHERE IS CINDERELLA?!?
HERE WE GO AGAIN.
HERE I AM, "SISTERS." NO NEED TO TERRORIZE THE STAFF.
YOU DARE TELL ME HOW TO TREAT THESE PEONS? WHO DO YOU THINK YOU ARE?
YEAH!

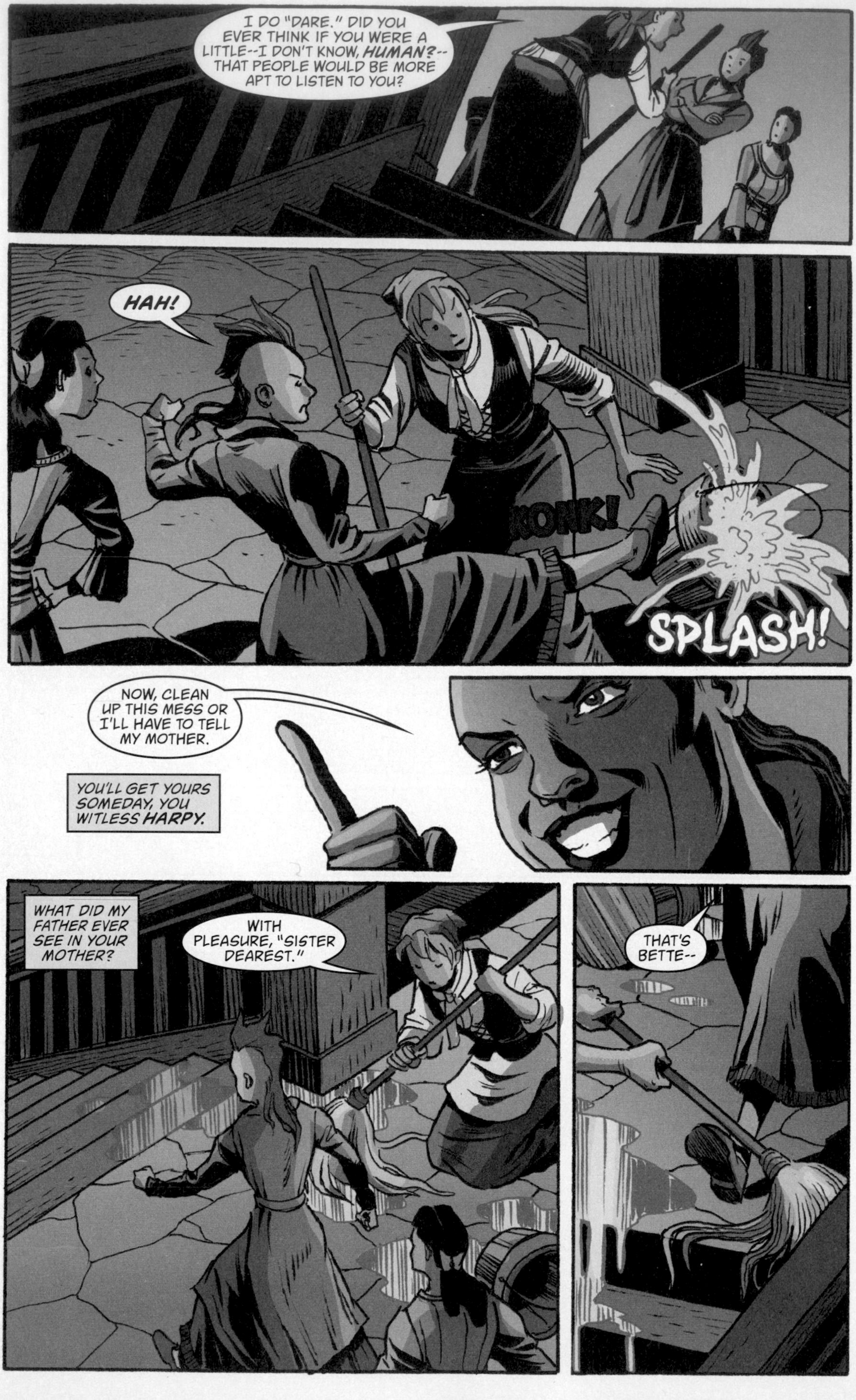
I DO "DARE." DID YOU EVER THINK IF YOU WERE A LITTLE--I DON'T KNOW, HUMAN?--THAT PEOPLE WOULD BE MORE APT TO LISTEN TO YOU?
HAH!
KONK!
SPLASH!
NOW, CLEAN UP THIS MESS OR I'LL HAVE TO TELL MY MOTHER.
YOU'LL GET YOURS SOMEDAY, YOU WITLESS HARPY.
WHAT DID MY FATHER EVER SEE IN YOUR MOTHER?
WITH PLEASURE, "SISTER DEAREST."
THAT'S BETTE--

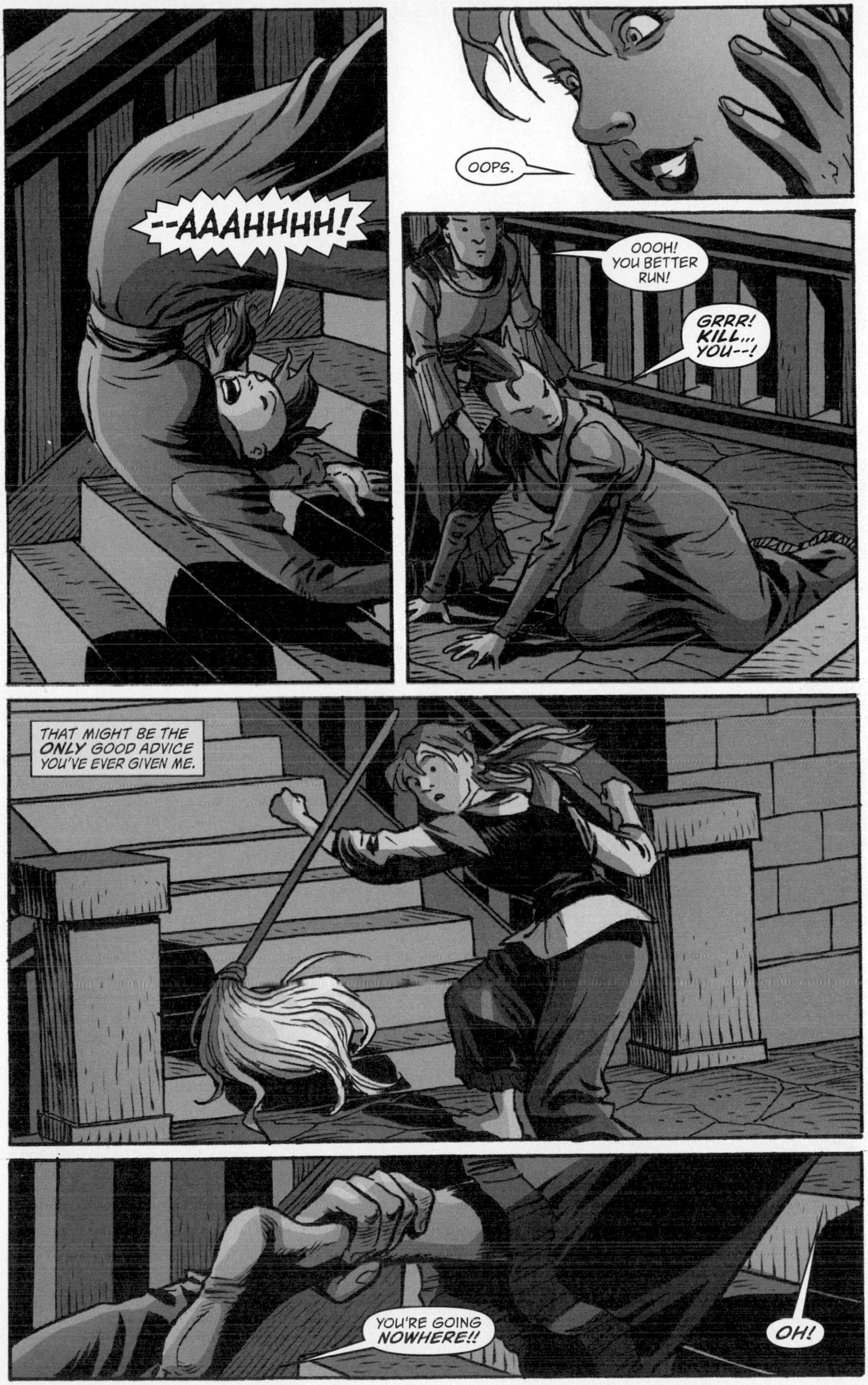

--AAAHHHH!
OOPS.
OOOH! YOU BETTER RUN!
GRRR! KILL... YOU--!
THAT MIGHT BE THE ONLY GOOD ADVICE YOU'VE EVER GIVEN ME.
YOU'RE GOING NOWHERE!!
OH!

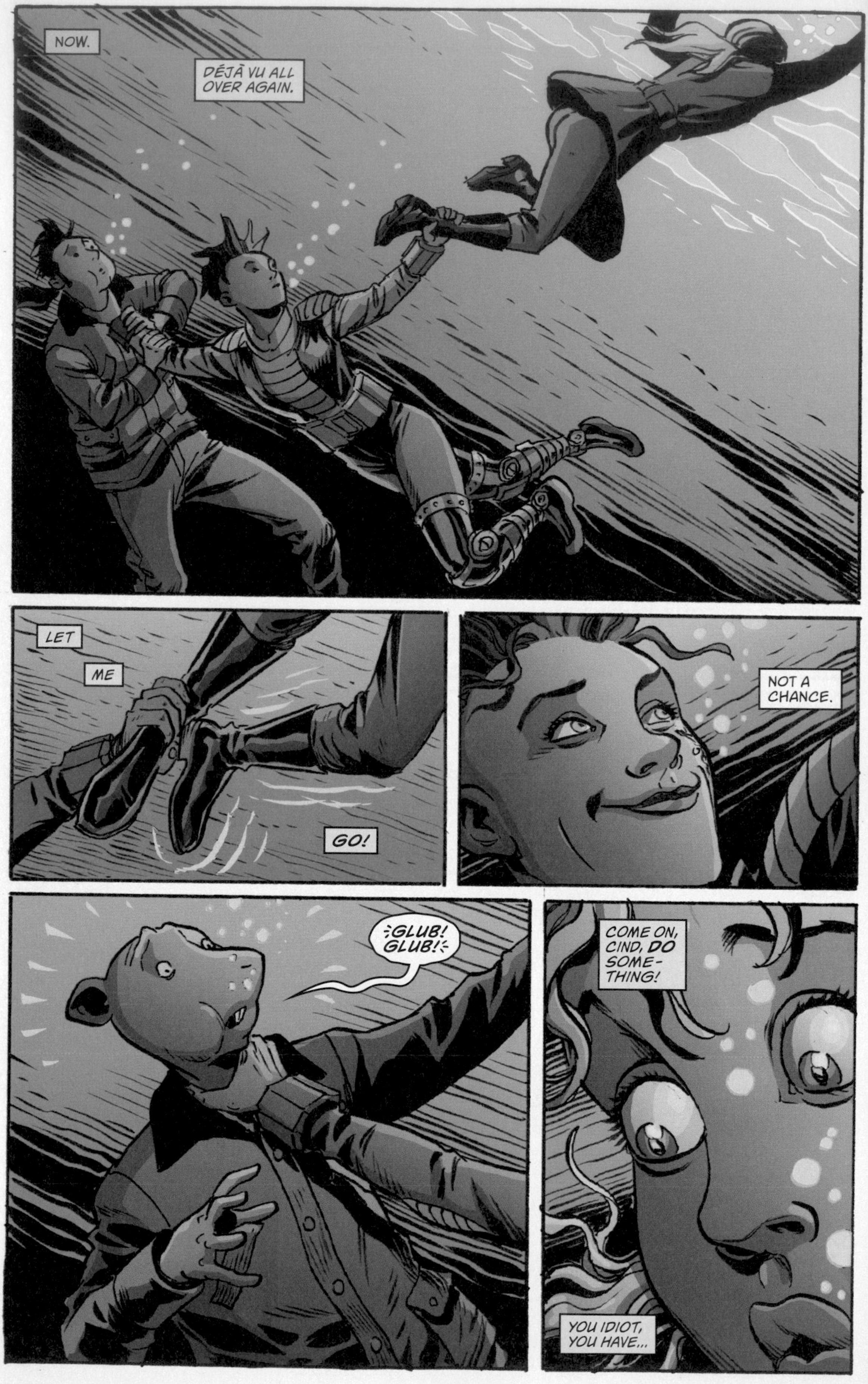
NOW.
DÉJÀ VU ALL OVER AGAIN.
LET
ME
GO!
NOT A CHANCE.
GLUB! GLUB!
COME ON, CIND, DO SOME-THING!
YOU IDIOT, YOU HAVE...

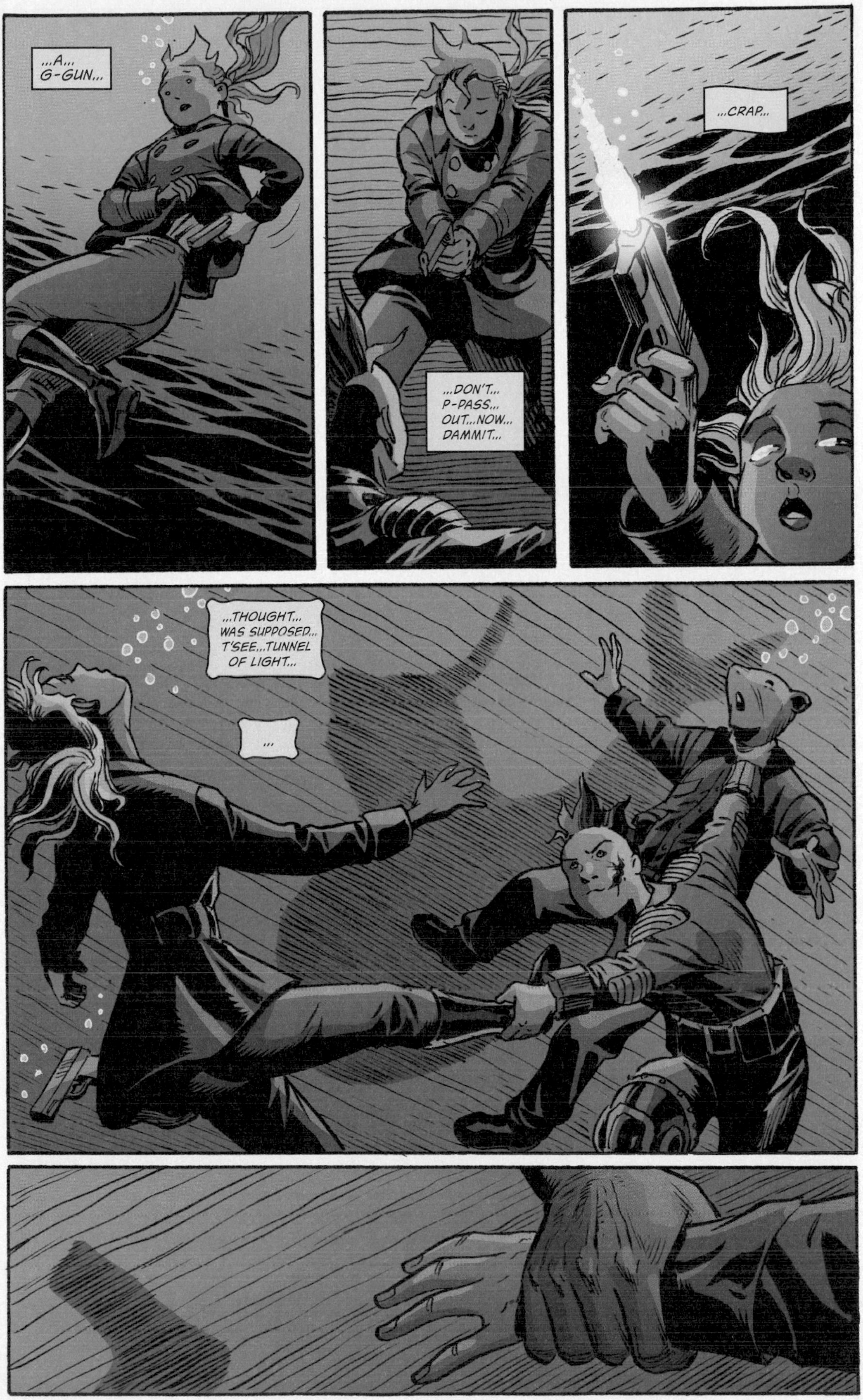
...A...
G-GUN...
...DON'T...
P-PASS...
OUT...NOW...
DAMMIT...
...CRAP...
...THOUGHT...
WAS SUPPOSED...
T'SEE...TUNNEL
OF LIGHT...
...

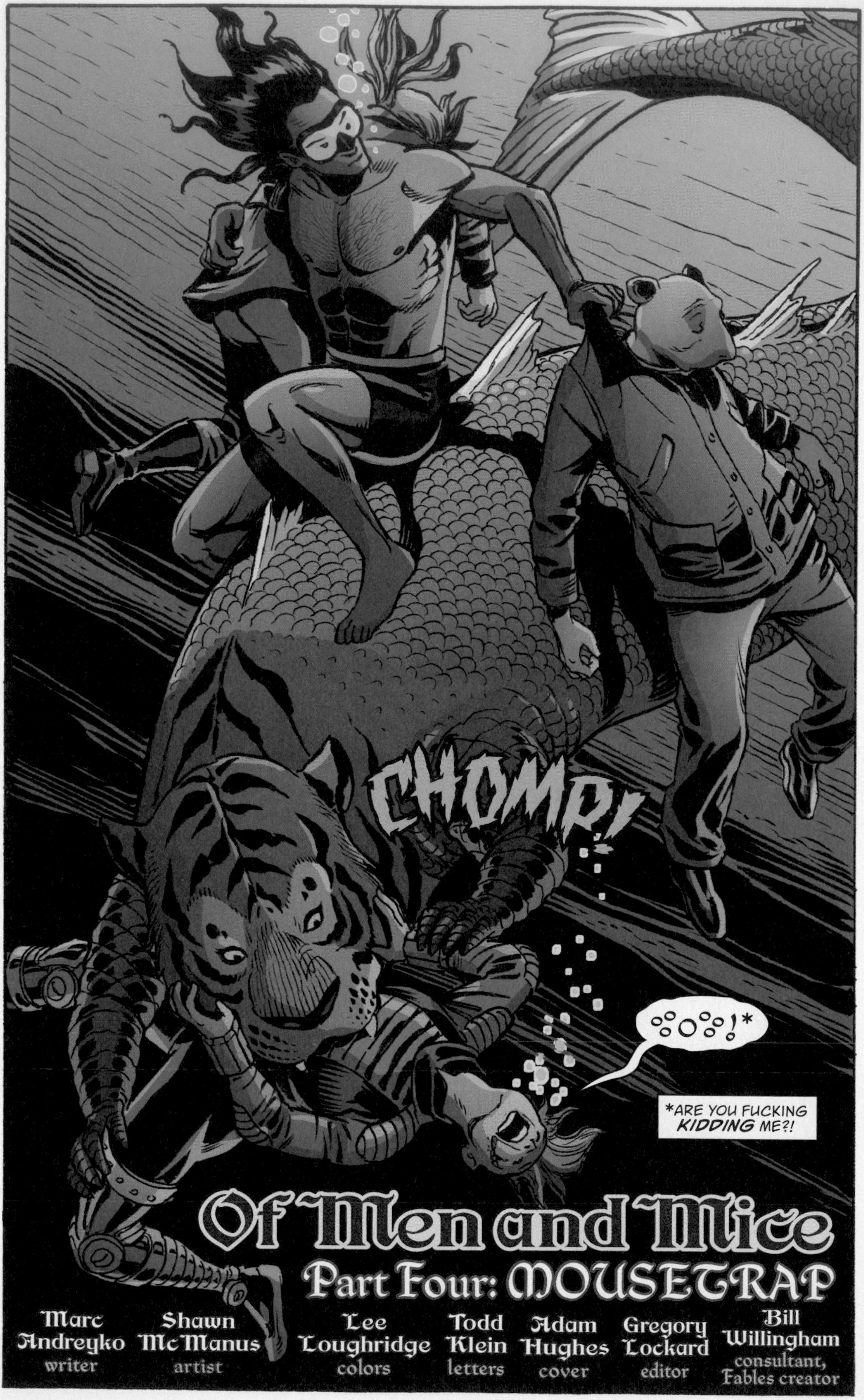
CHOMP!
°o°O°o°!*
*ARE YOU FUCKING KIDDING ME?!
Of Men and Mice
Part Four: MOUSETRAP
Marc Andreyko writer
Shawn McManus artist
Lee Loughridge colors
Todd Klein letters
Adam Hughes cover
Gregory Lockard editor
Bill Willingham consultant, Fables creator

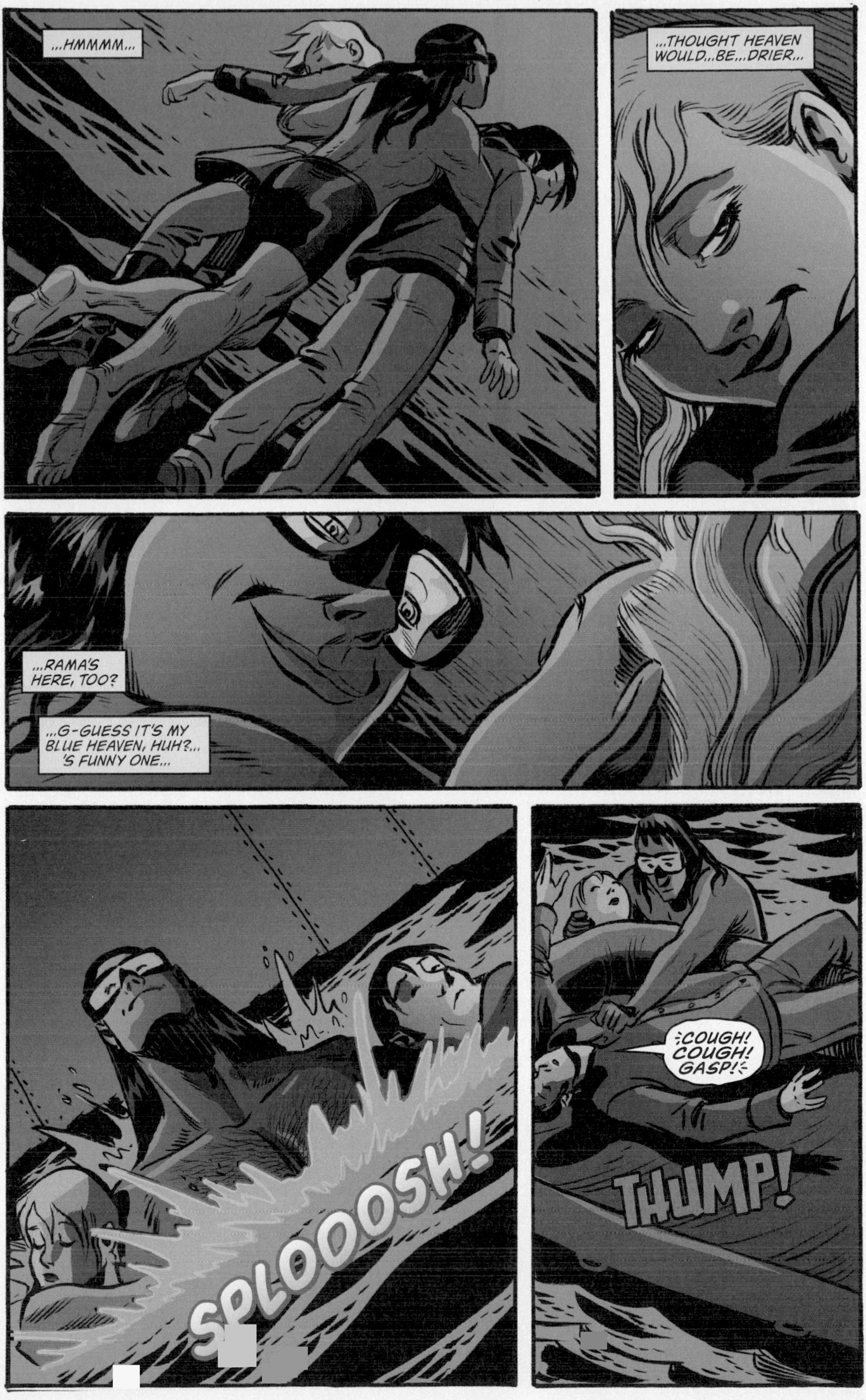
...HMMMM...
...THOUGHT HEAVEN WOULD...BE...DRIER...
...RAMA'S HERE, TOO?
...G-GUESS IT'S MY BLUE HEAVEN, HUH?... 'S FUNNY ONE...
SPLOOOSH!
COUGH! COUGH! GASP!
THUMP!

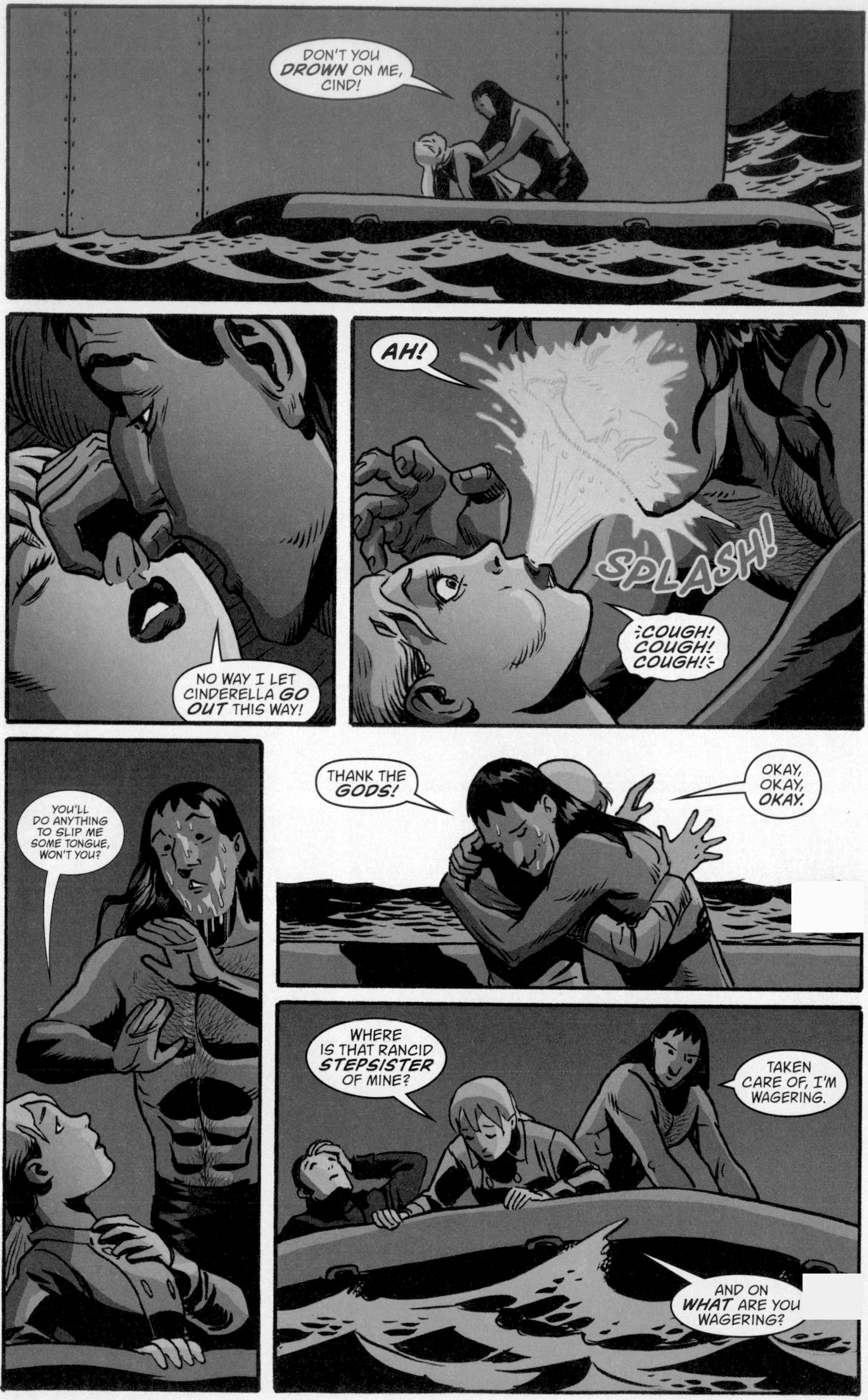
DON'T YOU DROWN ON ME, CIND!
NO WAY I LET CINDERELLA GO OUT THIS WAY!
AH!
SPLASH!
COUGH! COUGH! COUGH!
YOU'LL DO ANYTHING TO SLIP ME SOME TONGUE, WON'T YOU?
THANK THE GODS!
OKAY, OKAY, OKAY.
WHERE IS THAT RANCID STEPSISTER OF MINE?
TAKEN CARE OF, I'M WAGERING.
AND ON WHAT ARE YOU WAGERING?

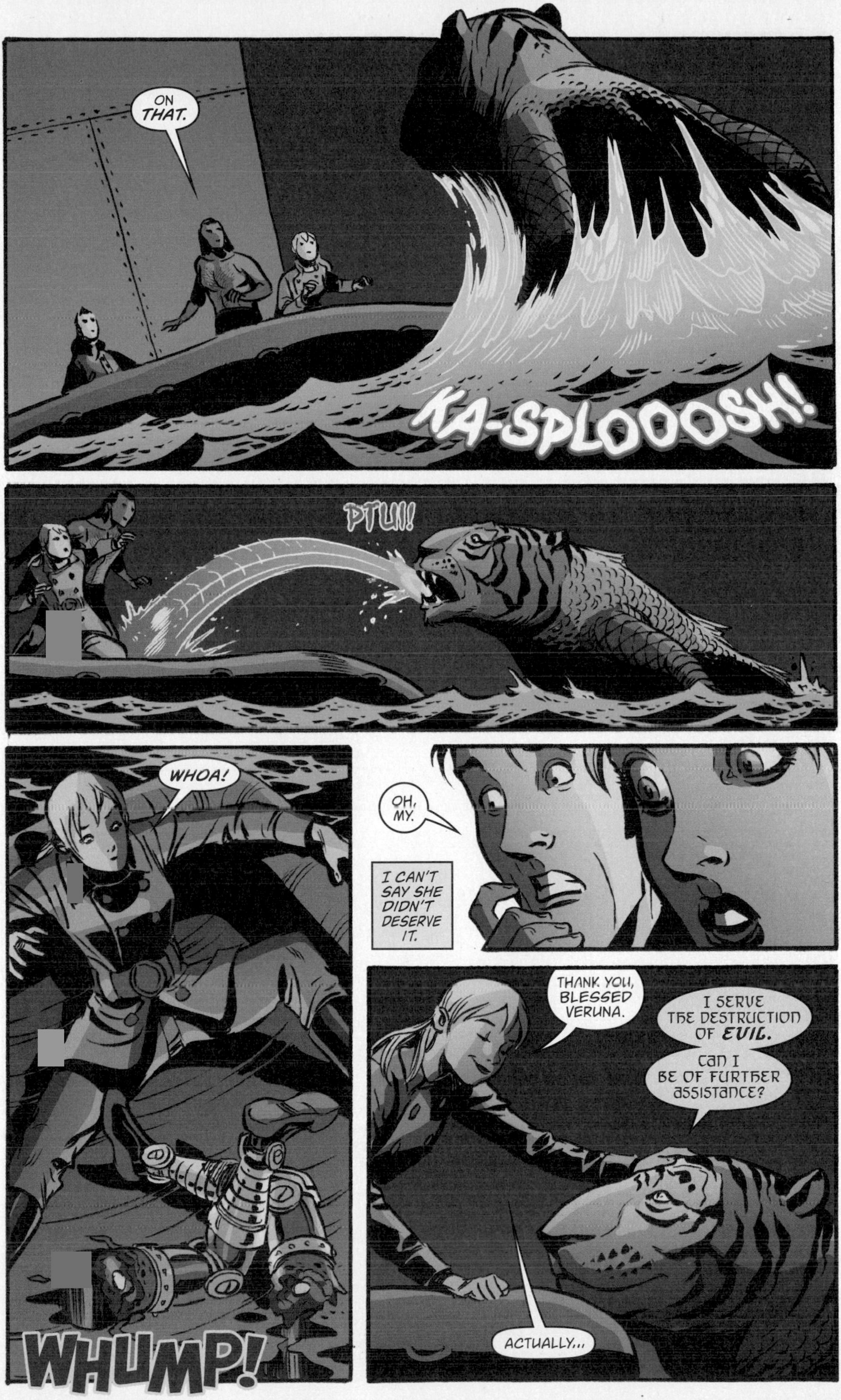

ON THAT.
KA-SPLOOOSH!
PTUI!
WHOA!
WHUMP!
OH, MY.
I CAN'T SAY SHE DIDN'T DESERVE IT.
THANK YOU, BLESSED VERUNA.
I SERVE THE DESTRUCTION OF EVIL.
CAN I BE OF FURTHER ASSISTANCE?
ACTUALLY...

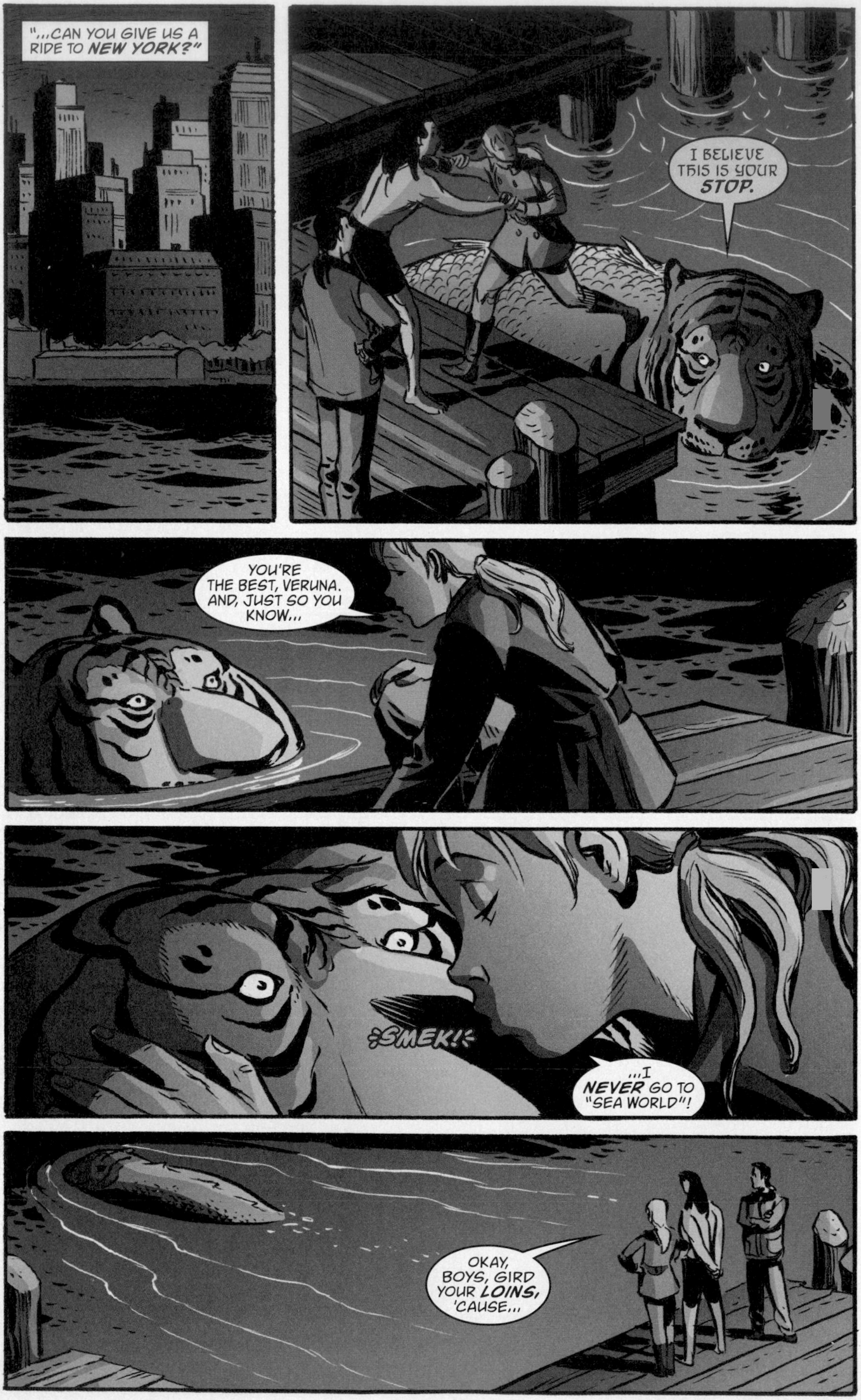
"...CAN YOU GIVE US A RIDE TO NEW YORK?"
I BELIEVE THIS IS YOUR STOP.
YOU'RE THE BEST, VERUNA. AND, JUST SO YOU KNOW...
SMEK!
...I NEVER GO TO "SEA WORLD"!
OKAY, BOYS, GIRD YOUR LOINS, 'CAUSE...

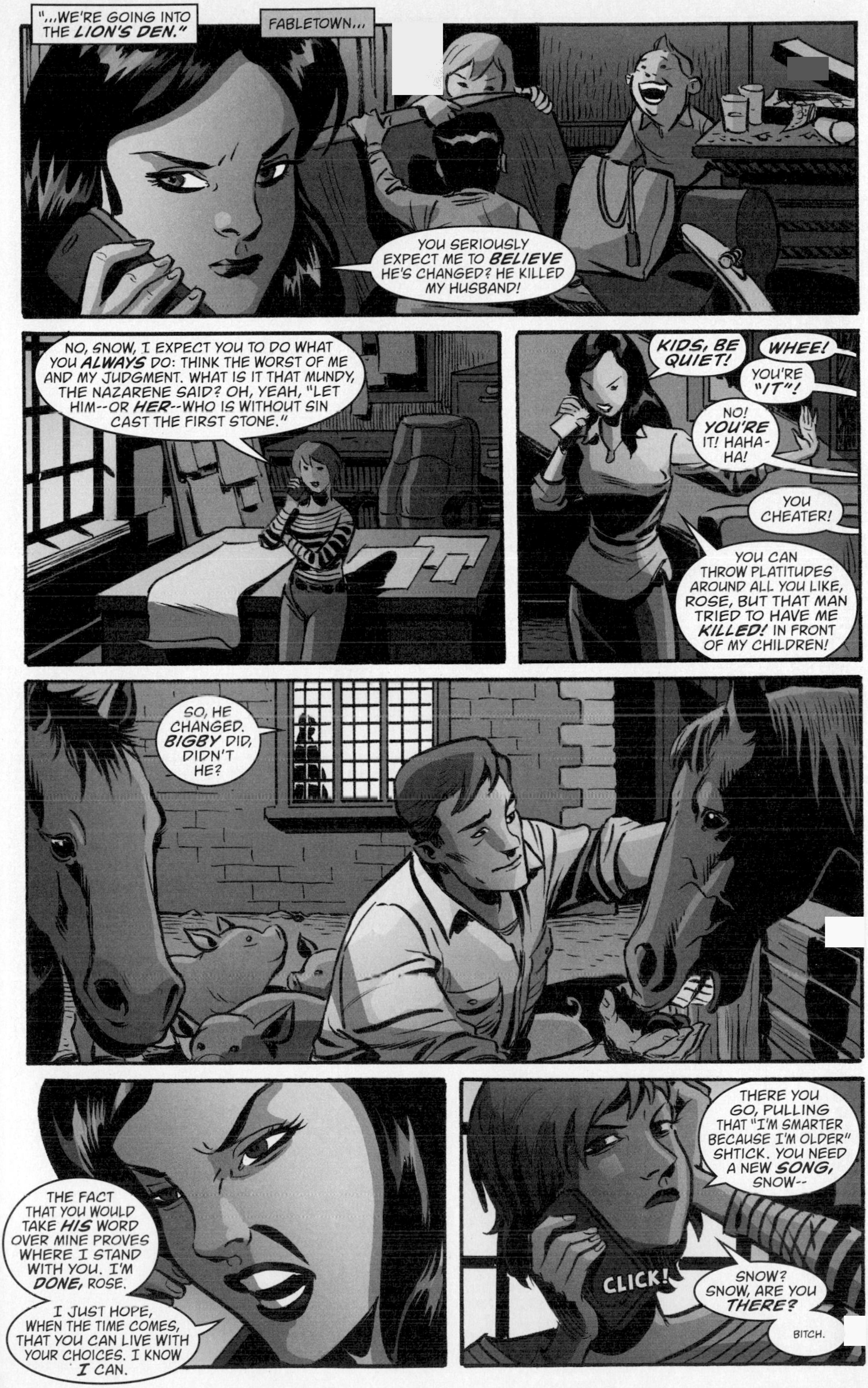
"...WE'RE GOING INTO THE LION'S DEN."
FABLETOWN...
YOU SERIOUSLY EXPECT ME TO BELIEVE HE'S CHANGED? HE KILLED MY HUSBAND!
NO, SNOW, I EXPECT YOU TO DO WHAT YOU ALWAYS DO: THINK THE WORST OF ME AND MY JUDGMENT. WHAT IS IT THAT MUNDY, THE NAZARENE SAID? OH, YEAH, "LET HIM--OR HER--WHO IS WITHOUT SIN CAST THE FIRST STONE."
KIDS, BE QUIET!
WHEE!
YOU'RE "IT"!
NO! YOU'RE IT! HAHA-HA!
YOU CHEATER!
YOU CAN THROW PLATITUDES AROUND ALL YOU LIKE, ROSE, BUT THAT MAN TRIED TO HAVE ME KILLED! IN FRONT OF MY CHILDREN!
SO, HE CHANGED. BIGBY DID, DIDN'T HE?
THE FACT THAT YOU WOULD TAKE HIS WORD OVER MINE PROVES WHERE I STAND WITH YOU. I'M DONE, ROSE.
I JUST HOPE, WHEN THE TIME COMES, THAT YOU CAN LIVE WITH YOUR CHOICES. I KNOW I CAN.
THERE YOU GO, PULLING THAT "I'M SMARTER BECAUSE I'M OLDER" SHTICK. YOU NEED A NEW SONG, SNOW--
CLICK!
SNOW? SNOW, ARE YOU THERE?
BITCH.

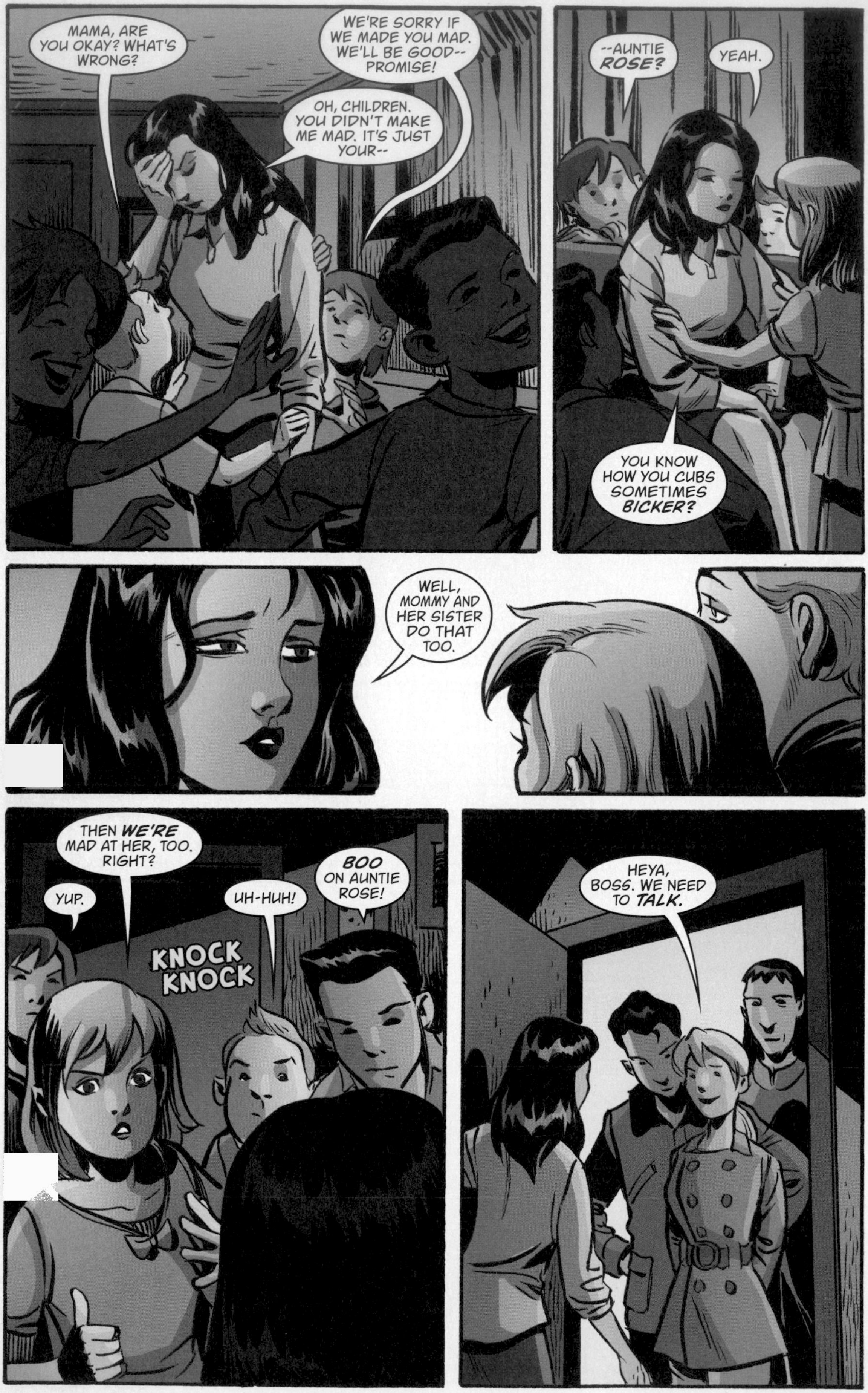
MAMA, ARE YOU OKAY? WHAT'S WRONG?
WE'RE SORRY IF WE MADE YOU MAD. WE'LL BE GOOD-- PROMISE!
OH, CHILDREN. YOU DIDN'T MAKE ME MAD. IT'S JUST YOUR--
--AUNTIE ROSE?
YEAH.
YOU KNOW HOW YOU CUBS SOMETIMES BICKER?
WELL, MOMMY AND HER SISTER DO THAT TOO.
THEN WE'RE MAD AT HER, TOO. RIGHT?
YUP.
UH-HUH!
BOO ON AUNTIE ROSE!
KNOCK KNOCK
HEYA, BOSS. WE NEED TO TALK.

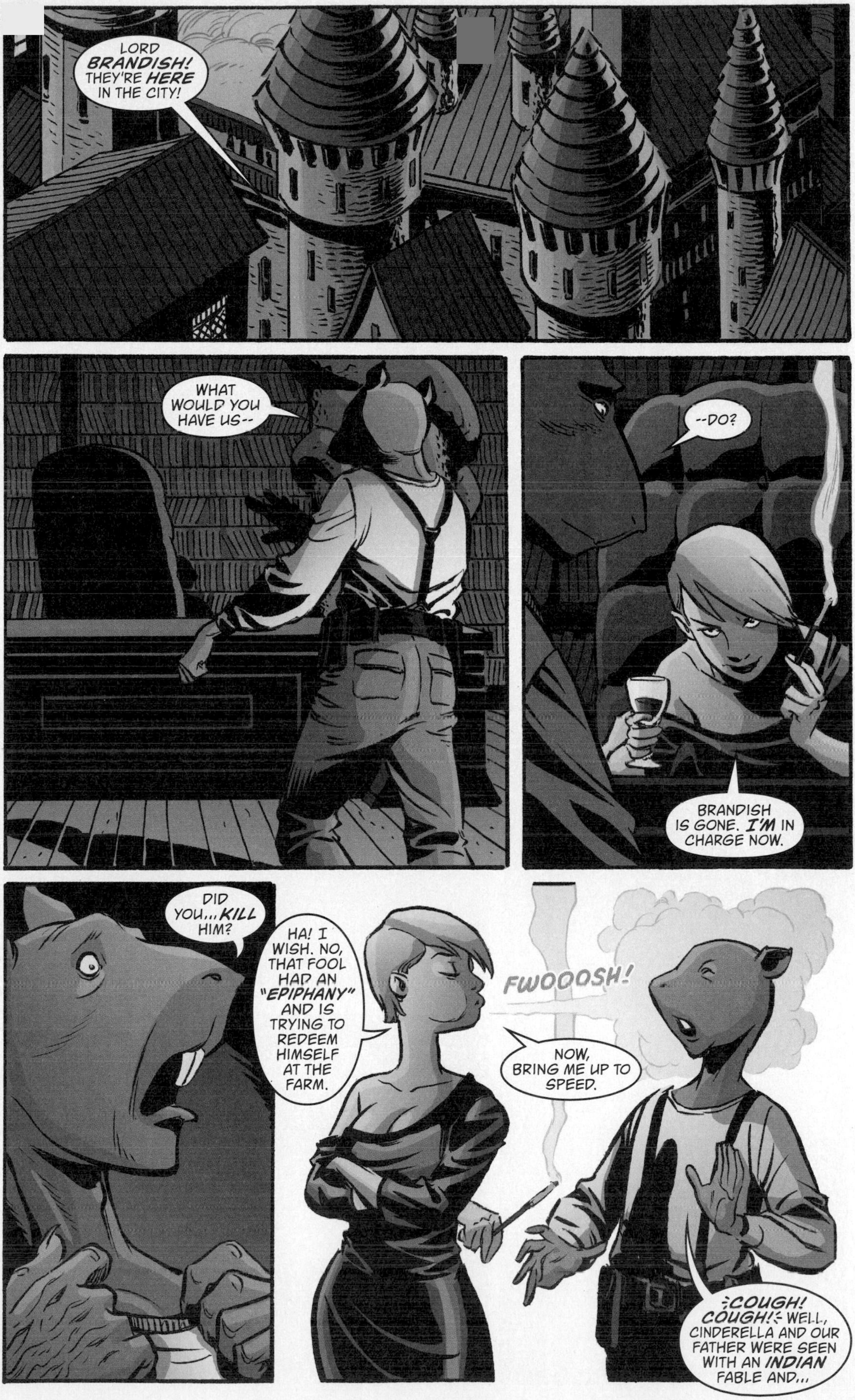
LORD BRANDISH! THEY'RE HERE IN THE CITY!
WHAT WOULD YOU HAVE US--
--DO?
BRANDISH IS GONE. I'M IN CHARGE NOW.
DID YOU...KILL HIM?
HA! I WISH. NO, THAT FOOL HAD AN "EPIPHANY" AND IS TRYING TO REDEEM HIMSELF AT THE FARM.
FWOOOSH!
NOW, BRING ME UP TO SPEED.
COUGH! COUGH! WELL, CINDERELLA AND OUR FATHER WERE SEEN WITH AN INDIAN FABLE AND...

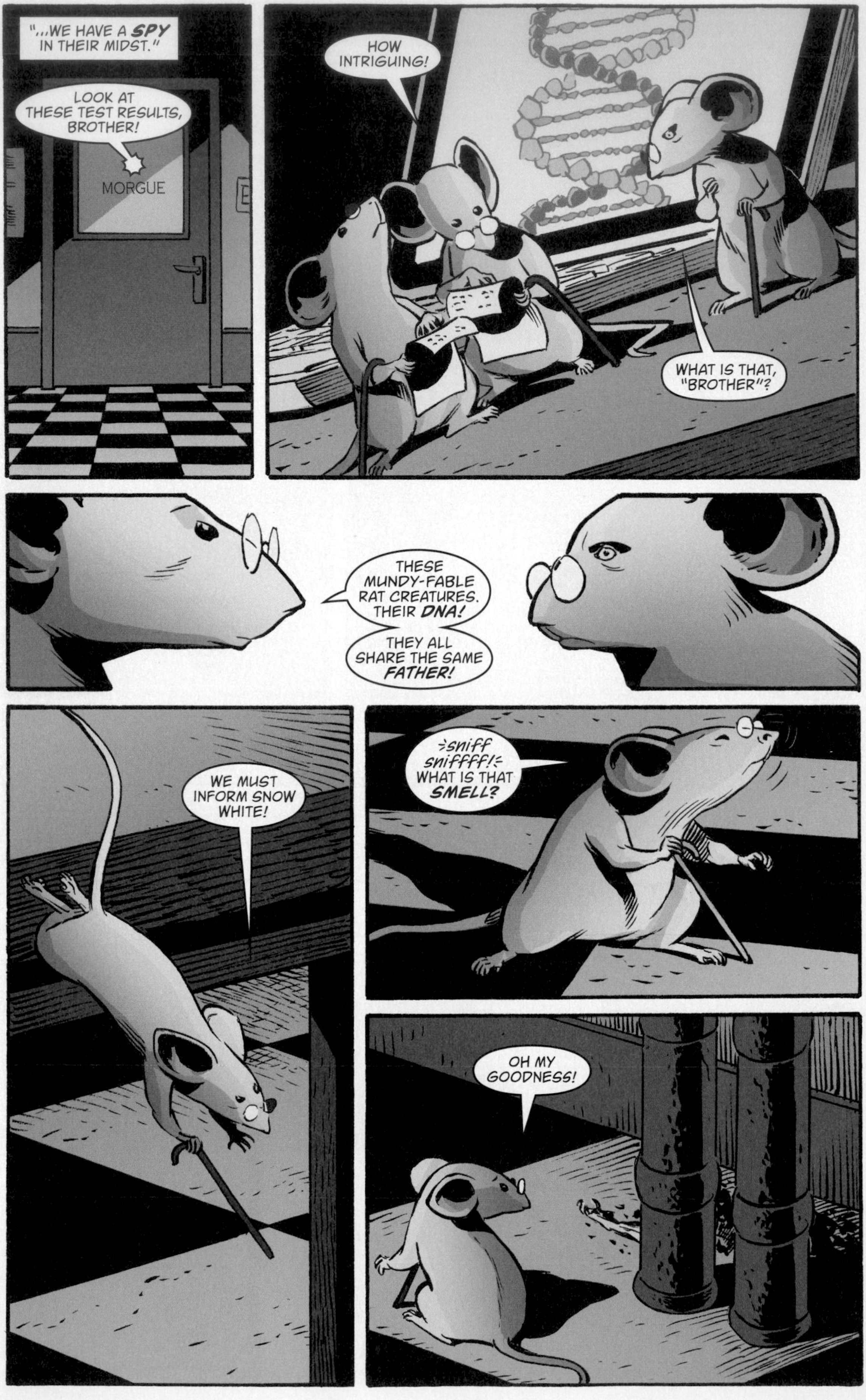
"...WE HAVE A SPY IN THEIR MIDST."
LOOK AT THESE TEST RESULTS, BROTHER!
MORGUE
HOW INTRIGUING!
WHAT IS THAT, "BROTHER"?
THESE MUNDY-FABLE RAT CREATURES. THEIR DNA!
THEY ALL SHARE THE SAME FATHER!
WE MUST INFORM SNOW WHITE!
sniff sniffff! WHAT IS THAT SMELL?
OH MY GOODNESS!

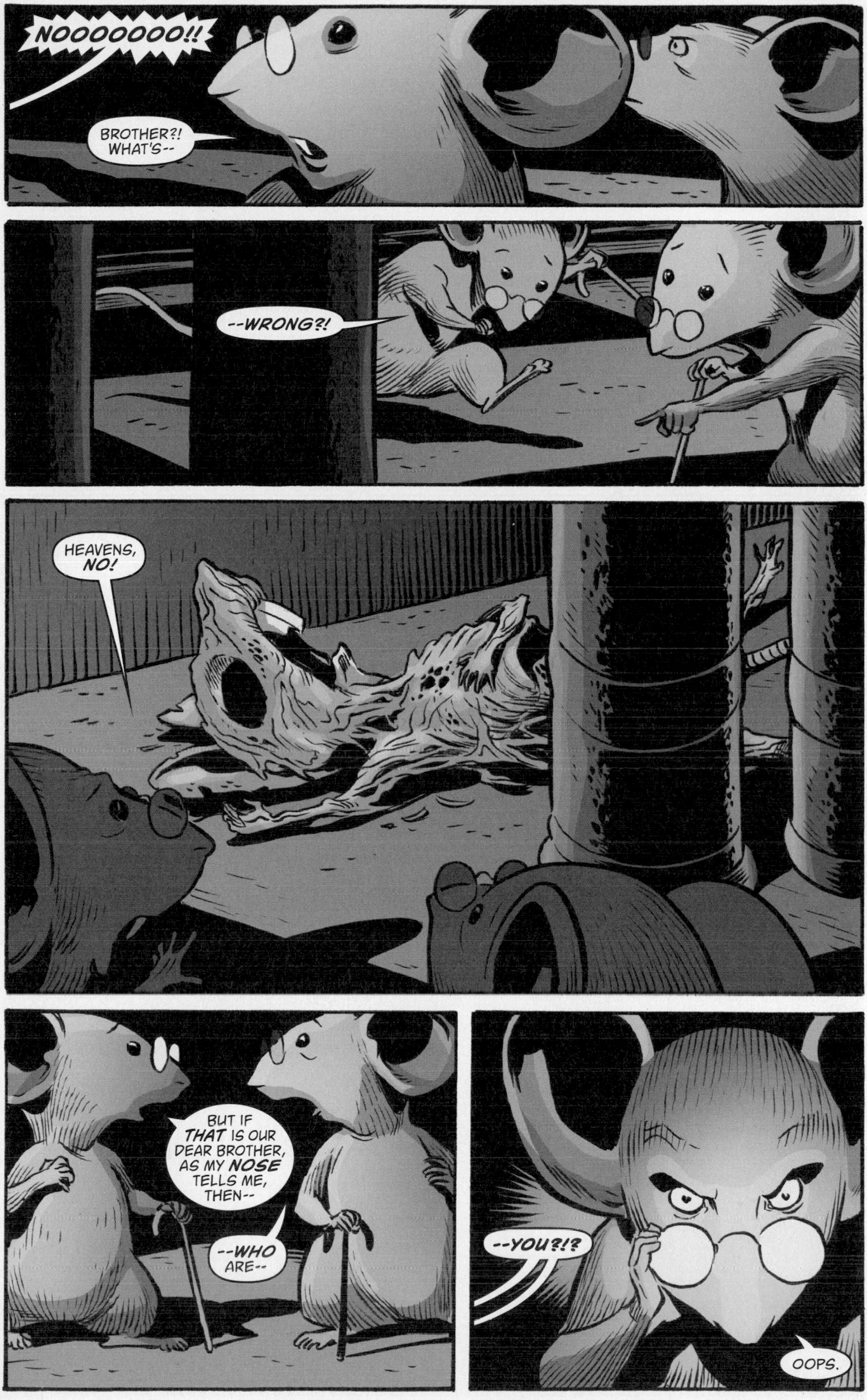
NOOOOOOO!!
BROTHER?! WHAT'S--
--WRONG?!
HEAVENS, NO!
BUT IF THAT IS OUR DEAR BROTHER, AS MY NOSE TELLS ME, THEN--
--WHO ARE--
--YOU?!?
OOPS.

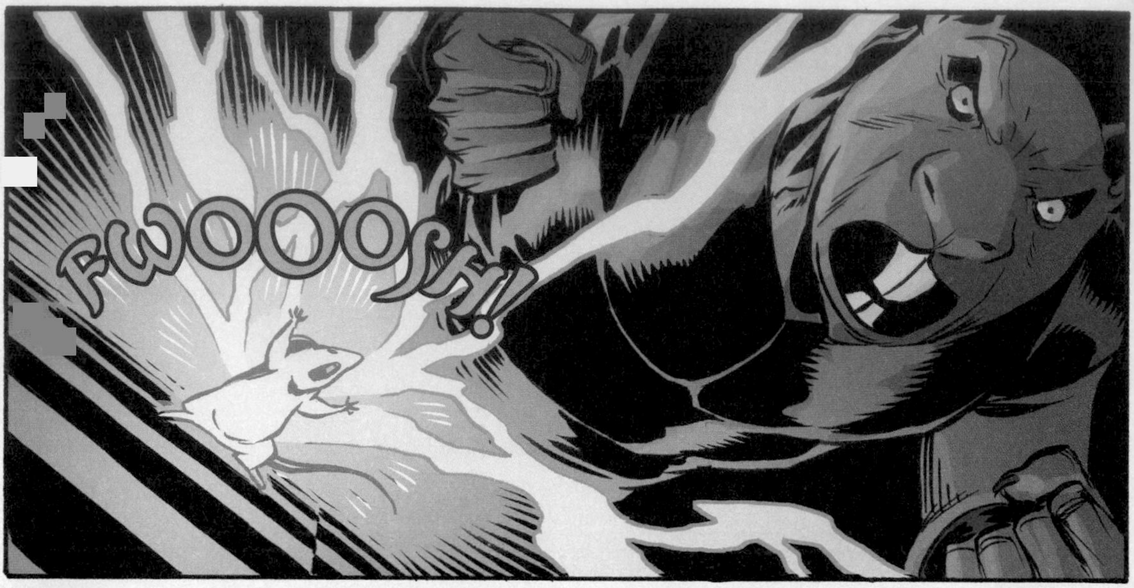
FWOOOSH!!

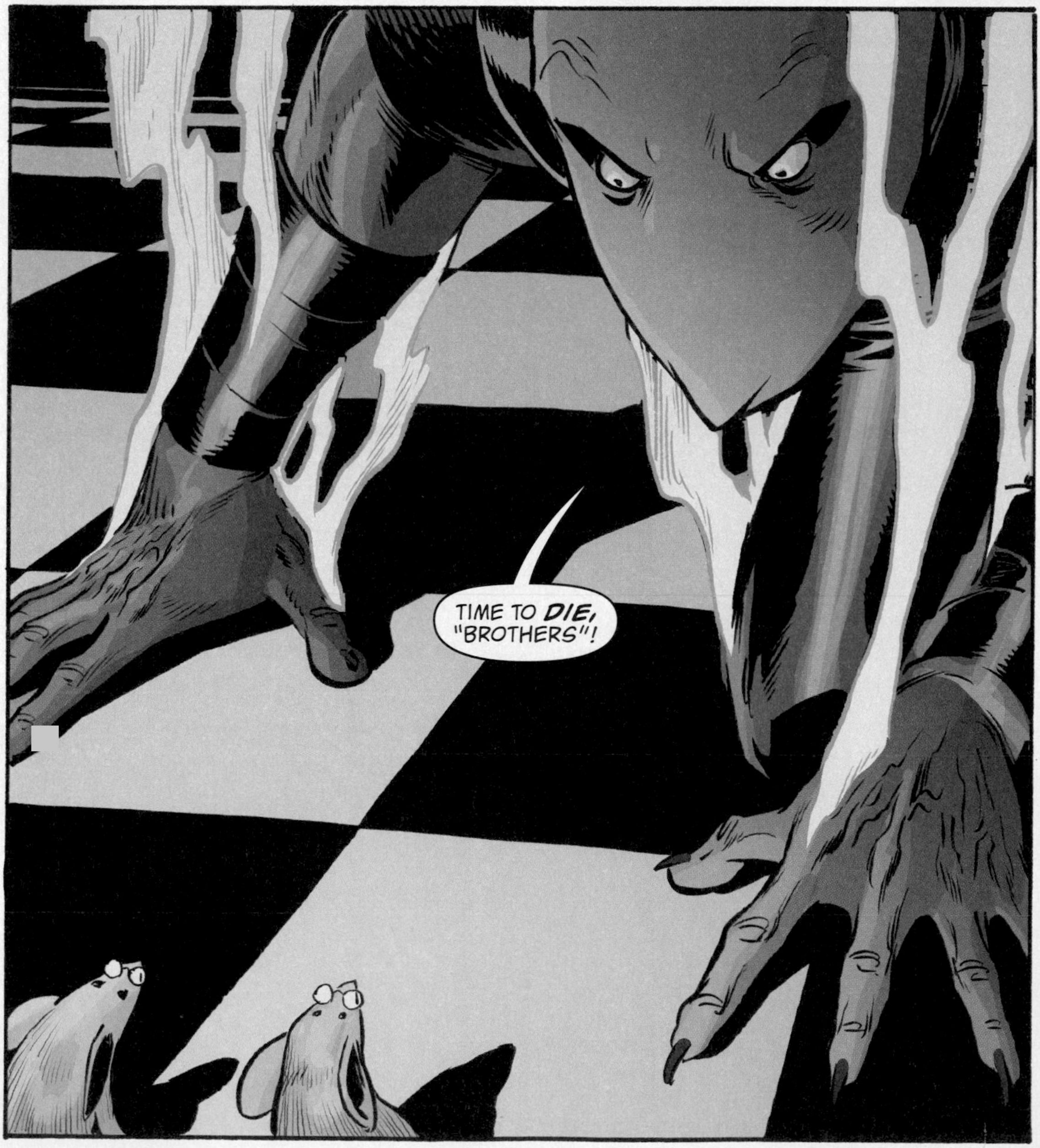
TIME TO DIE, "BROTHERS"!

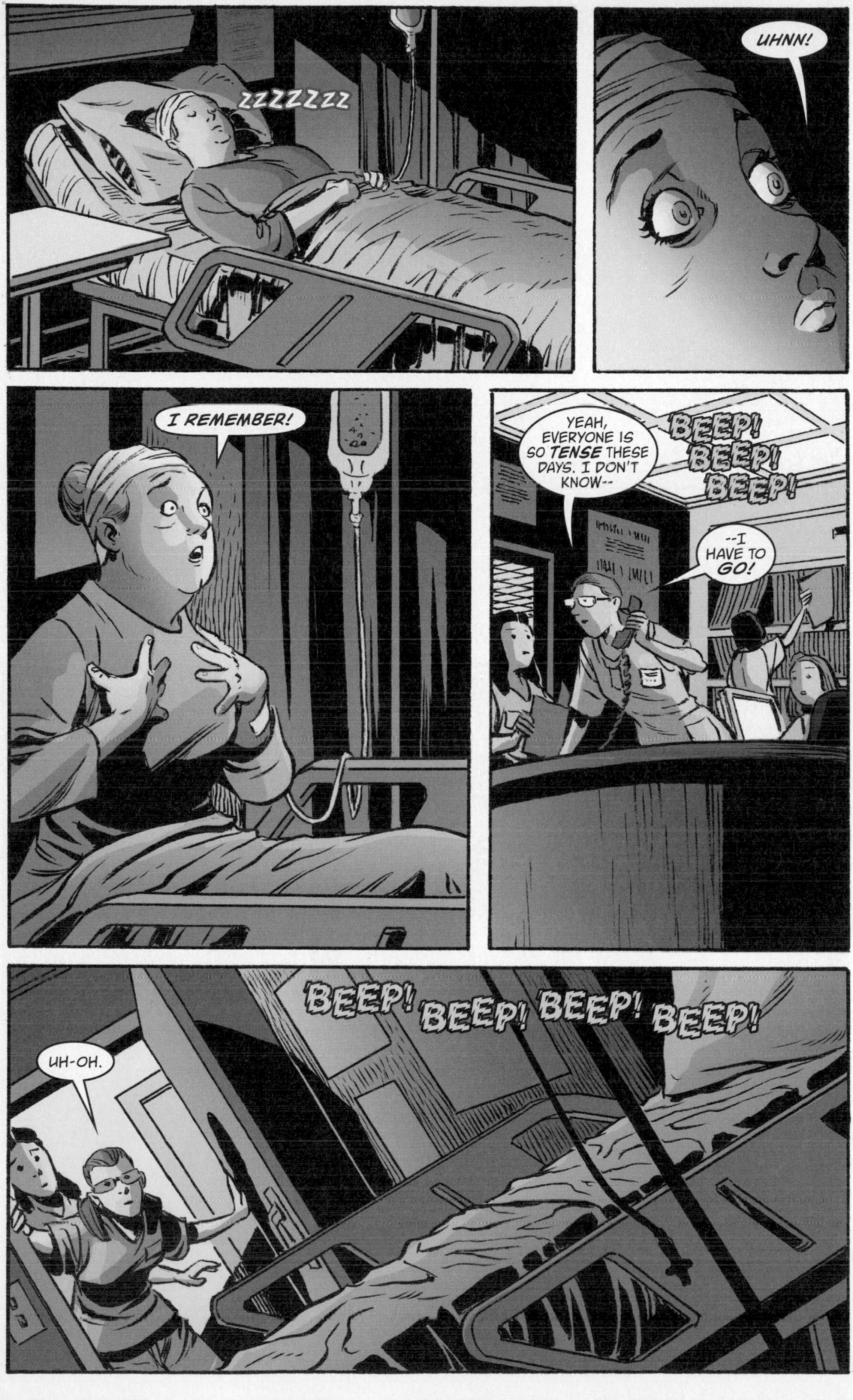
ZZZZZZZ
UHNN!
I REMEMBER!
YEAH, EVERYONE IS SO *TENSE* THESE DAYS. I DON'T KNOW--
BEEP! BEEP! BEEP!
--I HAVE TO *GO!*
BEEP! BEEP! BEEP! BEEP!
UH-OH.

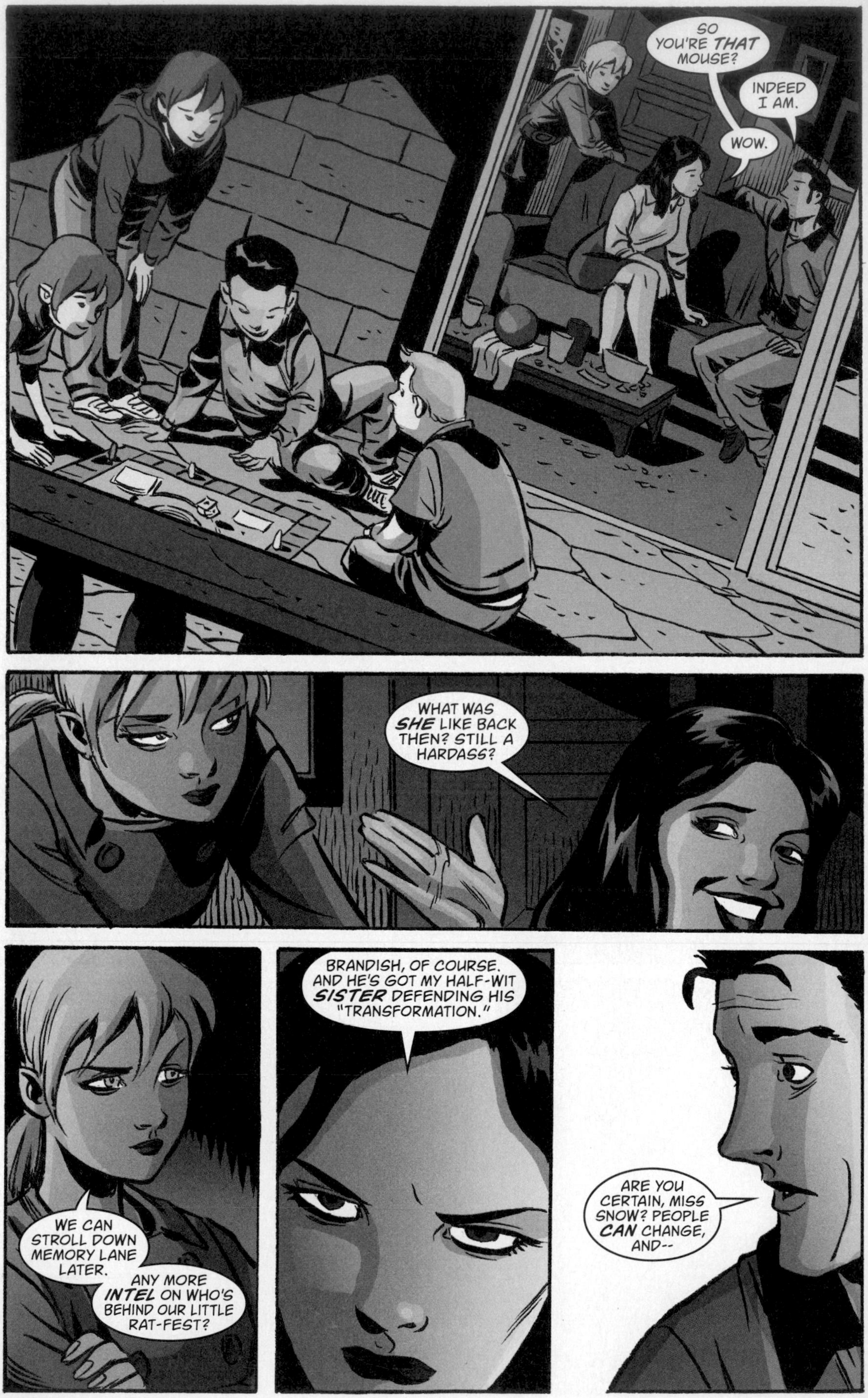

SO YOU'RE THAT MOUSE?
INDEED I AM.
WOW.
WHAT WAS SHE LIKE BACK THEN? STILL A HARDASS?
WE CAN STROLL DOWN MEMORY LANE LATER.
ANY MORE INTEL ON WHO'S BEHIND OUR LITTLE RAT-FEST?
BRANDISH, OF COURSE. AND HE'S GOT MY HALF-WIT SISTER DEFENDING HIS "TRANSFORMATION."
ARE YOU CERTAIN, MISS SNOW? PEOPLE CAN CHANGE, AND--

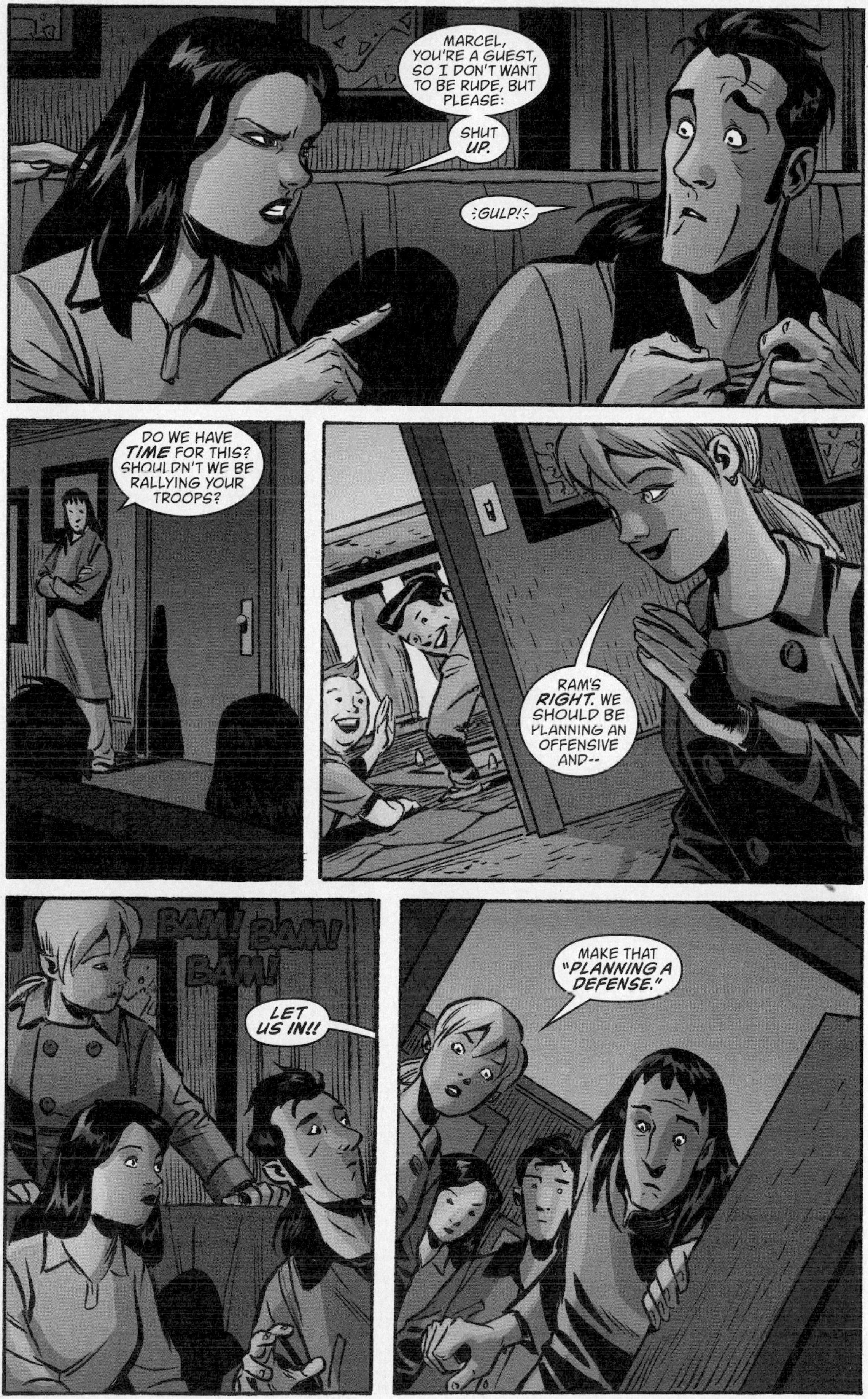
MARCEL, YOU'RE A GUEST, SO I DON'T WANT TO BE RUDE, BUT PLEASE:
SHUT UP.
GULP!
DO WE HAVE TIME FOR THIS? SHOULDN'T WE BE RALLYING YOUR TROOPS?
RAM'S RIGHT. WE SHOULD BE PLANNING AN OFFENSIVE AND--
BAM! BAM! BAM!
LET US IN!!
MAKE THAT "PLANNING A DEFENSE."

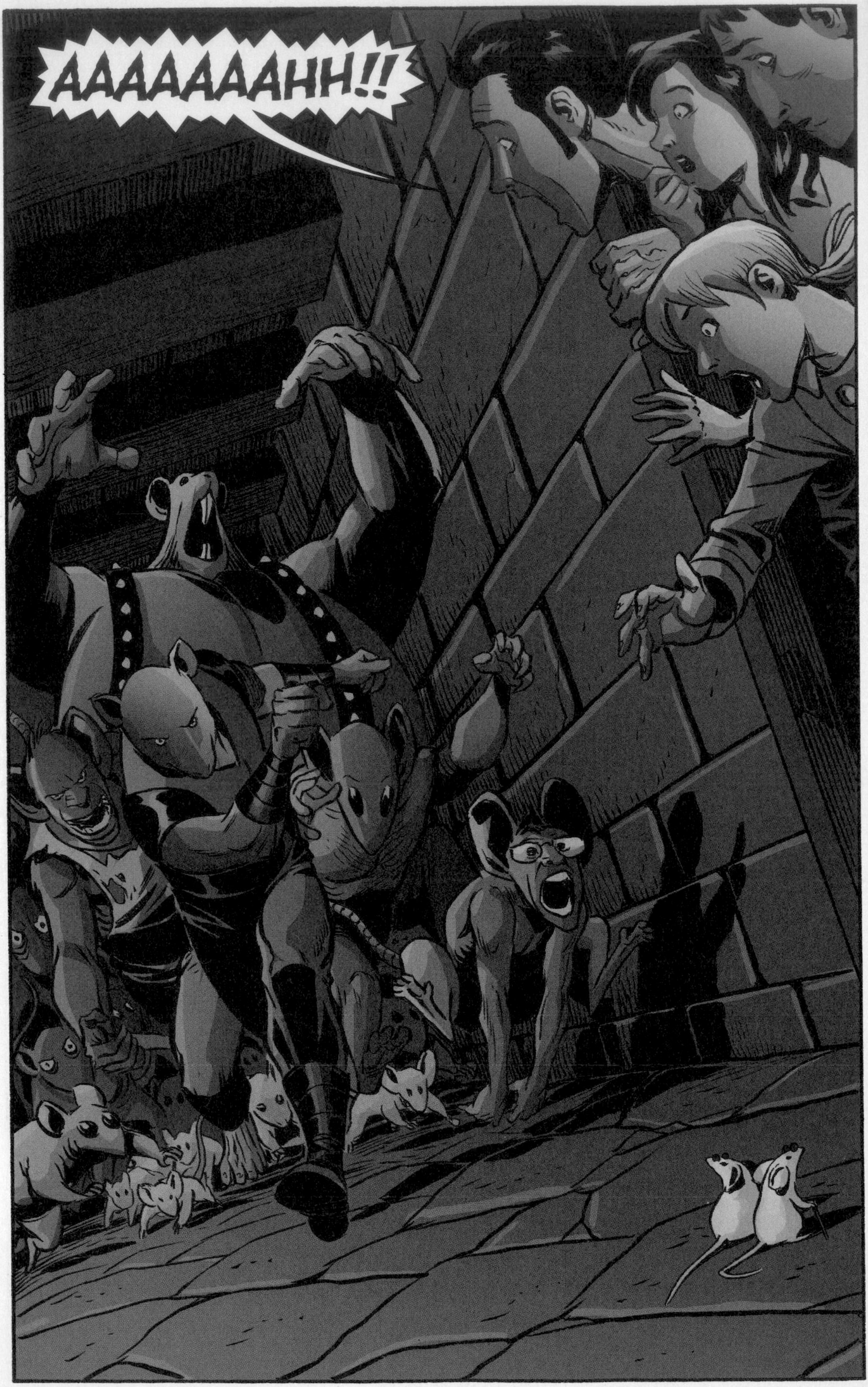
AAAAAAAHH!!

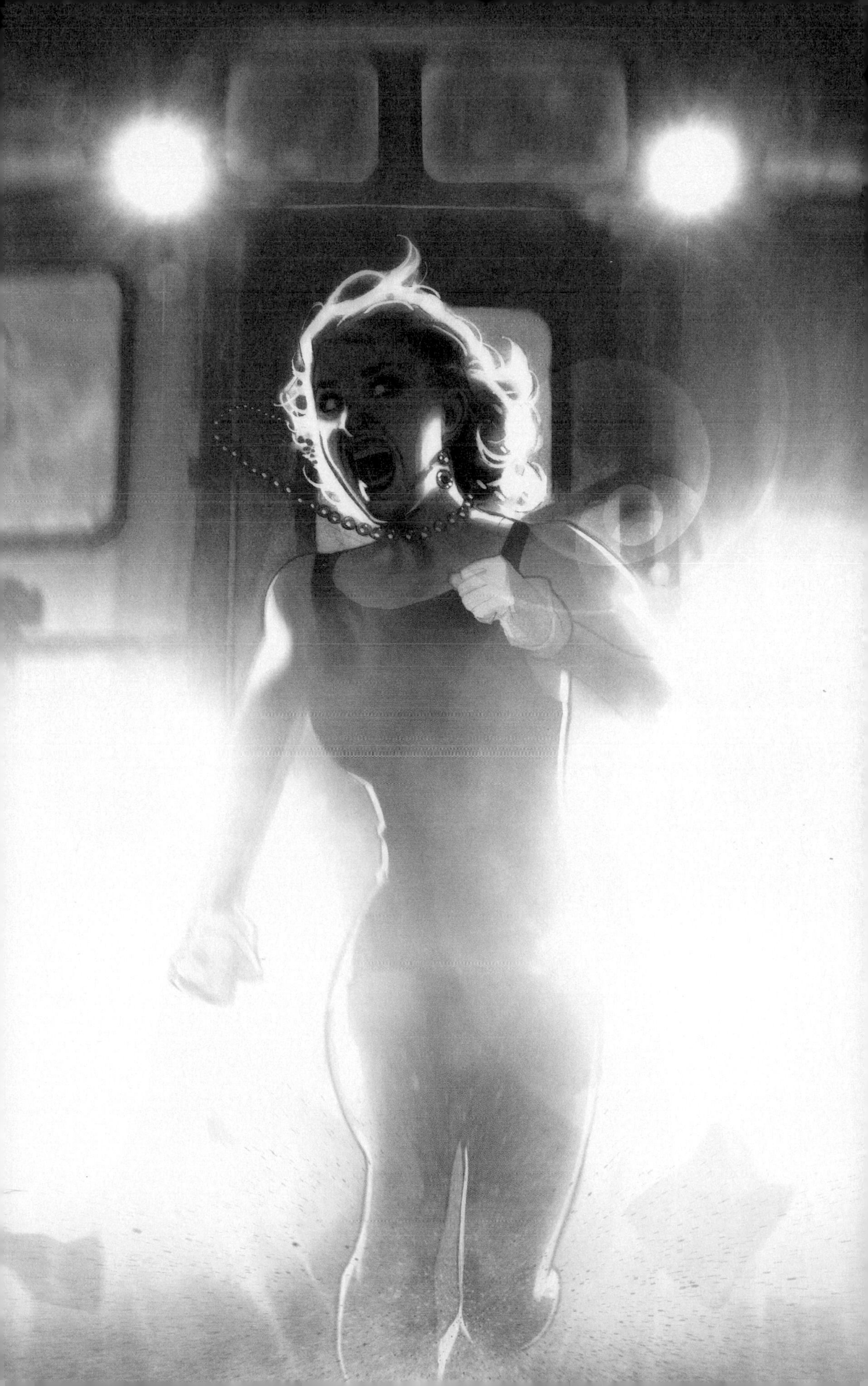

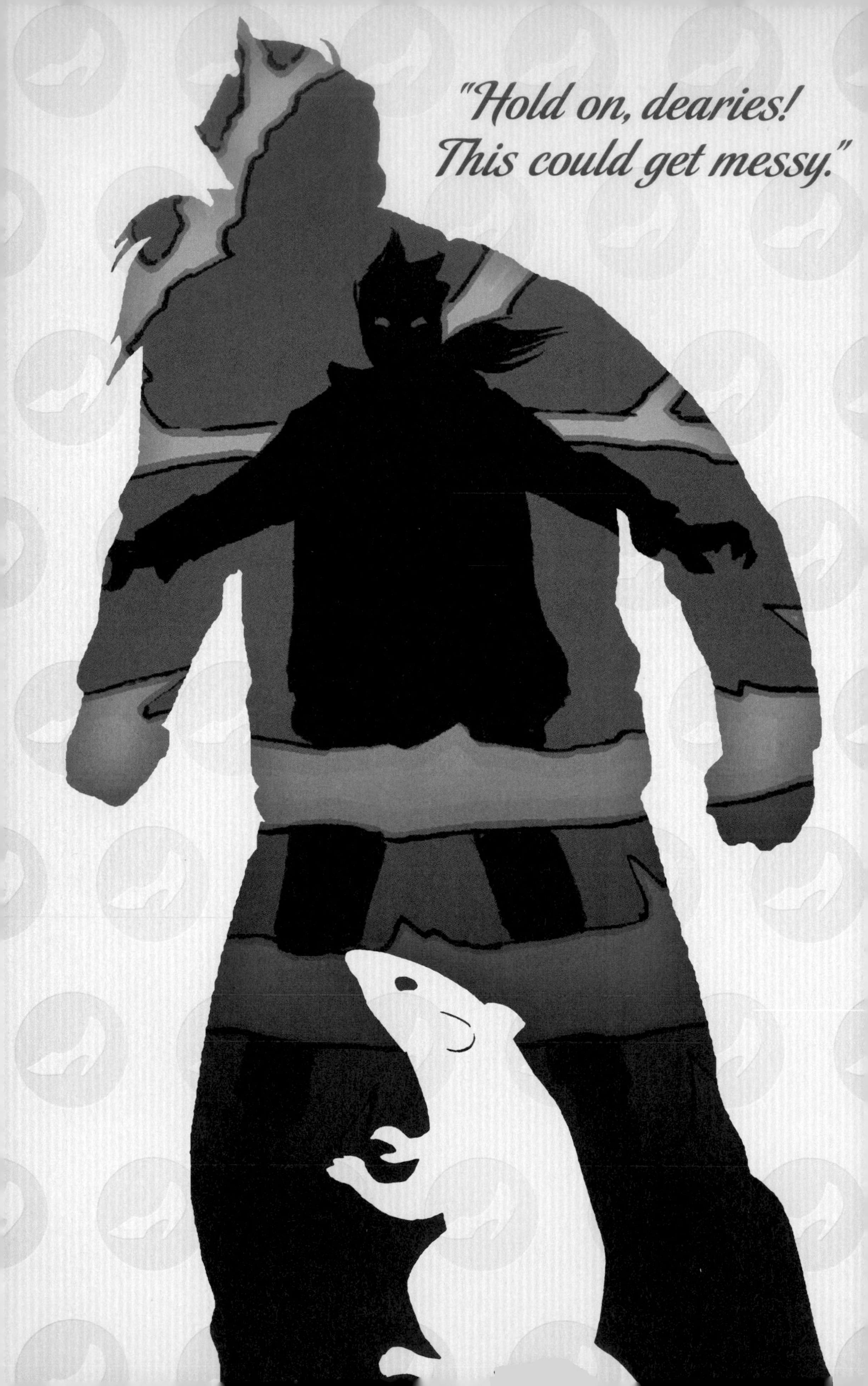
"Hold on, dearies!
This could get messy."

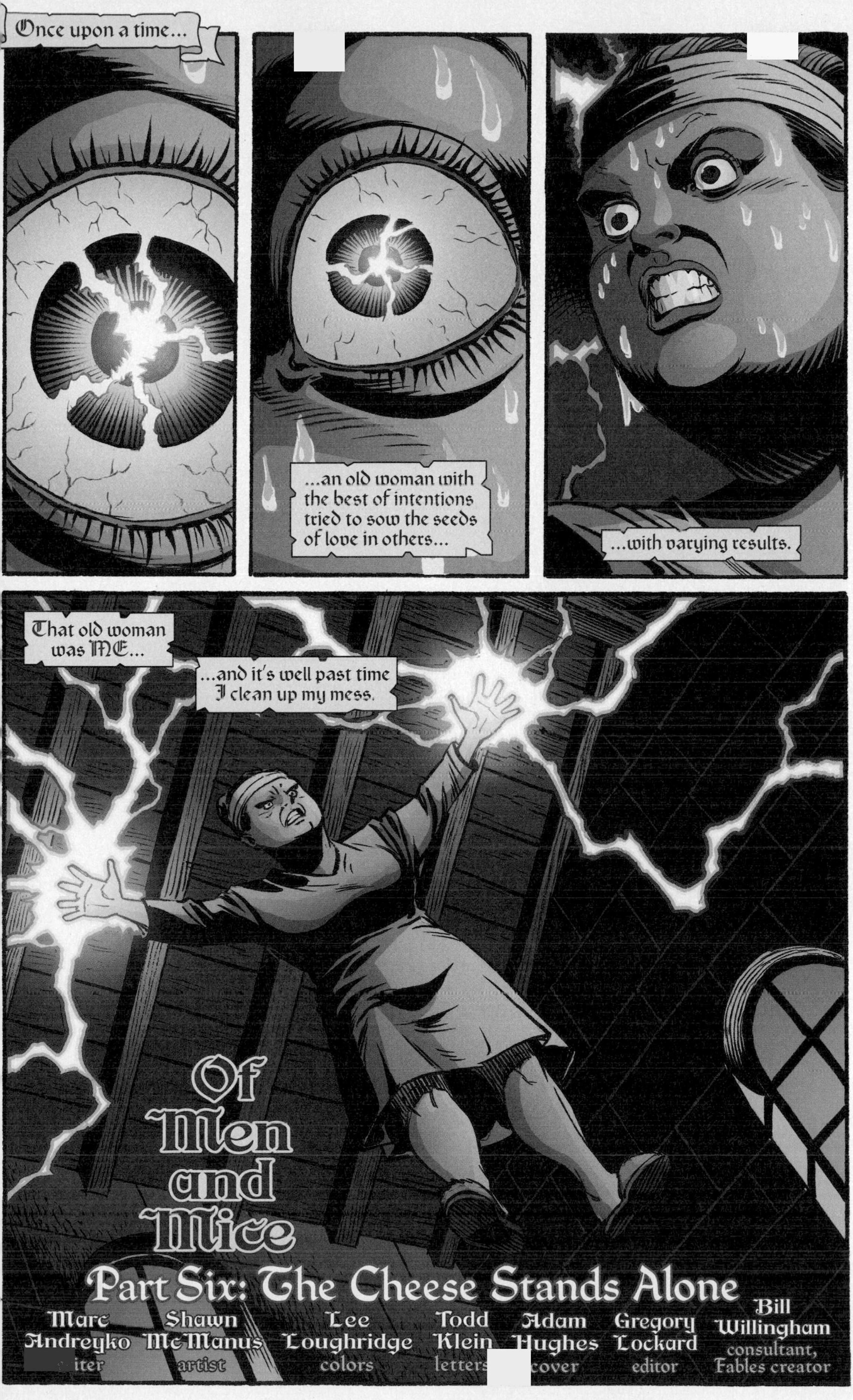
Once upon a time...
...an old woman with the best of intentions tried to sow the seeds of love in others...
...with varying results.
That old woman was ME...
...and it's well past time I clean up my mess.
Of Men and Mice
Part Six: The Cheese Stands Alone
Marc Andreyko [redacted]iter
Shawn McManus artist
Lee Loughridge colors
Todd Klein letters
Adam Hughes cover
Gregory Lockard editor
Bill Willingham consultant, Fables creator

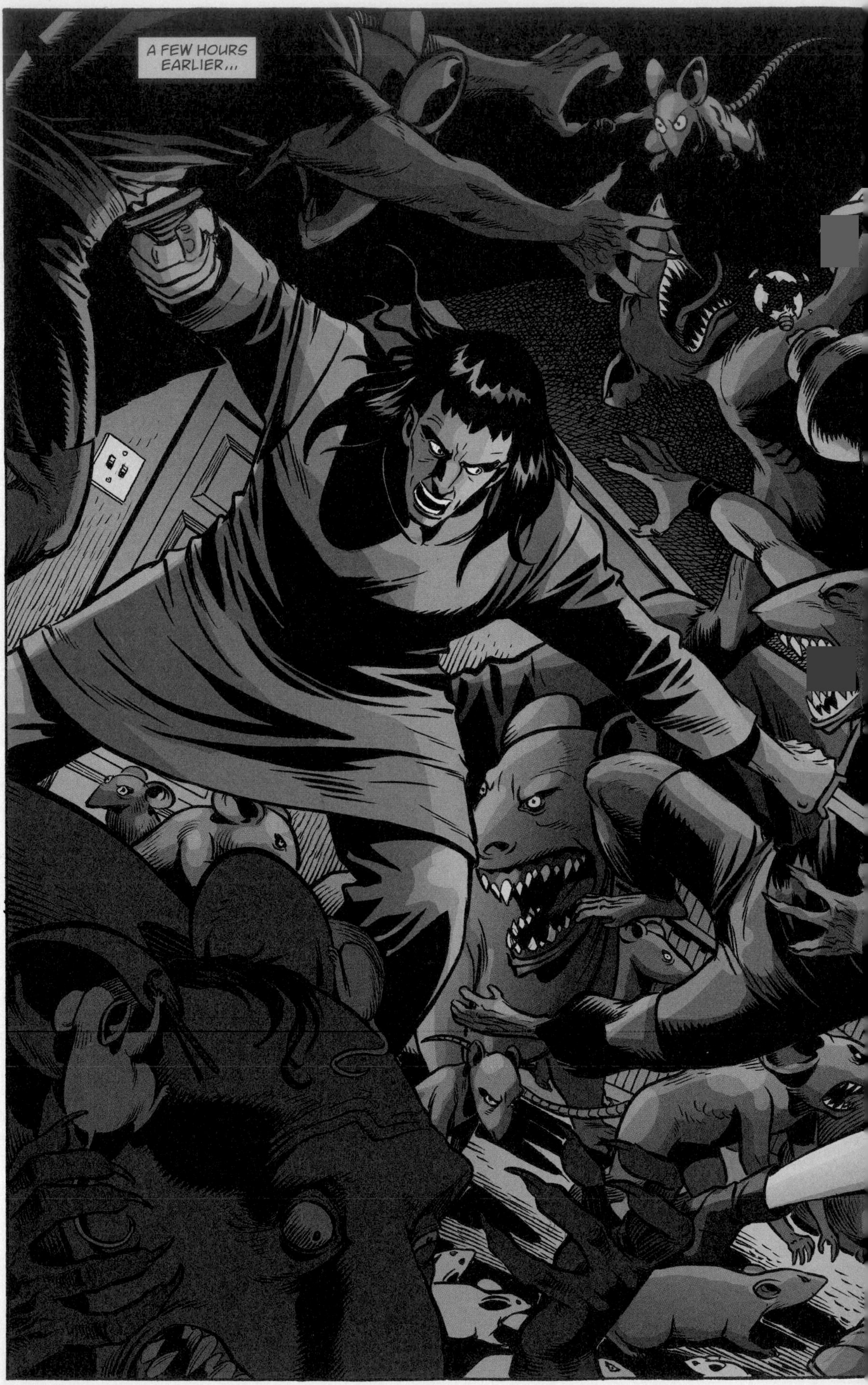
A FEW HOURS EARLIER...

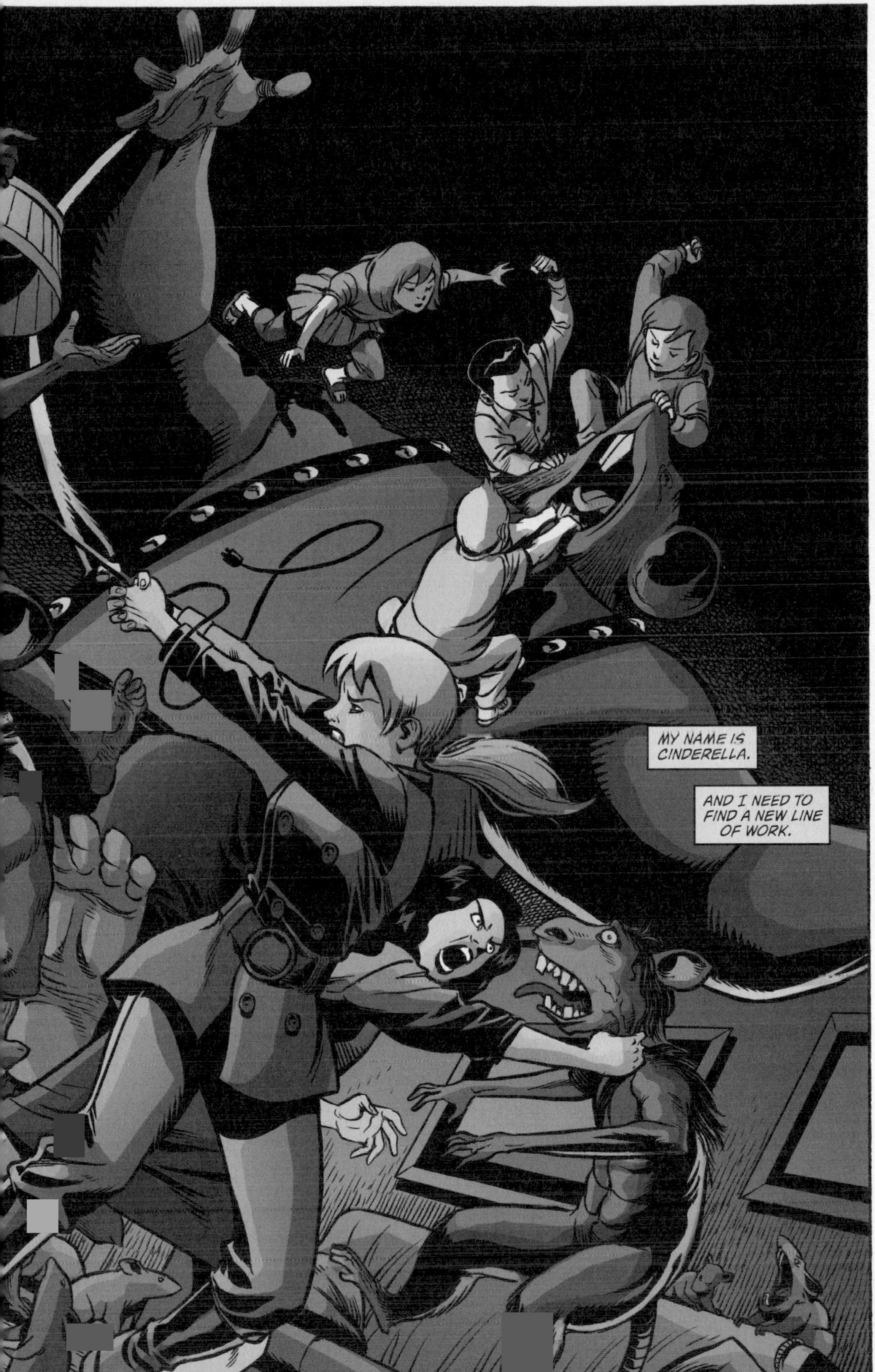
MY NAME IS CINDERELLA.
AND I NEED TO FIND A NEW LINE OF WORK.

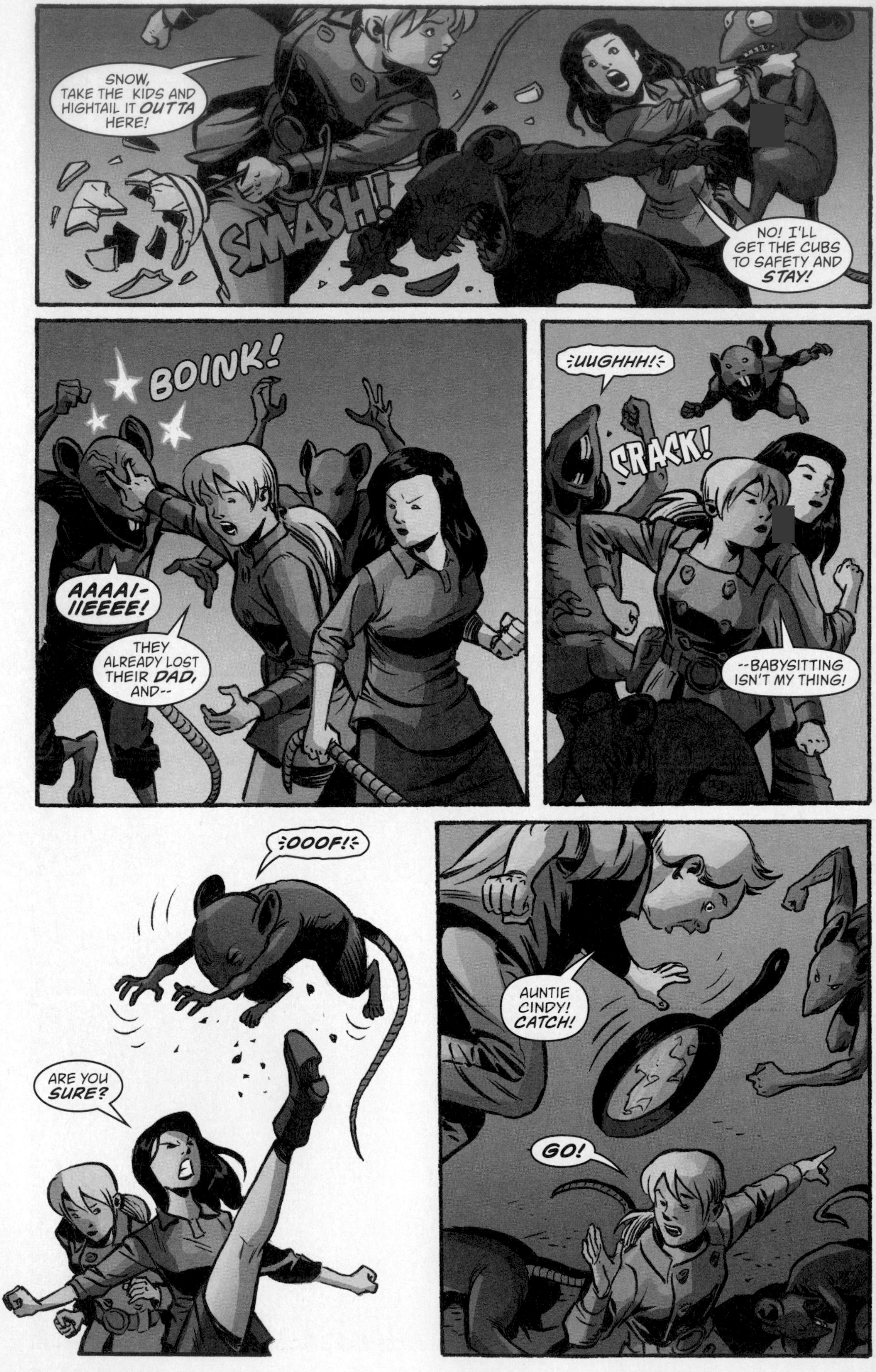
SNOW, TAKE THE KIDS AND HIGHTAIL IT OUTTA HERE!
SMASH!
NO! I'LL GET THE CUBS TO SAFETY AND STAY!
BOINK!
AAAAI-IIEEEE!
THEY ALREADY LOST THEIR DAD, AND--
UUGHHH!
CRACK!
--BABYSITTING ISN'T MY THING!
OOOF!
ARE YOU SURE?
AUNTIE CINDY! CATCH!
GO!

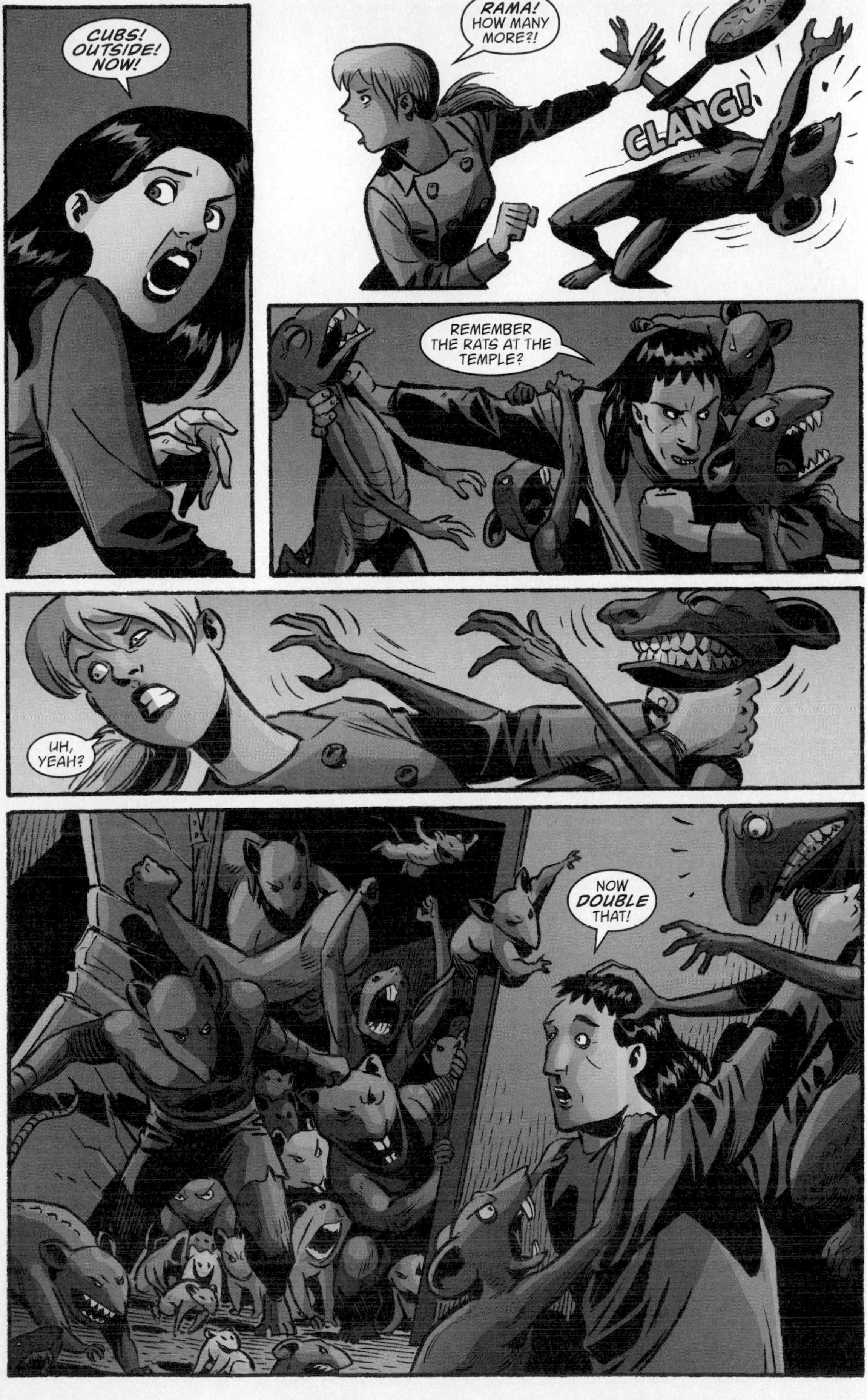
CUBS! OUTSIDE! NOW!
RAMA! HOW MANY MORE?!
CLANG!
REMEMBER THE RATS AT THE TEMPLE?
UH, YEAH?
NOW DOUBLE THAT!

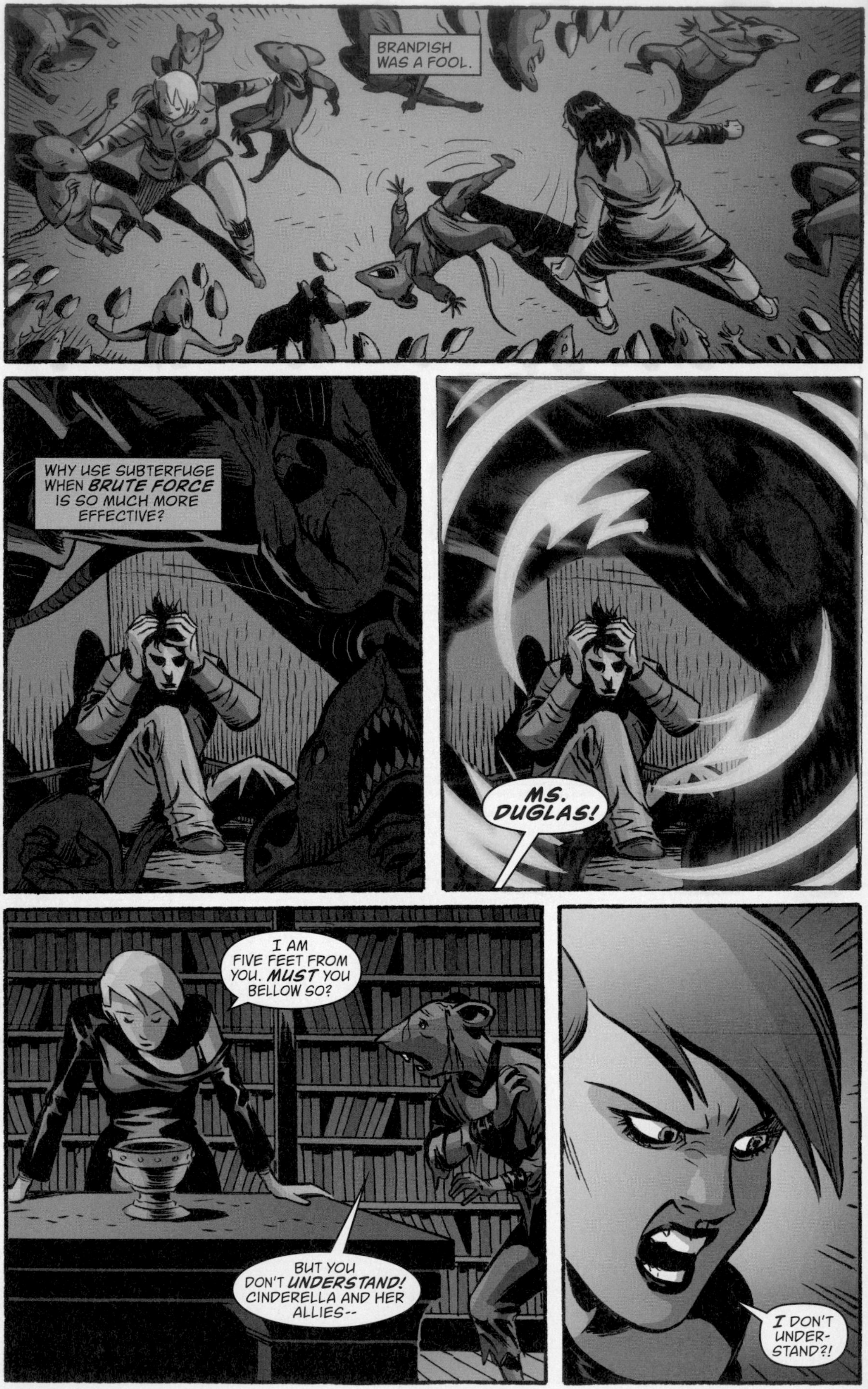
BRANDISH WAS A FOOL.
WHY USE SUBTERFUGE WHEN BRUTE FORCE IS SO MUCH MORE EFFECTIVE?
MS. DUGLAS!
I AM FIVE FEET FROM YOU. MUST YOU BELLOW SO?
BUT YOU DON'T UNDERSTAND! CINDERELLA AND HER ALLIES--
I DON'T UNDER-STAND?!

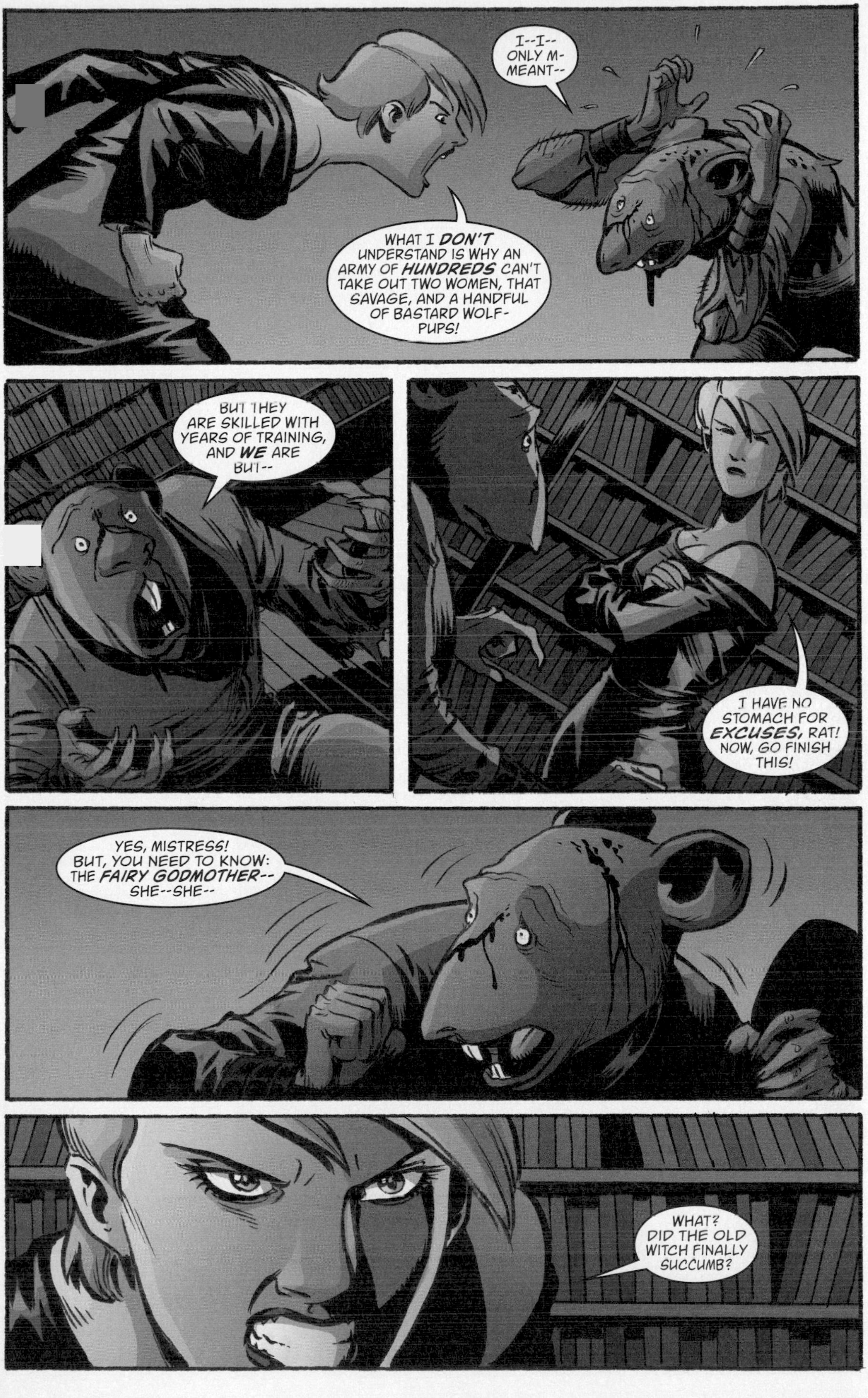
WHAT I DON'T UNDERSTAND IS WHY AN ARMY OF HUNDREDS CAN'T TAKE OUT TWO WOMEN, THAT SAVAGE, AND A HANDFUL OF BASTARD WOLF-PUPS!
I--I-- ONLY M-MEANT--
BUT THEY ARE SKILLED WITH YEARS OF TRAINING, AND WE ARE BUT--
I HAVE NO STOMACH FOR EXCUSES, RAT! NOW, GO FINISH THIS!
YES, MISTRESS! BUT, YOU NEED TO KNOW: THE FAIRY GODMOTHER-- SHE--SHE--
WHAT? DID THE OLD WITCH FINALLY SUCCUMB?

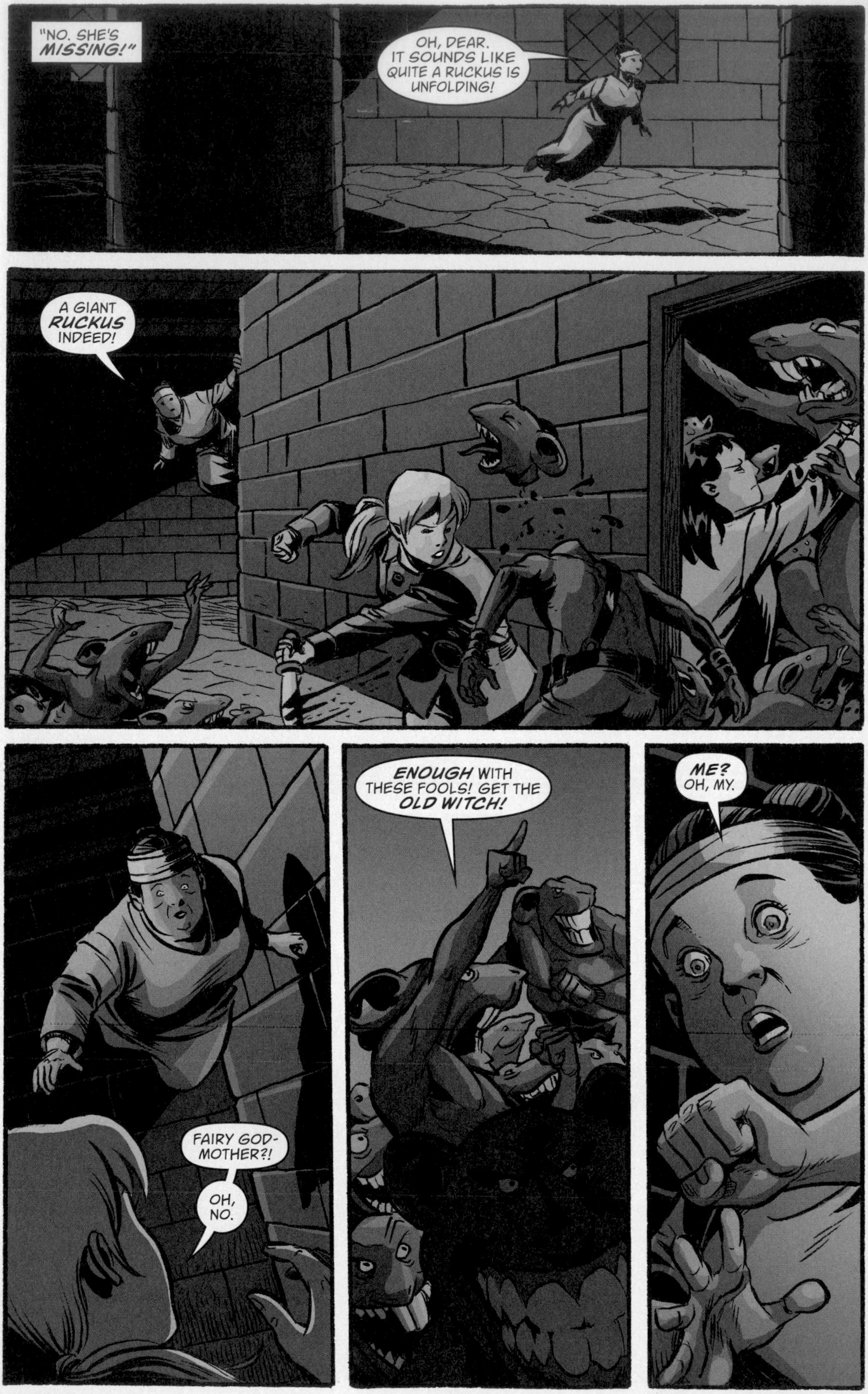
"NO. SHE'S MISSING!"
OH, DEAR. IT SOUNDS LIKE QUITE A RUCKUS IS UNFOLDING!
A GIANT RUCKUS INDEED!
FAIRY GOD-MOTHER?!
OH, NO.
ENOUGH WITH THESE FOOLS! GET THE OLD WITCH!
ME? OH, MY.

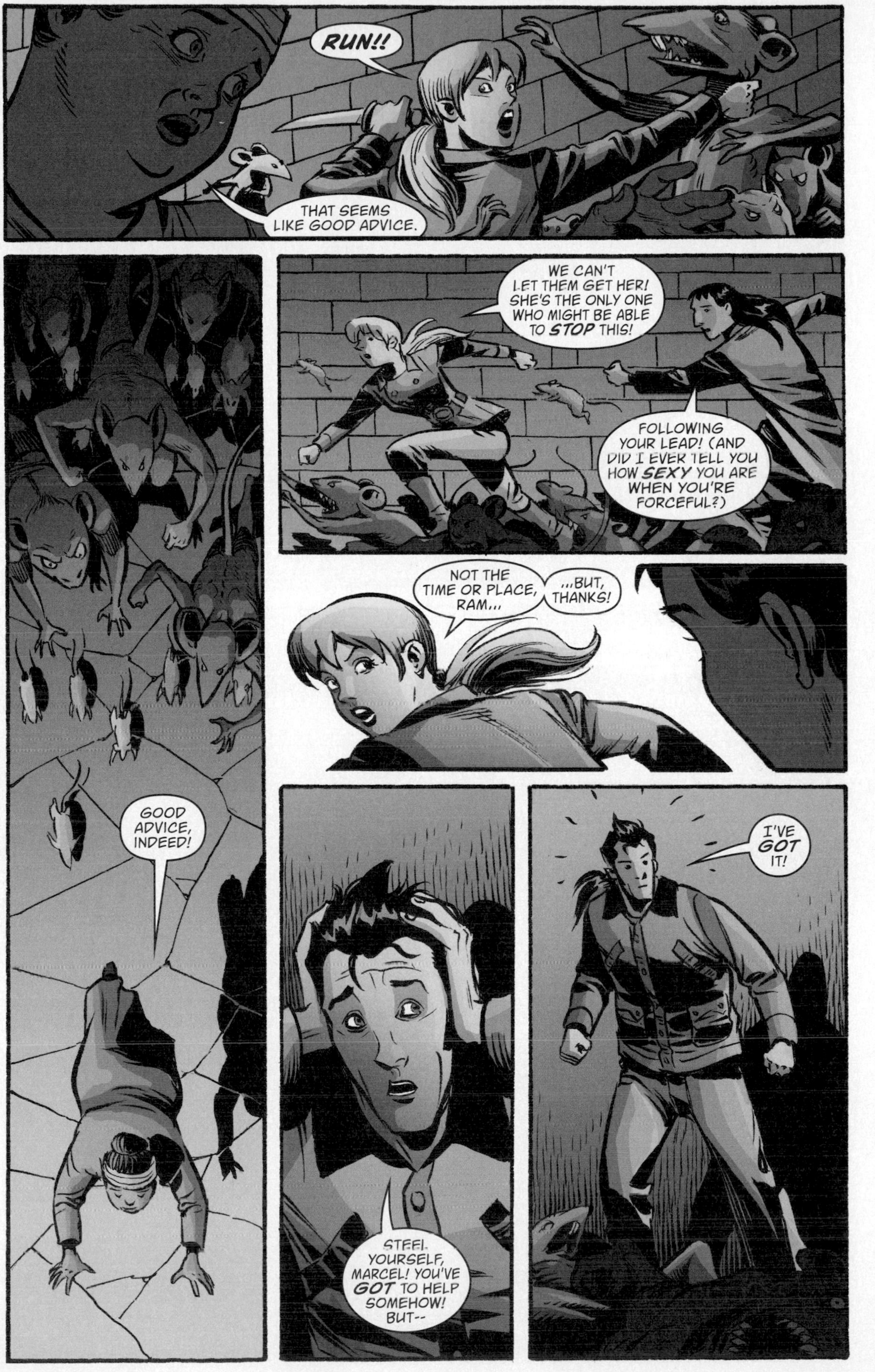
RUN!!
THAT SEEMS LIKE GOOD ADVICE.
GOOD ADVICE, INDEED!
WE CAN'T LET THEM GET HER! SHE'S THE ONLY ONE WHO MIGHT BE ABLE TO STOP THIS!
FOLLOWING YOUR LEAD! (AND DID I EVER TELL YOU HOW SEXY YOU ARE WHEN YOU'RE FORCEFUL?)
NOT THE TIME OR PLACE, RAM...
...BUT, THANKS!
STEEL YOURSELF, MARCEL! YOU'VE GOT TO HELP SOMEHOW! BUT--
I'VE GOT IT!

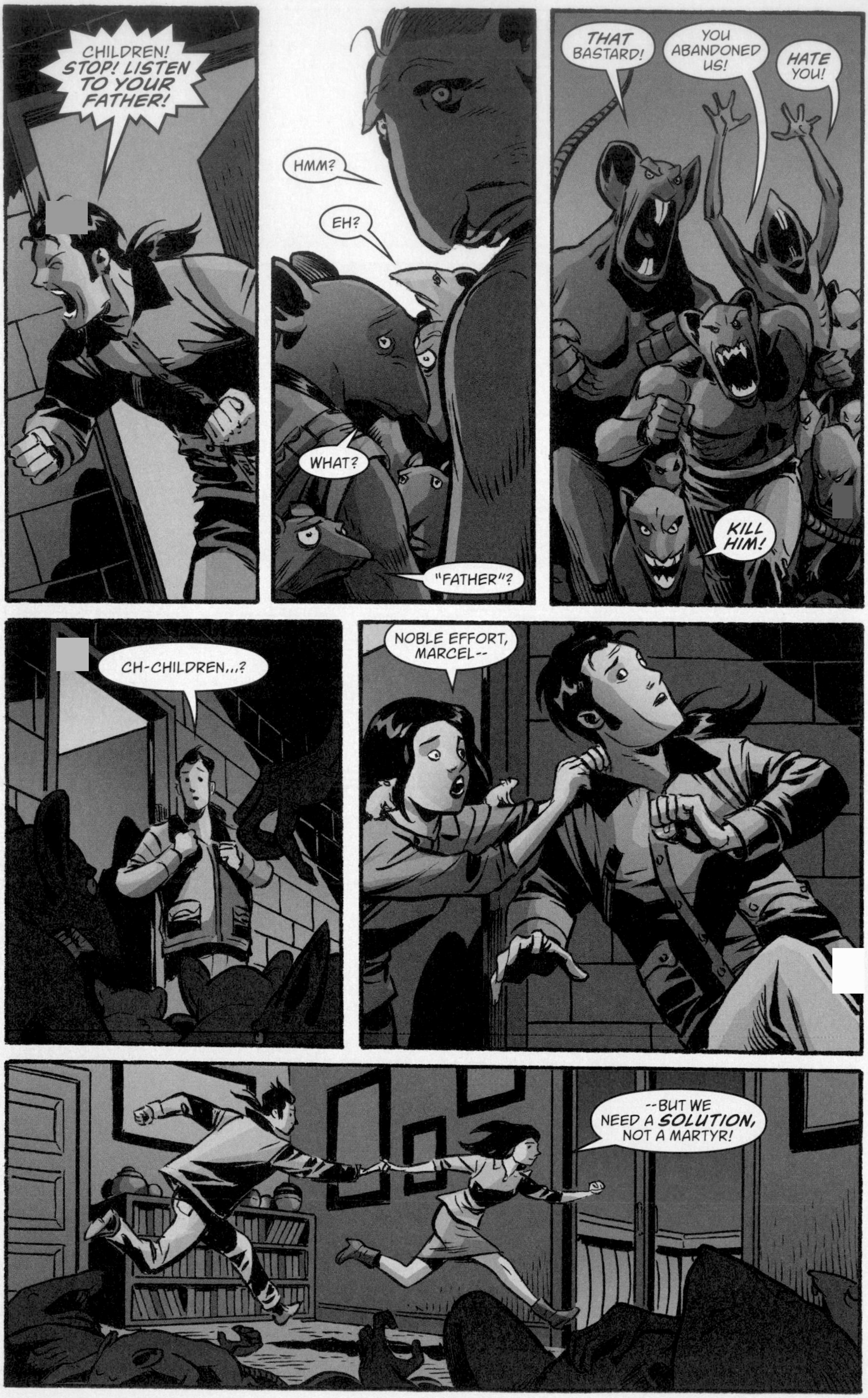
CHILDREN! STOP! LISTEN TO YOUR FATHER!
HMM?
EH?
WHAT?
"FATHER"?
THAT BASTARD!
YOU ABANDONED US!
HATE YOU!
KILL HIM!
CH-CHILDREN...?
NOBLE EFFORT, MARCEL--
--BUT WE NEED A SOLUTION, NOT A MARTYR!

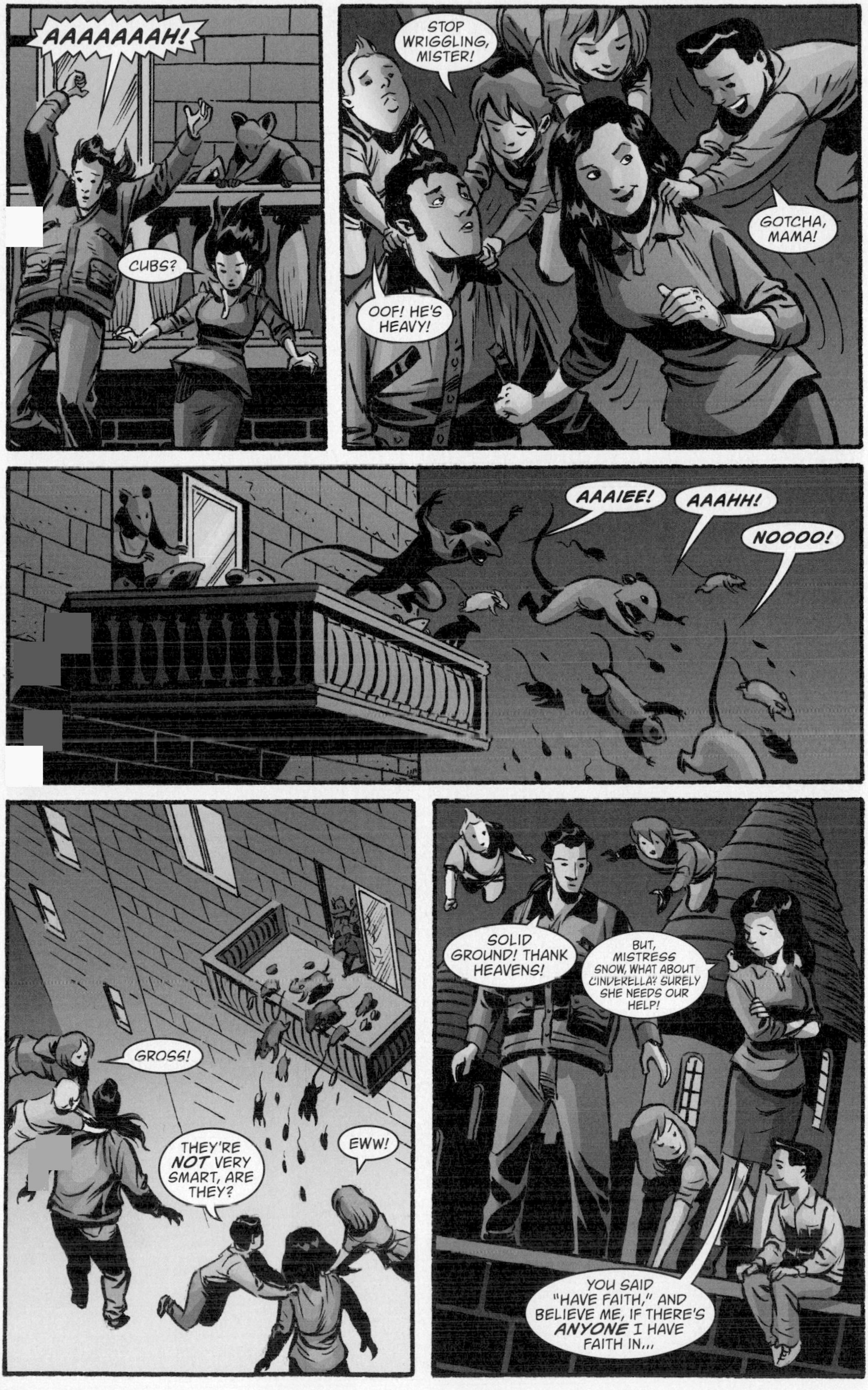
AAAAAAAH!
CUBS?
STOP WRIGGLING, MISTER!
GOTCHA, MAMA!
OOF! HE'S HEAVY!
AAAIEE!
AAAHH!
NOOOO!
GROSS!
THEY'RE NOT VERY SMART, ARE THEY?
EWW!
SOLID GROUND! THANK HEAVENS!
BUT, MISTRESS SNOW, WHAT ABOUT CINDERELLA? SURELY SHE NEEDS OUR HELP!
YOU SAID "HAVE FAITH," AND BELIEVE ME, IF THERE'S ANYONE I HAVE FAITH IN...

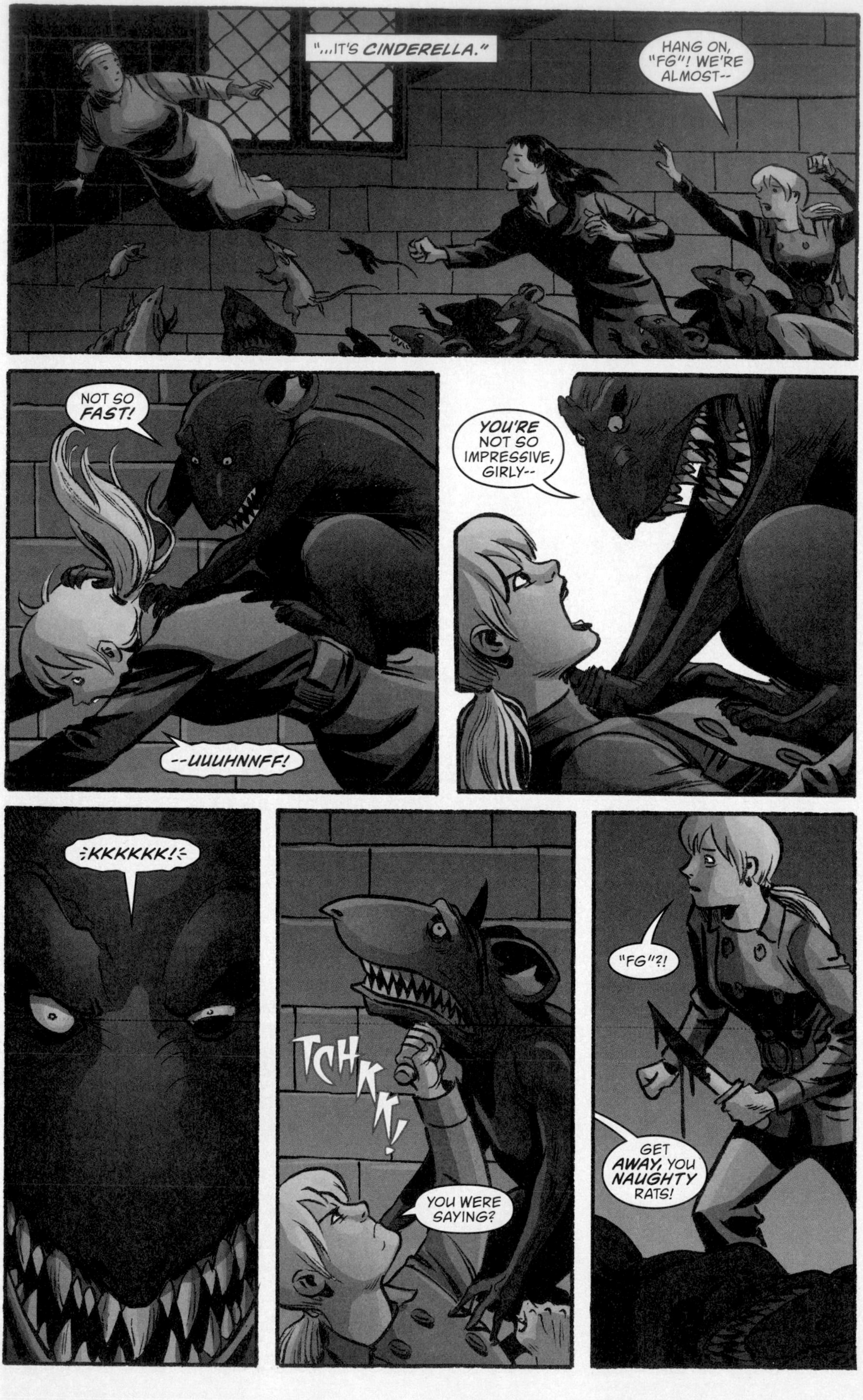
"...IT'S CINDERELLA."
HANG ON, "FG"! WE'RE ALMOST--
NOT SO FAST!
--UUUHNNFF!
YOU'RE NOT SO IMPRESSIVE, GIRLY--
KKKKKK!
TCHKK!
YOU WERE SAYING?
"FG"?!
GET AWAY, YOU NAUGHTY RATS!

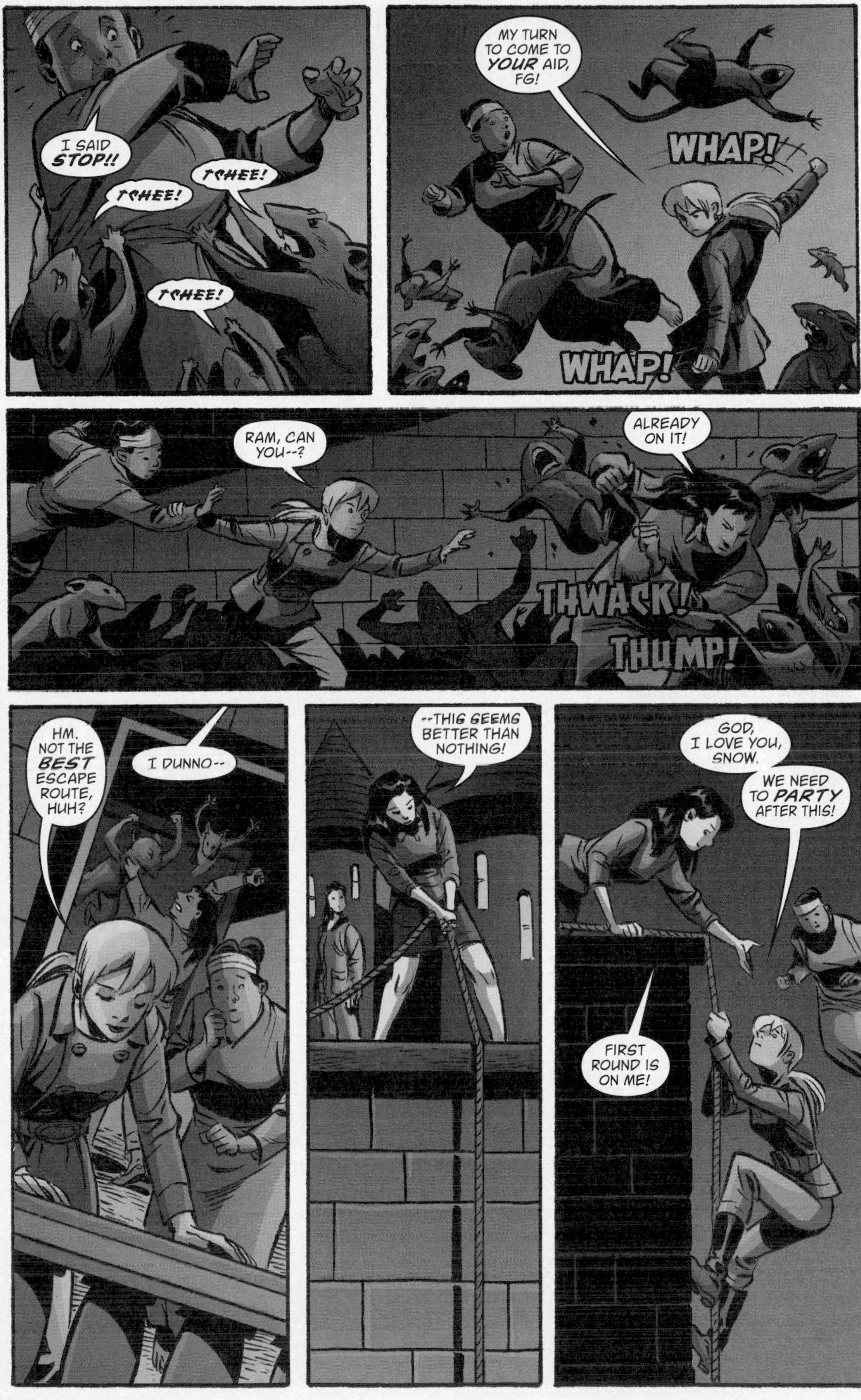
I SAID STOP!!
TCHEE!
TCHEE!
TCHEE!
MY TURN TO COME TO YOUR AID, FG!
WHAP!
WHAP!
RAM, CAN YOU--?
ALREADY ON IT!
THWACK!
THUMP!
HM. NOT THE BEST ESCAPE ROUTE, HUH?
I DUNNO--
--THIS SEEMS BETTER THAN NOTHING!
GOD, I LOVE YOU, SNOW.
WE NEED TO PARTY AFTER THIS!
FIRST ROUND IS ON ME!

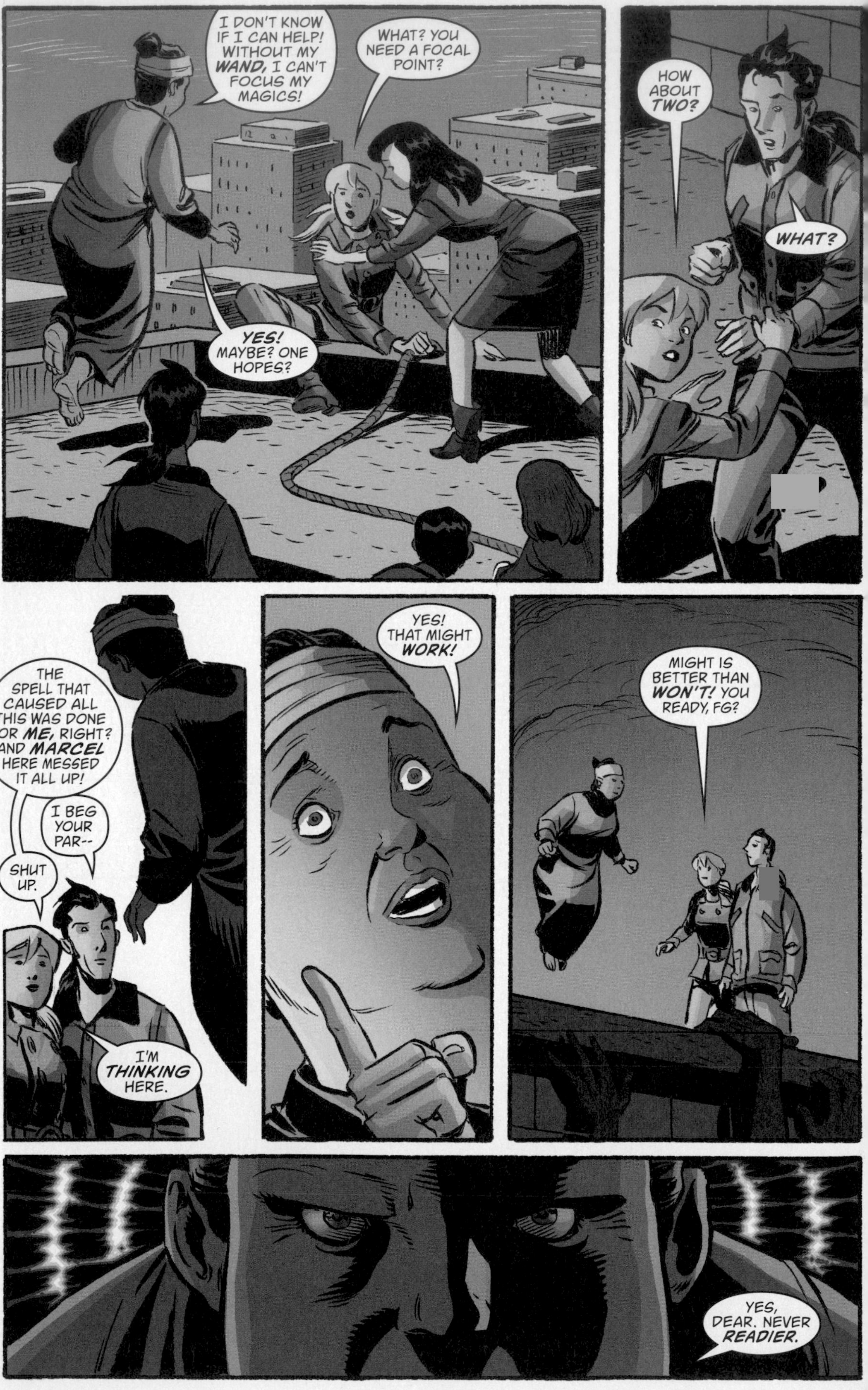

I DON'T KNOW IF I CAN HELP! WITHOUT MY WAND, I CAN'T FOCUS MY MAGICS!
WHAT? YOU NEED A FOCAL POINT?
YES! MAYBE? ONE HOPES?
HOW ABOUT TWO?
WHAT?
THE SPELL THAT CAUSED ALL THIS WAS DONE FOR ME, RIGHT? AND MARCEL HERE MESSED IT ALL UP!
I BEG YOUR PAR--
SHUT UP.
I'M THINKING HERE.
YES! THAT MIGHT WORK!
MIGHT IS BETTER THAN WON'T! YOU READY, FG?
YES, DEAR. NEVER READIER.

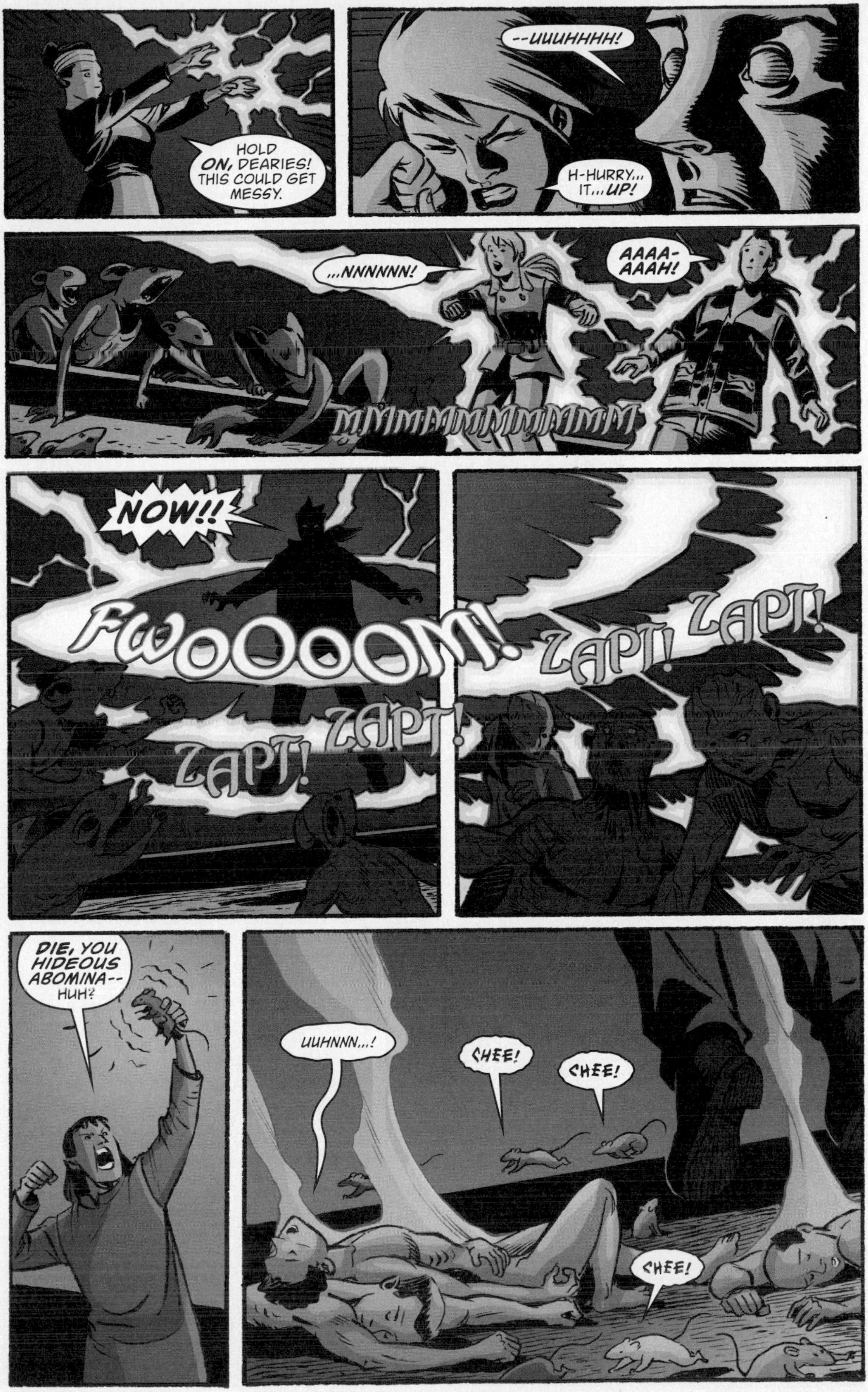
HOLD ON, DEARIES! THIS COULD GET MESSY.
--UUUHHHH!
H-HURRY... IT... UP!
...NNNNNN!
AAAA-AAAH!
MMMMMMMMMMMMMM
NOW!!
FWOOOOOM!
ZAPT! ZAPT!
ZAPT! ZAPT!
DIE, YOU HIDEOUS ABOMINA-- HUH?
UUHNNN...!
CHEE!
CHEE!
CHEE!

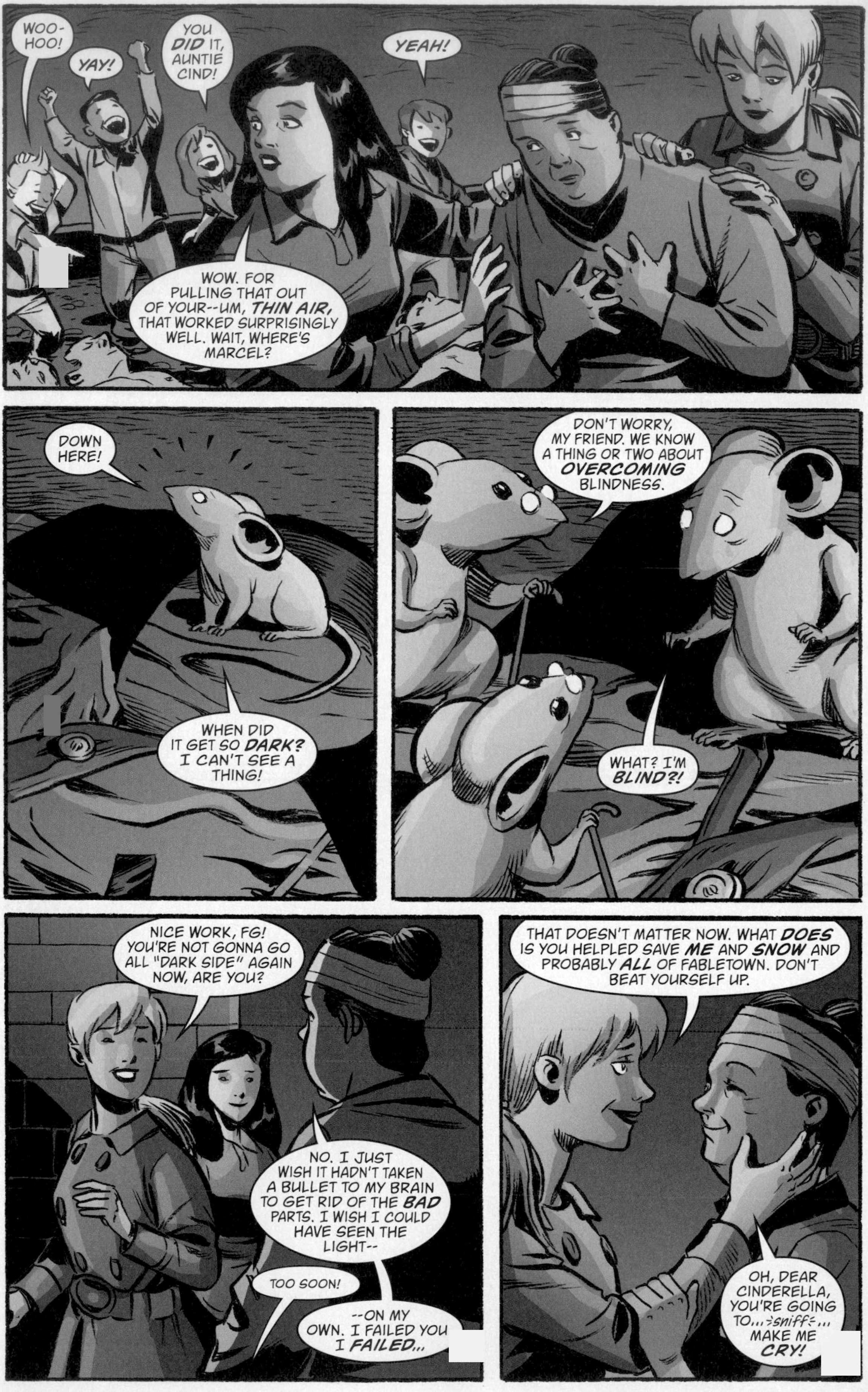

WOO-HOO!
YAY!
YOU DID IT, AUNTIE CIND!
YEAH!
WOW. FOR PULLING THAT OUT OF YOUR--UM, THIN AIR, THAT WORKED SURPRISINGLY WELL. WAIT, WHERE'S MARCEL?
DOWN HERE!
WHEN DID IT GET SO DARK? I CAN'T SEE A THING!
DON'T WORRY, MY FRIEND. WE KNOW A THING OR TWO ABOUT OVERCOMING BLINDNESS.
WHAT? I'M BLIND?!
NICE WORK, FG! YOU'RE NOT GONNA GO ALL "DARK SIDE" AGAIN NOW, ARE YOU?
NO. I JUST WISH IT HADN'T TAKEN A BULLET TO MY BRAIN TO GET RID OF THE BAD PARTS. I WISH I COULD HAVE SEEN THE LIGHT--
TOO SOON!
--ON MY OWN. I FAILED YOU I FAILED...
THAT DOESN'T MATTER NOW. WHAT DOES IS YOU HELPLED SAVE ME AND SNOW AND PROBABLY ALL OF FABLETOWN. DON'T BEAT YOURSELF UP.
OH, DEAR CINDERELLA, YOU'RE GOING TO... sniff... MAKE ME CRY!

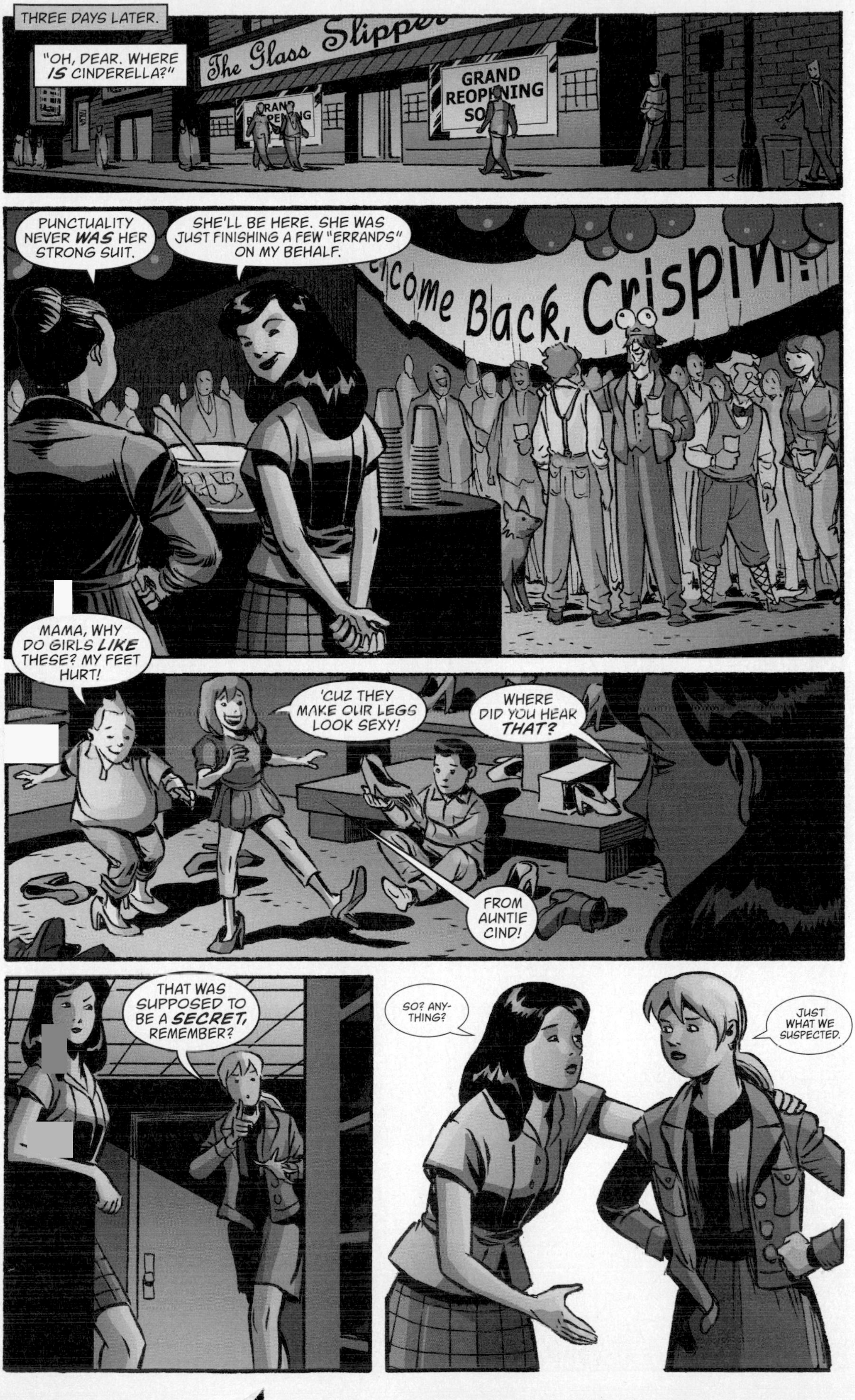
THREE DAYS LATER.
"OH, DEAR. WHERE IS CINDERELLA?"
The Glass Slipper
GRAND REOPENING SO
PUNCTUALITY NEVER WAS HER STRONG SUIT.
SHE'LL BE HERE. SHE WAS JUST FINISHING A FEW "ERRANDS" ON MY BEHALF.
come Back, Crispin
MAMA, WHY DO GIRLS LIKE THESE? MY FEET HURT!
'CUZ THEY MAKE OUR LEGS LOOK SEXY!
WHERE DID YOU HEAR THAT?
FROM AUNTIE CIND!
THAT WAS SUPPOSED TO BE A SECRET, REMEMBER?
SO? ANY-THING?
JUST WHAT WE SUSPECTED.

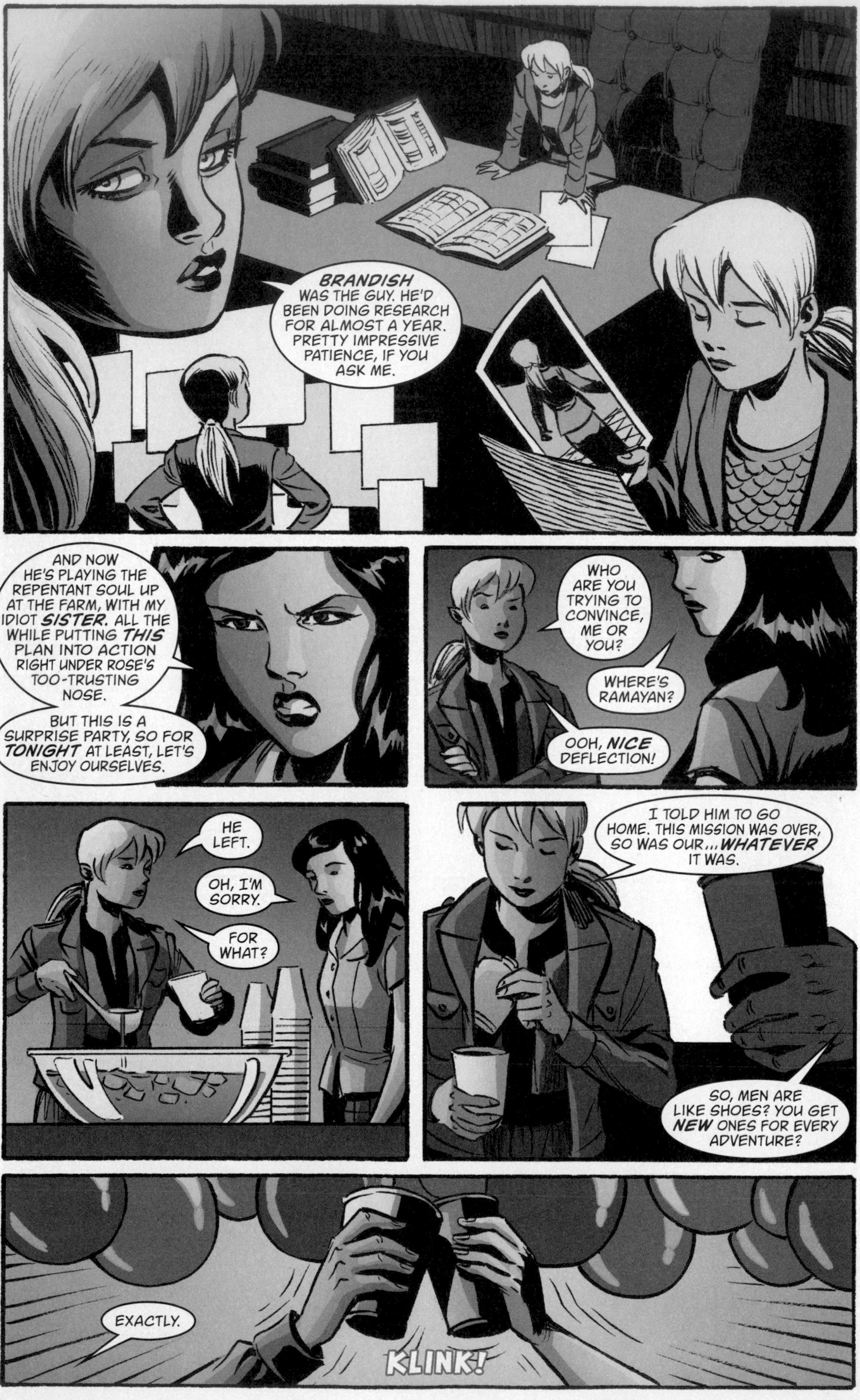
BRANDISH WAS THE GUY. HE'D BEEN DOING RESEARCH FOR ALMOST A YEAR. PRETTY IMPRESSIVE PATIENCE, IF YOU ASK ME.
AND NOW HE'S PLAYING THE REPENTANT SOUL UP AT THE FARM, WITH MY IDIOT SISTER. ALL THE WHILE PUTTING THIS PLAN INTO ACTION RIGHT UNDER ROSE'S TOO-TRUSTING NOSE.
BUT THIS IS A SURPRISE PARTY, SO FOR TONIGHT AT LEAST, LET'S ENJOY OURSELVES.
WHO ARE YOU TRYING TO CONVINCE, ME OR YOU?
WHERE'S RAMAYAN?
OOH, NICE DEFLECTION!
HE LEFT.
OH, I'M SORRY.
FOR WHAT?
I TOLD HIM TO GO HOME. THIS MISSION WAS OVER, SO WAS OUR... WHATEVER IT WAS.
SO, MEN ARE LIKE SHOES? YOU GET NEW ONES FOR EVERY ADVENTURE?
EXACTLY.
KLINK!

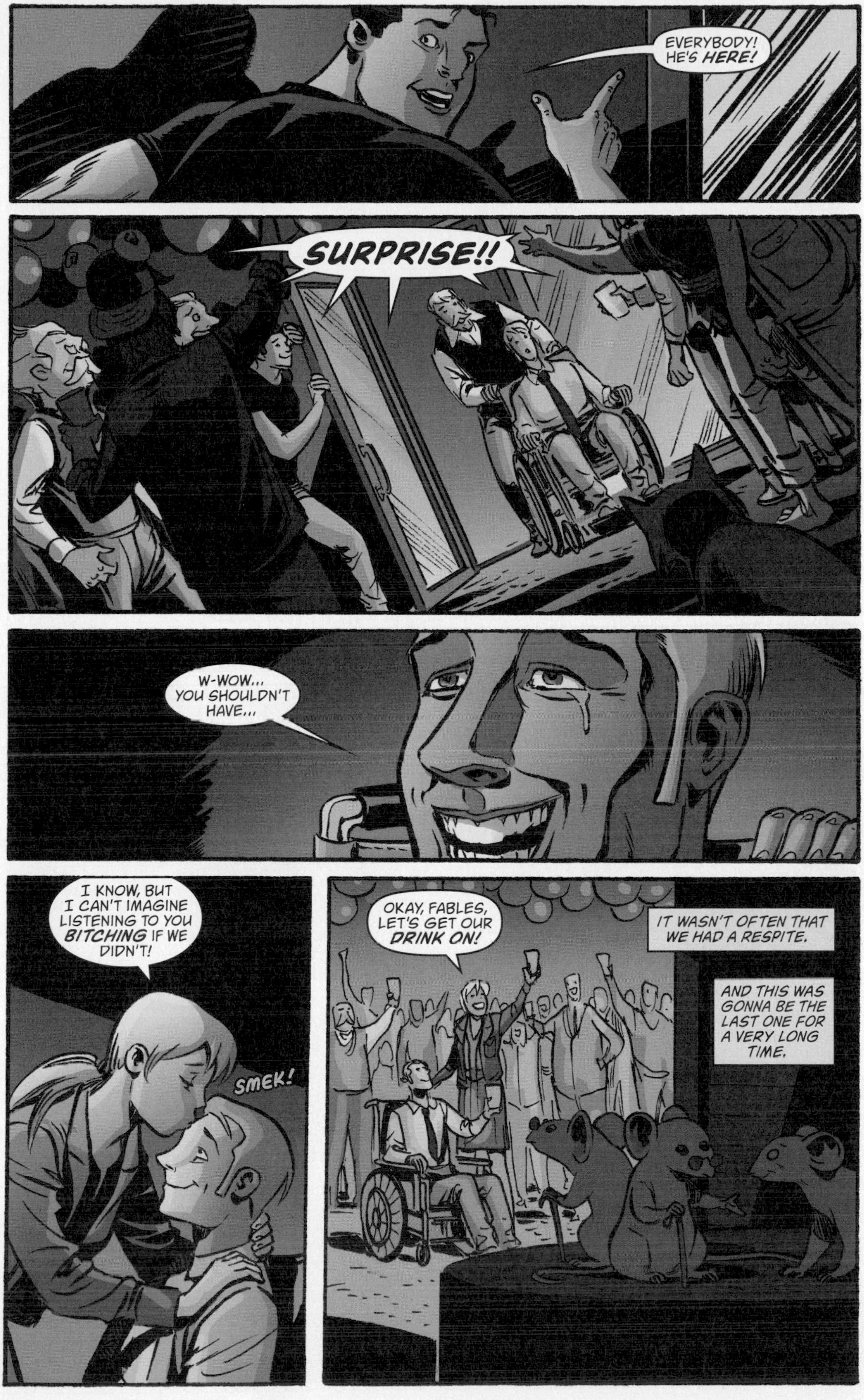
EVERYBODY! HE'S HERE!
SURPRISE!!
W-WOW... YOU SHOULDN'T HAVE...
I KNOW, BUT I CAN'T IMAGINE LISTENING TO YOU BITCHING IF WE DIDN'T!
SMEK!
OKAY, FABLES, LET'S GET OUR DRINK ON!
IT WASN'T OFTEN THAT WE HAD A RESPITE.
AND THIS WAS GONNA BE THE LAST ONE FOR A VERY LONG TIME.

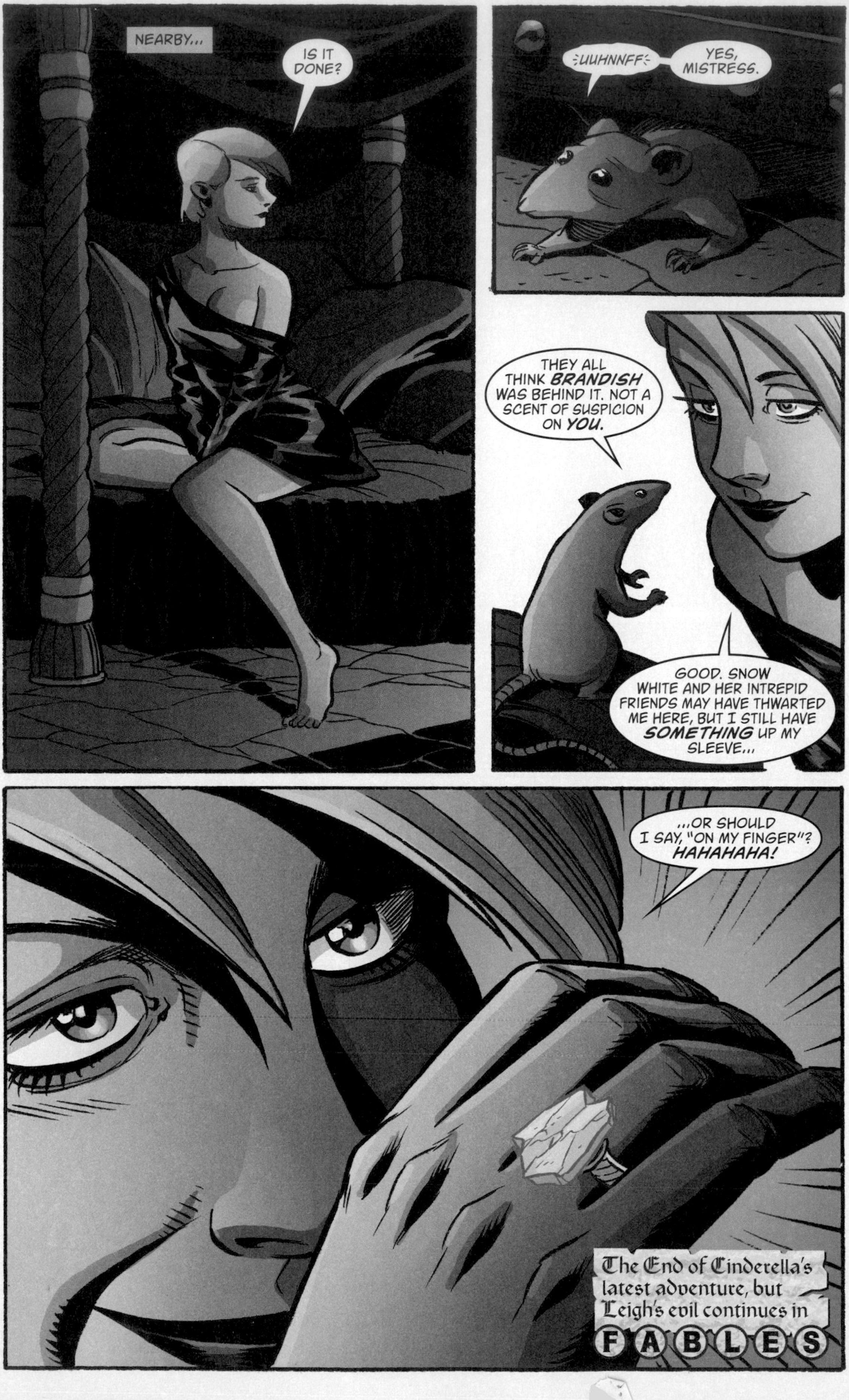
NEARBY...
IS IT DONE?
UUHNNFF
YES, MISTRESS.
THEY ALL THINK BRANDISH WAS BEHIND IT. NOT A SCENT OF SUSPICION ON YOU.
GOOD. SNOW WHITE AND HER INTREPID FRIENDS MAY HAVE THWARTED ME HERE, BUT I STILL HAVE SOMETHING UP MY SLEEVE...
...OR SHOULD I SAY, "ON MY FINGER"? HAHAHAHA!
The End of Cinderella's latest adventure, but Leigh's evil continues in
FABLES

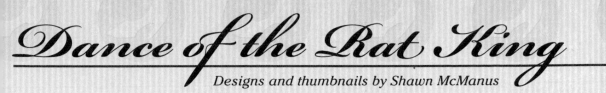

Dance of the Rat King

Designs and thumbnails by Shawn McManus

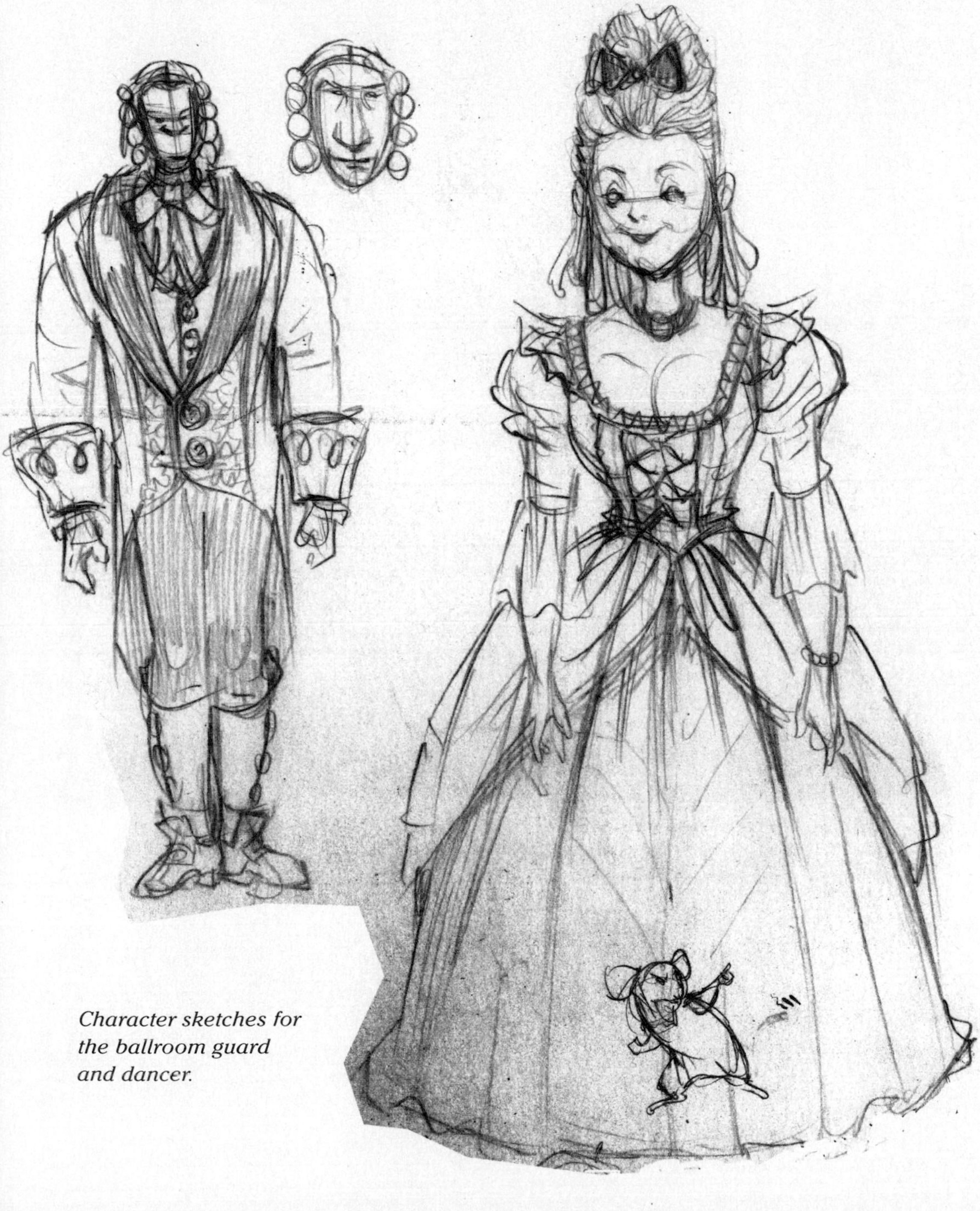

Character sketches for the ballroom guard and dancer.

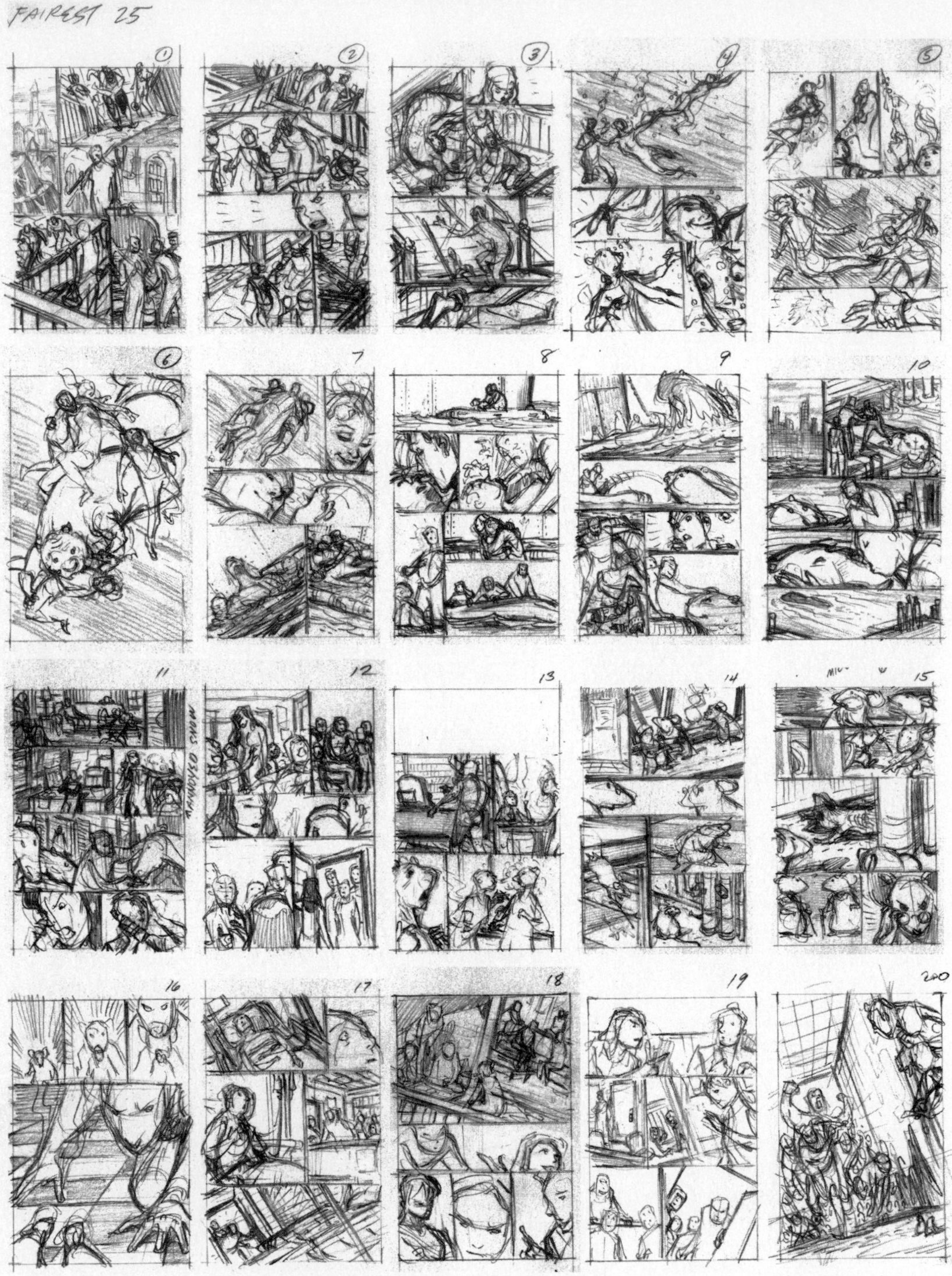
FAIREST 25

Page breakdowns for issue #25.

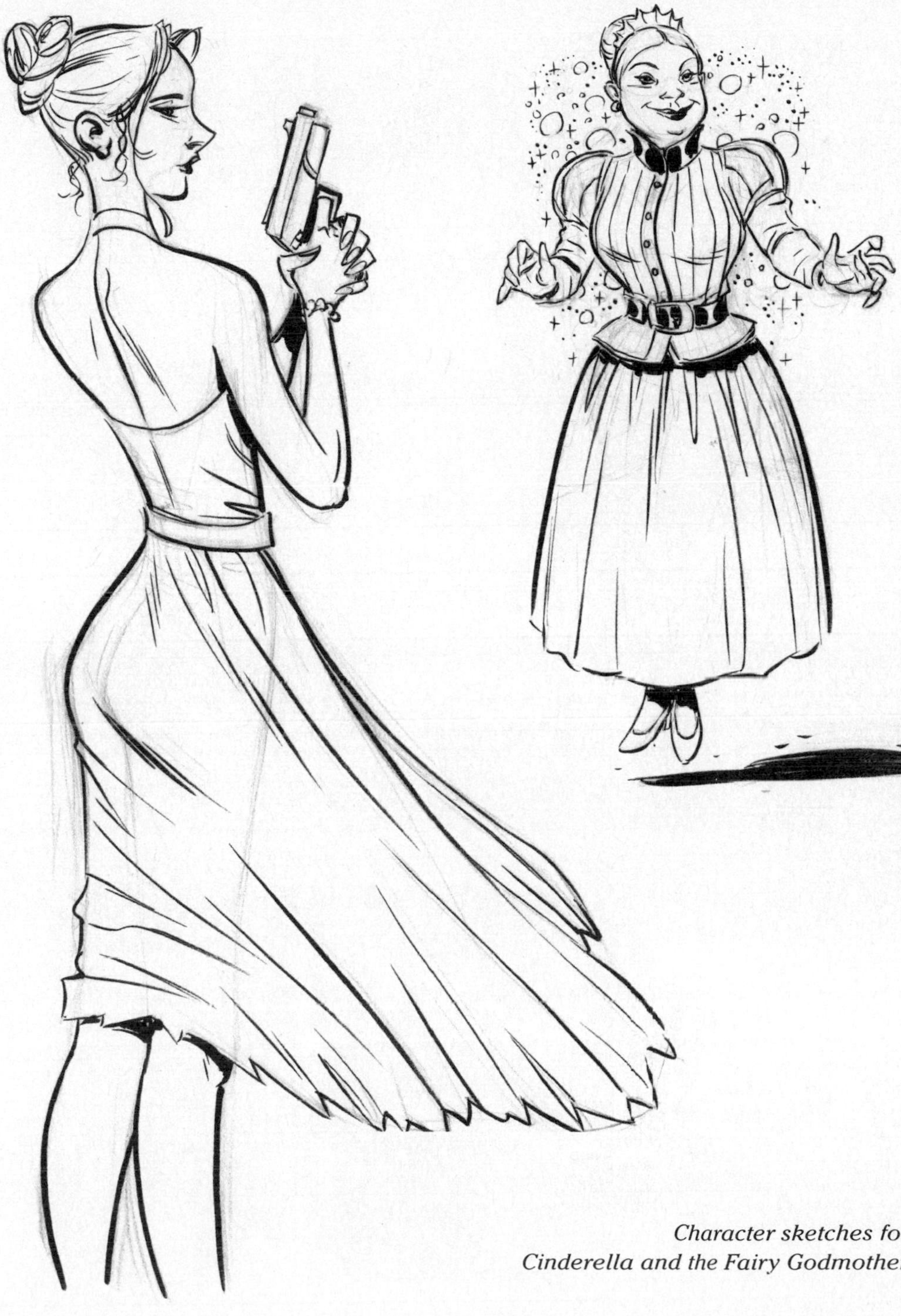

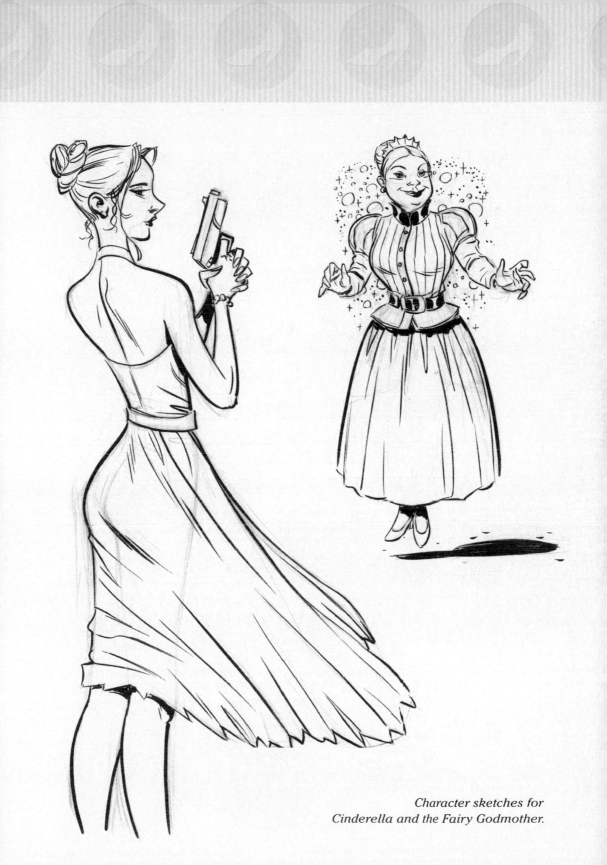

Character sketches for Cinderella and the Fairy Godmother.

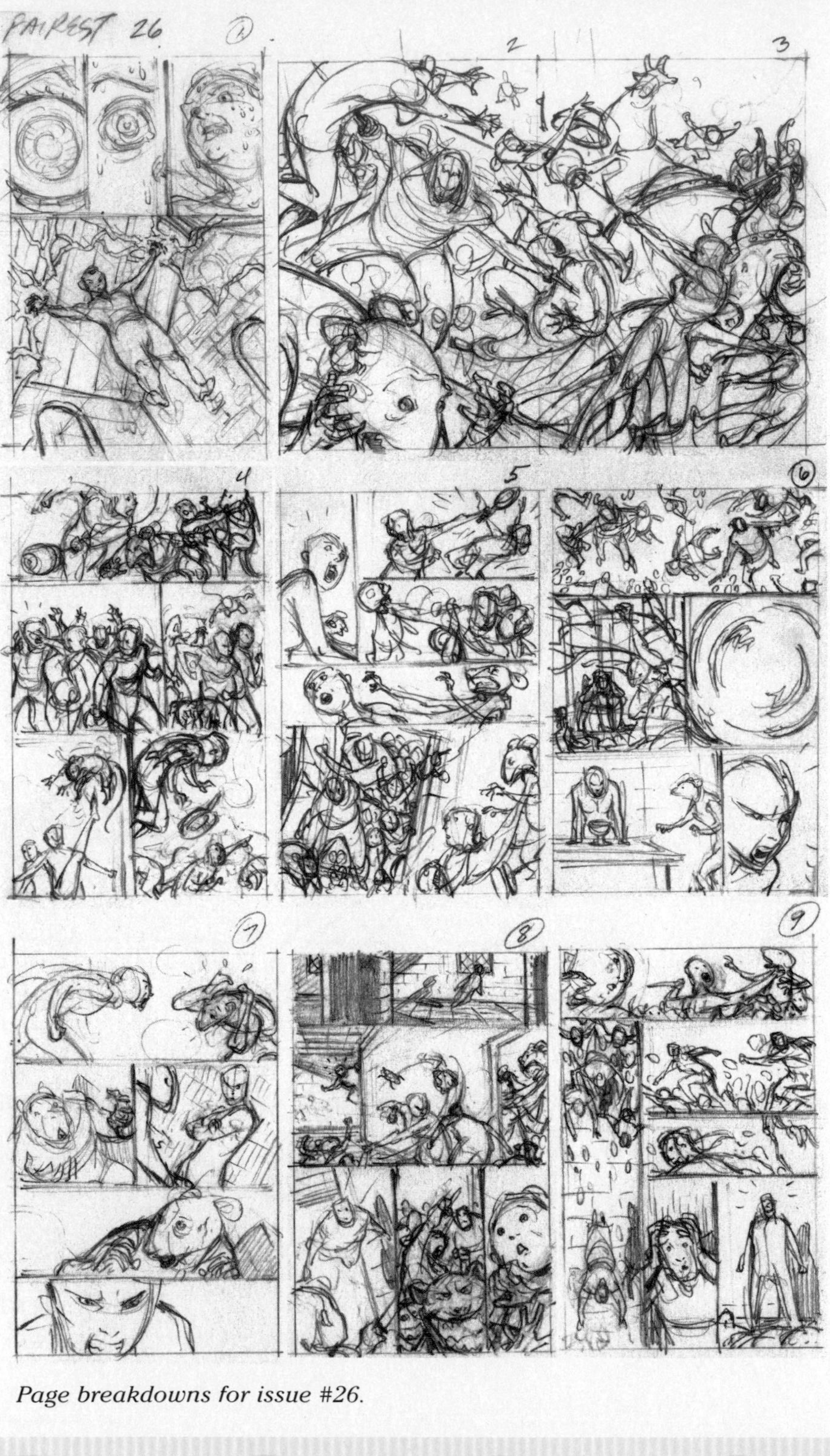
FAIREST 26

Page breakdowns for issue #26.

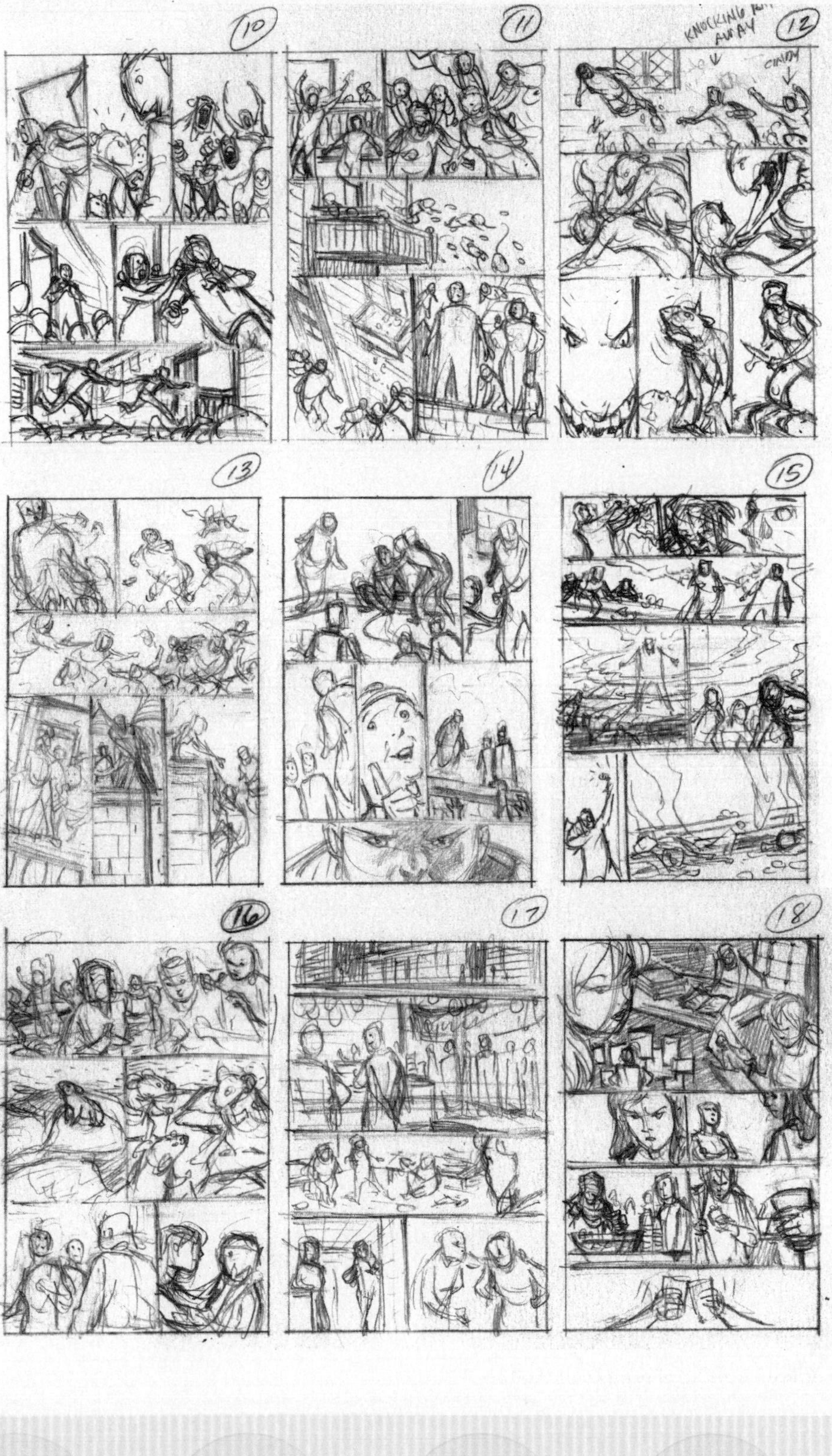
10
11
12
KNOCKING
AWAY
CINDY
13
14
15
16
17
18

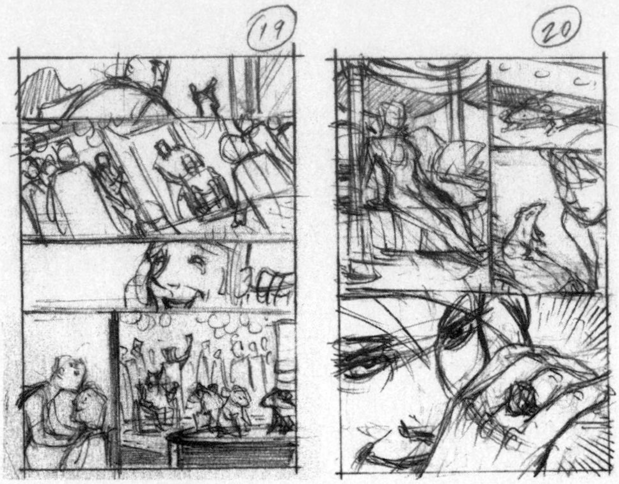
19
20

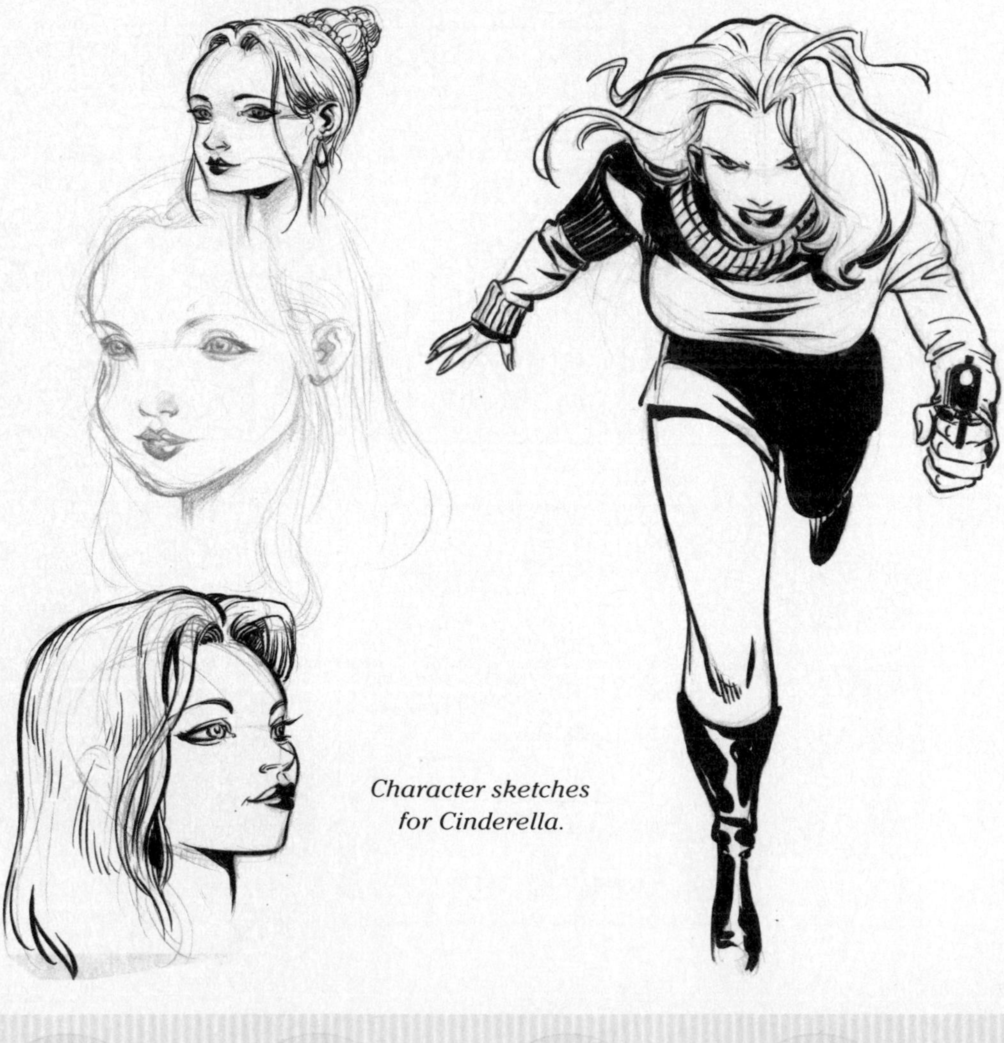

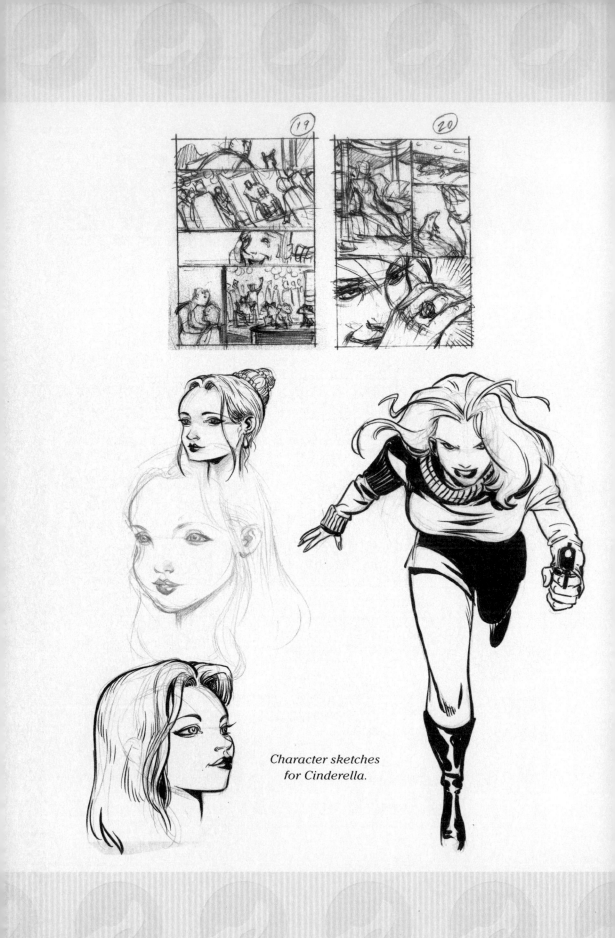

Character sketches for Cinderella.

"It's got a little bit of everything that any sophisticated comics fan will enjoy." —PUBLISHERS WEEKLY

"An unpredictable romp. It's a lot of fun." —THE ONION

"Sharp, quick-paced, fun-to-read stuff that is sure to impress." —METRO TORONTO

FROM THE PAGES OF *FABLES*

JACK OF FABLES

BILL WILLINGHAM, MATTHEW STURGES and TONY AKINS

JACK OF FABLES VOL. 7: THE NEW ADVENTURES OF JACK AND JACK

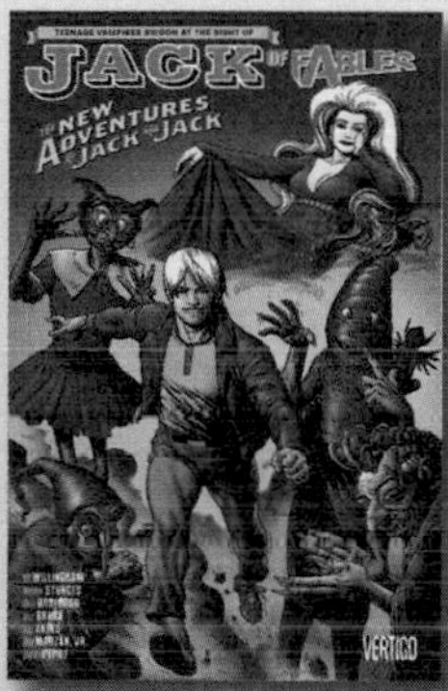

JACK
VERTIGO

READ THE ENTIRE SERIES!

JACK OF FABLES VOL. 1: THE (NEARLY) GREAT ESCAPE

JACK OF FABLES VOL. 2: JACK OF HEARTS

JACK OF FABLES VOL. 3: THE BAD PRINCE

JACK OF FABLES VOL. 4: AMERICANA

JACK OF FABLES VOL. 5: TURNING PAGES

JACK OF FABLES VOL. 6: THE BIG BOOK OF WAR

JACK OF FABLES VOL. 7: THE NEW ADVENTURES OF JACK AND JACK

JACK OF FABLES VOL. 8: THE FULMINATE BLADE

JACK OF FABLES VOL. 9: THE END

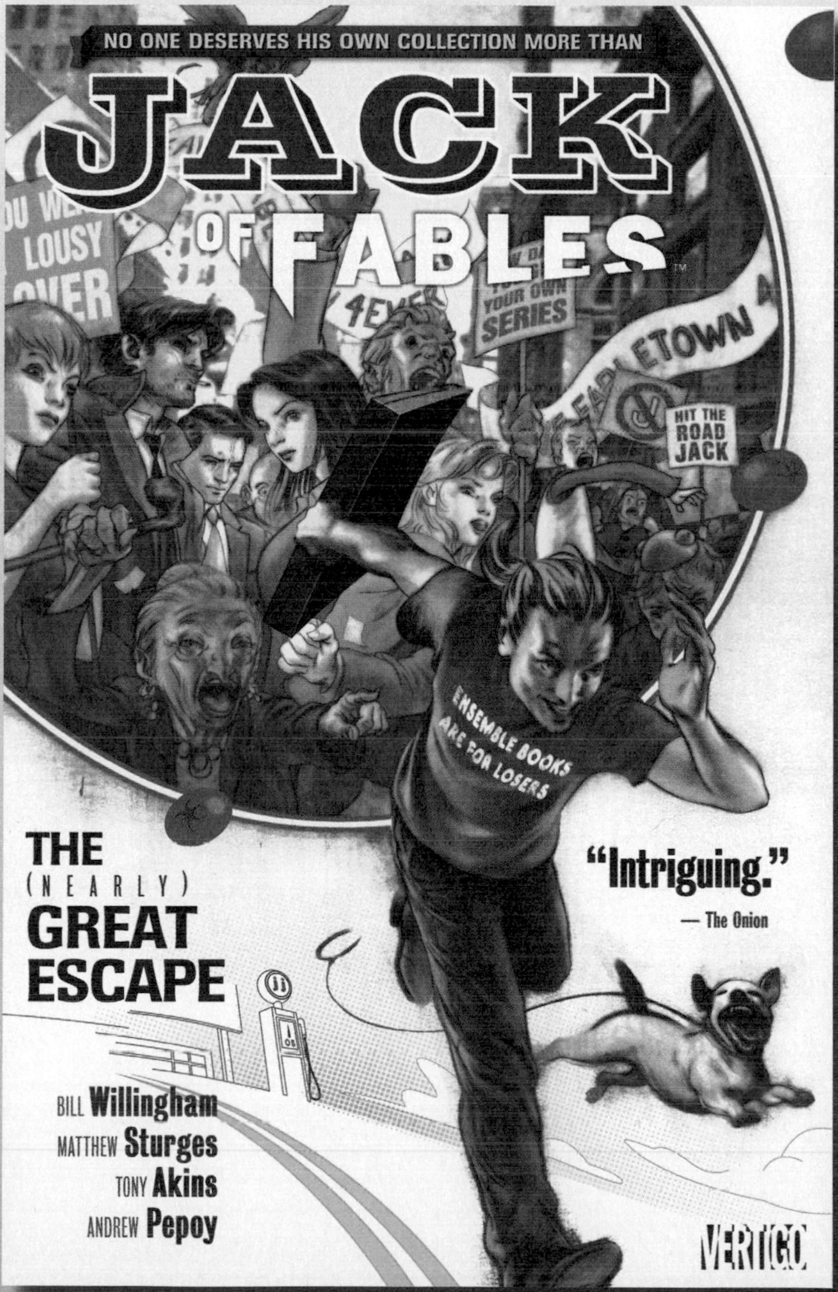

NO ONE DESERVES HIS OWN COLLECTION MORE THAN
JACK
OF FABLES
LOUSY
YOUR OWN SERIES
HIT THE ROAD JACK
ENSEMBLE BOOKS ARE FOR LOSERS
THE (NEARLY) GREAT ESCAPE
"Intriguing."
— The Onion
BILL Willingham
MATTHEW Sturges
TONY Akins
ANDREW Pepoy
VERTIGO